# THE EVERYTHING
## Coaching & Mentoring Book,
### 2nd Edition

Dear Reader,

My life experiences have placed me in a wide range of business environments, including the hustle and bustle of retail, the often fickle world of publishing, and even a couple of independent entrepreneurial adventures and misadventures. Along the way, I observed manager-employee relations that ran the gamut from the mutually respectful to the pitifully poisonous. I gleaned from all of this that there's most definitely a right way to manage people and a wrong way.

This is precisely where coaching and mentoring and their enlightened managerial practices come in. The philosophies of coaching and mentoring view employees as individuals—as, believe it or not, real people. There's no reason why managers and their staff cannot work together in productive harmony.

I've seen it happen. And, when all is said and done, the beauty of coaching and mentoring applications are that they can effortlessly transcend the office environs. They are relevant, too, in retail and service businesses, and a whole host of places outside of the push and shove of big business.

Straight Ahead.

*Nicholas Nigro*

# Welcome to the EVERYTHING® Series!

These handy, accessible books give you all you need to tackle a difficult project, gain a new hobby, comprehend a fascinating topic, prepare for an exam, or even brush up on something you learned back in school but have since forgotten.

You can read an *Everything*® book from cover to cover or just pick out the information you want from our four useful boxes: e-questions, e-facts, e-alerts, e-ssentials. We give you everything you need to know on the subject, but throw in a lot of fun stuff along the way, too.

We now have more than 400 *Everything*® books in print, spanning such wide-ranging categories as weddings, pregnancy, cooking, music instruction, foreign language, crafts, pets, New Age, and so much more. When you're done reading them all, you can finally say you know *Everything*®!

**QUESTIONS?**
Answers to
common questions

**FACTS**
Important snippets
of information

**ALERTS!**
Urgent
warnings

**ESSENTIALS**
Quick
handy tips

## Editorial

Director of Innovation: Paula Munier

Editorial Director: Laura M. Daly

Executive Editor, Series Books: Brielle K. Matson

Associate Copy Chief: Sheila Zwiebel

Acquisitions Editor: Lisa Laing

Associate Development Editor: Katie McDonough

Production Editor: Casey Ebert

## Production

Director of Manufacturing: Susan Beale

Production Project Manager: Michelle Roy Kelly

Prepress: Erick DaCosta, Matt LeBlanc

Design Manager: Heather Blank

Senior Book Designer: Colleen Cunningham

Interior Layout: Heather Barrett, Brewster Brownville

*Visit the entire Everything*® *series at* www.everything.com

# THE
# EVERYTHING®
# COACHING & MENTORING BOOK

## 2ND EDITION

Increase productivity, foster talent,
and encourage success

Nicholas Nigro

Avon, Massachusetts

*To Michael Siconolfi,*
*an artist at his craft and pillar of his profession.*

———————————

An Everything® Series Book.
Everything® and everything.com® are registered trademarks of F+W Publications, Inc.

Published by Adams Media, an F+W Publications Company
57 Littlefield Street, Avon, MA 02322 U.S.A.
*www.adamsmedia.com*

ISBN 10: 1-59869-450-2
ISBN 13: 978-1-59869-450-5

Printed in the United States of America.

J   I   H   G   F   E   D   C   B

**Library of Congress Cataloging-in-Publication Data**
is available from the publisher.

This publication is designed to provide accurate and authoritative information with regard to the subject matter covered. It is sold with the understanding that the publisher is not engaged in rendering legal, accounting, or other professional advice. If legal advice or other expert assistance is required, the services of a competent professional person should be sought.

—From a *Declaration of Principles* jointly adopted by a Committee of the American Bar Association and a Committee of Publishers and Associations

Many of the designations used by manufacturers and sellers to distinguish their products are claimed as trademarks. Where those designations appear in this book and Adams Media was aware of a trademark claim, the designations have been printed with initial capital letters.

*This book is available at quantity discounts for bulk purchases.*
*For information, please call 1-800-289-0963.*

# Contents

# Acknowledgments

Foremost, many thanks to editor Lisa Laing and the people at Adams Media for affording me the opportunity to do this book. These opportunities are what writers live for. And, although not the literary agent of record for this project, I'd like to express my gratitude to June Clark for encouraging me to take it on while simultaneously writing another book. Writers can successfully multitask.

Special thanks to Bill Lipman, Joe Nigro, Rosanne D'Esposito, Remy D'Esposito, Tom Nigro, Frank Rosa, Rich Covello, Nick Checki, and, last but not least, the trio of wise elders: Nicholas, Agnes, and Rose. These fine folks provided me food, transportation, and—most importantly— succor when I was laid up for a spell after an unanticipated medical moment. I couldn't have written this book without their selfless assistance.

## Top Ten Reasons Why Coaching and Mentoring Bests Traditional Managing

1.  It maximizes overall performance results by appreciating each employee as an individual with unique talents and possibilities.

2.  It delegates challenging job roles and tasks, while setting bold but realistic goals for every employee.

3.  It expands knowledge and grows skills of employees and managers alike, thus enhancing their job futures.

4.  It establishes and maintains an open work environment with free-flowing dialogue and constructive feedback.

5.  It enhances communication abilities, both written and oral.

6.  It seeks solutions and positive outcomes to any and all workplace situations, including conflicts.

7.  It links workplace performance growth with personal growth.

8.  It recognizes the need for properly balanced work and home lives.

9.  It works with comprehensible, achievable performance plans for employees so they always know where they stand.

10. It sweetens company bottom lines and efficiency.

# Introduction

▶ GETTING PERSONS OF any age to perform at their utmost is a bona fide challenge for those in tutelage roles, be they in the home, on the sports field, or at the workplace. Keeping a diverse staff of employees both contented and focused on the work at hand is a job that's not for the faint-hearted. As fate would have it, there is an increasingly utilized managerial methodology that meets these weighty challenges head-on and with a proven track record of success. This coveted managerial road map, known as coaching and mentoring, essentially asks that its devotees conscientiously manage men and women as distinct individuals with unique talents and possibilities.

With the baby boom generation poised to retire en masse from the workforce in the coming years, businesses will need to replace a wholesale brain drain of knowledge and skills. They will accomplish this in part by requiring their managers to be coaches. They will also need organizational mentors to pass down wisdom and know-how to the younger crowd. Right now, locating and maintaining the necessary critical talent to keep companies at once profitable and competitive is a huge concern. Thus, coaching and mentoring as a far-sighted replacement for the old style of managing has assumed center stage. Unlike traditional managerial ways and means, coaching and mentoring instills in employees knowledge and skills that both enhance the present and augment the future.

Successful managing in any venue is an art form. In the new millennium, managing men and women demands a whole lot more than technical proficiency and a loud, booming voice. To get the most out of their people, managers must appreciate the intricacies and depth of the human condition. A one-size-fits-all approach to managing staff just doesn't cut it anymore. In fact, it never really did make much sense—

nor did it maximize dollars and cents—and that's what more and more executive decision makers are seeing.

To maximize the performance of your team you must uncover what makes each and every one of your players tick. You've got to locate the keys that unlock their drive to succeed. And the only way you can possibly realize this goal is by closely working with every person in your charge—on an individual basis. From the many on your team, you can accomplish one very satisfying result.

Sure, coaching and mentoring as managerial disciplines aren't textbook solutions to every problem. People are, after all, a very imperfect and unpredictable bunch. Ironically, though, this is an essential tenet of coaching and mentoring. Yes, you heard it right. Coaching and mentoring tools and techniques are people-driven—warts and all. Their managerial formulas are firmly grounded in fashioning contented and personally nourishing work atmospheres, while simultaneously making employees more productive. This highly resourceful and enlightening approach to managing individuals fully understands that these two positive results are not mutually exclusive.

In fact, the chief reason that coaching and mentoring in management are becoming more widespread as accepted business approaches is precisely because their implementation is proving highly effective in spurring employees to produce favorable results. Companies that employ coaches as managers, bring in external coaches as consultants, or utilize mentors are not motivated by mere altruism. No matter what anybody says, businesses exist—first and foremost—to sweeten bottom lines.

Coaches and mentors in management roles seek to amplify human possibilities, while simultaneously recognizing the consequence of profit maximization. By accepting the connection between employee job satisfaction and overall performance and level of productivity, coaching and mentoring offer new and improved ways of managing human beings. What it all comes down to is coaching and mentoring endeavors to find solutions and positive outcomes—anywhere and everywhere. This is the foundation upon which this innovative managerial art rests.

Chapter 1

# The Brave New World of Coaching and Mentoring

Coaching and mentoring have been getting a lot of positive press lately. The tools and techniques of this fresh and intriguing managerial methodology are taking root in both the private and public sectors. This introductory chapter reveals the myriad benefits of coaching and mentoring and elucidates why this forward-looking brand of managing is the perfect fit for the twenty-first century.

## Building a Coaching Vocabulary

There are coaches who operate as independent consultants (and rather high-paid ones at that). Brought into companies from the outside, these are men and women who address specific problems ranging from the highly technical to the more abstract, like communication deficiencies and morale issues. And then there are mentors within companies (usually highly regarded top managers) who take carefully selected subordinates "under their wings" and groom them for "bigger and better things" in a rather informal, open-ended relationship.

**FACT**

The English word "mentor" is derived from Homer's *Odyssey*. In this literary classic, Odysseus ventures off to war and turns the guidance of his young son Telemachus over to his friend Mentor. In the absence of his father, the boy is "mentored" by Mentor in the ways of the world.

The sum and substance of this book revolves around coaching and mentoring applied to managing on a day-to-day basis. That is, on the ABCs of coaching as a managerial art that distinguishes itself from traditional managing. Indeed, coaching and daily managing are no longer strangers, but a very compatible, happy couple.

So, from this point onward, sole references to "coaches," without any qualifiers, will refer to the managers who are employing—or hope to employ—this enlightened and fast-spreading managerial methodology on a daily basis. As a matter of fact, coaching is grounded in continuity and consistency across the board. It is not a pick-and-choose managerial approach, but a way of life in the office, or wherever else it is practiced. A manager who says to an employee, "Let's have a coaching session now" is not engaged in the art of coaching.

Throughout this book, you will also encounter perpetual references to "coaching and mentoring" to depict an all-inclusive managerial discipline, even though "coaching" and "mentoring" are not exactly the same thing (see Chapter 4).

## *Understanding the Benefits of Coaching*

Exactly what are the benefits of being a manager and a coach at the same time? For starters, coaches who get the utmost out of their employees realize the personal and professional satisfaction of seeing their managerial talents bear real fruit. Additional benefits that accrue to successful coaches include a pat on the head from the executive class (nice), financial remuneration (nicer still), and sometimes even a promotion (how sweet it is!).

And, if none of these things come your way, battle-tested and results-oriented coaches can always take their formidable track records of managerial accomplishments somewhere else. Capable coaches, with tried-and-true accomplishments on their resumes, are in high demand on the corporate frontier. They are rare birds indeed. When you demonstrate that you can manage men and women with supreme confidence, as well as deliver the goods, you can—in effect—write your own career script.

If New York is the "city that never sleeps," then coaching and mentoring are the managerial methods that never sleep. Their tools and techniques are rooted in never-ending learning. And this continuous learning requires that coaches, mentors, and employees alike view the workplace as a learning hub without knowledge boundaries.

The *pièce de résistance* of first-rate coaching is its many tentacles. That is, high-performing employees are similarly put on the fast track of personal growth and career advancement. If you boldly delegate real responsibilities and challenge your employees to better themselves, you—as a conscientious coach—grow their skills and make them more self-sufficient and productive workers. In other words, employees who respond favorably to a coach's guardianship are destined to rise in the company or—perhaps—in another company that is on the prowl for self-motivated, solid talent.

In the big picture, coaching and mentoring methods are designed to better the lot of one and all under their attentive thumb. Simply stated, the coaching and mentoring learning tree avails its fruit to those who are willing to sample it. Adept coaches, as well as those on the receiving end of their intelligent, devoted leadership, are always poised to move on to the next level of learning and of skills. The coach-employee relationship, and the learning environment that's part and parcel of it, embodies not only career growth and, hopefully, a fatter paycheck, but a rewarding interior journey as well, where all concerned feel better about themselves and what they do. And this job satisfaction cuts across their professional lives and into their personal lives. The bottom line: Reliable, results-oriented coaches can always take pride in the knowledge that they inspired people to perform at higher levels than they otherwise would have if left to their own devices.

## Coaching and Mentoring Is Teaching

Coaching and mentoring are for all intents and purposes teaching tools and techniques. In the classroom, first-rate teaching entails more than just imparting facts and figures, although that's very important. Inspired teaching—both in school settings *and* in the workplace—is really about stimulating students to desire learning on their own. The best educators plant the seeds of learning and hope that they get enough water and sunshine over time to sprout and grow trees of knowledge.

**FACT**

Coaching and mentoring are art forms that unceasingly endeavor to expand everyone's knowledge base and skill levels. Knowledge is the ability to organize information into a context and practical perspective. Skills embody the application of this knowledge in performing specific tasks or job roles.

The principal mission of this book is to reveal coaching and mentoring and their increasingly important role in the business sphere, as well as in offices in the sprawling public sector of the economy. Until relatively recently (let's say before 1990), the workplace was clearly differentiated from "home sweet home." It was a rigidly structured environment—almost antiseptic in its activities and schedules. Generally speaking, the boss was the boss and you did what you were told to do. You performed your everyday workload and went home near suppertime. And maybe—in time—you became the boss.

That was then and this is now—the twenty-first century.

For the preponderance of the twentieth century, it was not unusual for a man or woman to labor in one job—and one job only—for an entire working life. It happened all the time: Young, wet-behind-the-ears adults graduated from high school or college, found work with a company, and were still around for their retirement parties forty and fifty years later. And for their longstanding and loyal toiling, they received engraved wristwatches and pensions to live on until the Grim Reaper came calling.

Indeed, these dedicated souls, who stayed in one place from the beginning to the end of their working life, were once upon a time lauded for their steadfastness and allegiance to the companies that employed them. And, in turn, many of these employers reciprocated this dedication by not casting them aside when they sprouted their first gray hairs. It is an epoch that is long gone.

## *Twenty-First Century Workplace Challenges*

Today it's counterproductive to debate whether the sedentary but stable old business world just described was somehow better than the more dynamic and unstable business world of today. No doubt, this is a highly competitive and technological age. But this high-tech world notwithstanding, no time machine has yet been invented that can shuttle us back to the days when everything, it seemed, cost a nickel. So let's live our lives and move forward in the present realities.

While not completely ancient history, the days of moving up the corporate ladder in the same company are fast becoming the exception rather than the rule. Nowadays, employee advancement is more often a lateral movement. Moving on up, yes, but in different companies—and sometimes in totally different professions—in a dizzying zigzag rather than a straight line.

## Technological Competency

We've established that there are no time machines on the market. There are, however, these curious contraptions called computers that are omnipresent in business environs (and everywhere else for that matter). And courtesy of this technological marvel that has spawned the expansive Internet, the corporate world is in a constant state of flux.

The information age makes it altogether more imperative that businesses never rest on their laurels. Every business, big and small, must adapt to perpetually and rapidly changing market conditions, or risk falling by the wayside.

To err is human; to forgive is being a coach. Forgive, yes, but coaching doesn't ever amount to overlooking performance lapses! As a coach, you must swiftly identify missteps and correct them at the source. You don't do this to embarrass a particular person, but to impart valuable lessons on avoiding similar foul-ups, bleeps, and blunders in the future.

So, what exactly does this spanking new business-world order mean for you, a manager or manager of tomorrow? In essence, it means that you must be a sponge for learning with a nimble capacity to adapt to changing circumstances at a moment's notice. The new skills that are needed to keep up with all of these inevitable technological advances must become your skills.

## Continuous Growth

Learning new skills throughout your entire work life is not only recommended, it is indispensable. College knowledge is merely the beginning, not the end of the learning curve. By keeping up with the fast-changing times, you prepare yourself to effortlessly slide into another job role. And, if and when a job termination occurs (voluntarily or involuntarily), you don't emerge shell-shocked and stuck in quicksand. You come out of it all adept at moving on to bigger and better things because your knowledge base and skill level are in great demand.

Coaching and mentoring in today's dog-eat-dog corporate environs attempts to counterbalance, as much as humanly possible, the sometimes very unpleasant twenty-first-century realities of work life. As a coach, your predominant mission is to at once broaden your own abilities along with those who work alongside you. To accomplish this noble mission, you must ply your team with substantive responsibilities, genuine challenges, and ceaseless opportunities for career growth and development of their skills.

## Preparing Employees for a Future of Changes

The Boy Scouts' motto is "be prepared." That is, don't go out into the wilderness without the accouterments of survival (food, bandages, mosquito spray, snake bite kit, and so on). And it's an adage applicable to the coaching and mentoring approach to managing. As already touched upon, in the contemporary work environment, you had better be prepared to one day lose your job or change jobs by choice—and possibly in the proverbial New York minute. But, as this whole book will demonstrate, coaching and mentoring methodologies can transform seemingly negative work circumstances into very positive experiences.

Coaches recognize that employee turnover is a fact of life in the modern workplace. This sober reality, however, makes it even more vital that they fashion a work environment chock full of genuine challenges and opportunities for advancement. Coaches are charged with keeping dependable and skilled employees in the fold and encouraging outsiders to want in.

## *Fashioning Resilient Workers*

If you haven't been "downsized," "rightsized," laid off, or given a pink slip yourself, you've perhaps witnessed what happens to some of the terminated minions on the corporate landscape these days. They're often given no warning at all, their computers are unplugged, and they're summarily and unceremoniously escorted out of the workplace by dour-faced security guards.

Some of the dismissed minions depart with a quiet dignity; some leave the premises with tears freely flowing; and still others part in a pique of rage, threatening retaliation against the company or a particular manager or executive. It's the complete human spectrum of personalities and emotions revealed in a moment of crisis. Whatever the means or reasons for the discharge, it is—to be sure—a humiliating affair for all concerned.

As already alluded to, coaching and mentoring practices strive to fashion an army of resilient workers proficient at quickly getting up off the ground when they get knocked for a loop. In the final analysis, coaching and mentoring tools and techniques are all about empowering people to move forward—to take the knocks and disappointments of life on the job without looking back and without ever wallowing in debilitating recriminations.

## *Empowering Employees with Knowledge and Skills*

Ideally, coaching and mentoring in managerial circles furnish employees with a cornucopia of knowledge and skills that those without such leadership will never receive. Why? Because those who work with a qualified coach or mentor more fully understand and appreciate the ways and means of the twenty-first-century working world.

In order to consider yourself a coach in good standing, you must always lead by example, delegate important responsibilities, listen to and freely communicate with your staff, and treat each and every one of your employees as individuals with distinct personalities and unique abilities.

That is, they are not ignorant of the trials and tribulations that come with the territory, and they fully understand what is required of them to succeed. Contentedly lumbering about may suit manatees in the wide-open waters of the ocean. It doesn't, however, suit employees in the demanding, results-oriented, and often very stressful workplace of today.

## Putting Out the Welcome Mat

Individuals on the move reign supreme in the workforce these days, assuring that the labor pool is in a perpetual state of motion. Thus, coaching and mentoring seek to fashion, as much as is humanly possible, workplace climes that encourage employees to stay put—that is, to remain in the companies that put a high premium on learning. When companies actively provide employees training in cutting-edge skills, place them in challenging job roles, and offer opportunities for promotion, relative stability is the natural byproduct.

**FACT**

Coaching and mentoring are not some mushy managerial dictums akin to cheerleading. They are, in fact, action-oriented and engaged approaches to managing employee performance. Coaches take the tested managerial model of plan, do, check, act, and raise it to a higher level by focusing on the maximization of individual productivity.

Vague promises to employees of what may, might, or could happen don't cut it anymore. While it's certainly unavoidable that there will be many changes in personnel in the overall life of any enterprise, this isn't meant to imply that fast-paced employee turnover is a positive thing and welcomed in any way, shape, or form. Both the retention and the attraction of the best and the brightest from the employee pool are coaching and mentoring's desired endgame. Enlightened management gives rise to loyalty by creating work environments that are magnets for employees with solid skills, self-motivation, and a hearty appetite for career growth and development. A business atmosphere that genuinely values and rewards achievement is where everyone wants to be, whether in managerial roles or in fledgling positions on the bottom rung of a corporate ladder.

Now more than ever, there is a bromide that rings truer with each passing day: "Good help is hard to find." So, when you, as a coach, find employees who get the job done, you want to keep them in your fold for as long as is humanly possible. And, simultaneously, you always want to be on the lookout for fresh, energized talent. A wise coach always keeps one eye focused on today's work situation and the other eye on tomorrow's.

# How Coaching and Mentoring Delivers

Why are coaching and mentoring managerial methods achieving such positive results in the most diverse places? Why are they becoming increasingly the rule and not the exception in work environments in both the private and public sectors? There are some very considerable factors why there is all this fuss about coaching and mentoring.

## Technology Gets More Technical Every Day

As previously noted, technological advancement is moving faster than a speeding bullet. This means that vital, in-demand job skills are constantly evolving, too, as a natural byproduct of these fast and furious advances in computer programming and other information technologies. Your technical proficiency today may well be obsolete tomorrow.

And then there's the darkest side yet to this technological evolution. Computers and machines are eliminating many jobs and performing many tasks formerly the sole province of the living and breathing. Yes, it's true.

## Mergers and Acquisitions

It seems that almost every minute of every day you hear about one business buying out another, or merging with another, to maximize their profitability. They accomplish this one-two punch by combining both their resources and know-how. Shareholders cheer, but this invariably leads to serious streamlining. That is, elimination of human resources—real people's jobs.

Delegating important job responsibilities is fundamental to good coaching. It's the best evidence there is that you believe in your employees' talents. It also means that you, the coach, are maximizing your resources—your people—while simultaneously maximizing the company's bottom line.

More and more public companies these days have more and more antsy investors needing constant reassurance that they are making the right and proper financial moves. Too often, shareholder pressure results in serious cost cutting. And you know what this means. Layoffs. Sweetening the bottom line frequently placates apprehensive investors but leaves a lot of men and women on the unemployment line. Coaching and mentoring methods reduce both the likelihood and magnitude of such job loss, as well as cushion the shock of it when it does occur.

Chapter 2

# Coaching and Mentoring: Art, Not Science

There are essential principles that make coaching and mentoring more of a managerial art form than a dry science. This chapter not only details what these principles are but also elaborates on why they are at the heart and soul of coaching and mentoring. From the significance of respect and trust in the workplace, to the emphasis on virtuous behaviors all around, to the establishment of ethical boundaries, coaching and mentoring in action is revealed here as the ultimate in leadership by example.

## Why Coaching Is Not Therapy

What some would call "psychobabble" is ubiquitous in countless quarters in today's society. So, it should come as no great shock to you that some people equate coaching and mentoring with corporate managers and consultants engaged in roles more suited for psychotherapists than business professionals. This misconception has coaches and mentors handling questions and dispensing counsel far removed from job-related concerns.

Coaches and mentors are not psychotherapists and should be careful not to venture down this analytical path. Even a management style that accentuates a highly personal approach should leave serious emotional and behavioral problems to those professionals specifically trained in handling them.

Well, if that's what you think coaching and mentoring on the business frontier is all about, it's time to disabuse yourself of the notion. Granted, coaching is not a paint-by-numbers, rigid style of managing. Far from it! And yes, it traverses the borders of traditional managing by appreciating individuals as unique personalities with unique abilities. That is, coaching and mentoring puts a high premium on interacting with employees on a one-to-one basis to maximize their potential both on and, by osmosis, off the job. Nevertheless, this plainly people-oriented managerial methodology is a far cry from managing with a therapy couch in the office.

## Good Coaches Produce Results

At the risk of sounding a tad snide here, one obvious difference between coaches in business and licensed therapists is that coaches have to produce results—or else. Even if they call themselves "coaches," managers who don't deliver the goods will be out of a job in a heartbeat. And with all due respect to the honorable profession of psychiatry, therapists do not have to realize any kind of quantifiable results to get paid for their services—and well paid at that. Patients can be in therapy for years—even decades—and still be struggling with the same issues. In business settings, however, success today is the key to success tomorrow and to the tomorrow after that. Be you a fossil manager or cutting-edge coach, you've got to get results in the here and now to ensure both a future for you and those who work for you.

Coaching and mentoring practices focus on self-development. And, coaches and mentors, too, are expected to be in a perpetual state of learning. As a coach, you should always be "coachable" and open to new possibilities. The best and the brightest coaches and mentors don't ever put a cork in their thirst to acquire more knowledge and new skills.

Keep in mind that coaching is results-oriented from the get-go. It is not some namby-pamby version of management. Coaching in management demands high performance and asks that you deliver it by fully unleashing your human resources. But, you ask, aren't all managerial approaches committed to such strong performance and getting the best possible productivity out of employees? The answer, of course, is "yes," but it's the avenues to those positive outcomes that put coaching and mentoring on a much higher plane. For instance, you can travel long distances in your car via the back roads in small towns, twisting and turning, encountering endless stoplights, getting lost, and eventually running out of gas. Or you can take the interstate. You'll get to your destination more swiftly using the interstate. You'll use less of that overpriced petrol, too. Consider coaching and mentoring as the interstates of managing—fast and focused on reaching the final destination.

## The Personal-Professional Life Connection

Coaching and mentoring are firmly committed to grappling with human behavior and understanding what motivates people, but they are decidedly not about getting employees' romantic lives in order, dealing with their eating disorders, forging close personal friendships, or any such intimate connections. Nonetheless, coaching and mentoring managerial methods fully accept that dissatisfaction in employees' personal lives directly impact their professional performances.

The managerial tools and techniques applied by coaches seek to increase employees' insight into what makes them tick. Coaching and mentoring methods endeavor to strengthen employees' personal wellness by making their job experiences more satisfying than they would otherwise be. Still, the coach or mentor always—without exception—operates within the parameters of the professional business environment. Performance on the job is job one.

## Coaching Is Being There

There's no getting around the fact that you will be judged by the overall performance of your employees and the results that they ultimately deliver. In the end, the buck stops on your desk. Coaching, and the delegating of the genuine responsibilities that come with the territory, doesn't amount to distancing yourself from the final results. Sorry, but it's the results that count— even in the halls of coaching and mentoring. To maximize these results, there are a few key things you should always "be" in your job role and vis-à-vis your relationship with your employees:

- **Be aware.** Be aware of precisely what you've got to accomplish and what you have to work with in both personnel and time constraints.
- **Be fair.** Be fair with your employees at all times, never losing sight of the fact that things don't always run as planned and that individuals are unique personalities who work at different paces and sometimes in very distinct ways.
- **Be there.** Be there for them in the work environment—from point A to point Z—of any office task or project.

## Virtue Matters Most: Respect Breeds Respect

If you've had the good fortune of working alongside a manager with indisputable integrity, you noticed it, appreciated it, and in all likelihood respected that individual. Respect breeds respect. And those whom you respect, you trust. When you place your trust in a manager, you generally want to please that individual. Respect and trust are the two best motivating factors in town. Conversely, if you've worked in an office or on a team run by a less than stellar soul, you've no doubt experienced the complete opposite feeling. When laboring for a manager whom you hold in utter contempt, there's no warm, fuzzy feeling in the air. Managers who are not respected by their employees invariably preside over offices rife with dissension and assembly-line personnel turnover.

## You Don't Have to Be Mother Teresa

This little discourse on virtue does not mean you, as a coach and manager of people, need be an ethical Mother Teresa to pass muster. Naturally, many managers have topsy-turvy personal lives for one reason or another. Indeed, we are all human beings walking around with our various faults and skeletons rattling around in our closets.

And, if you haven't noticed, very few folks are sporting halos. But the fact remains, morally bankrupt persons away from the job are not about to find their morals in desk drawers at the office. Shallow and insincere individuals, without the capacity to grasp the interior needs of their fellow human beings, always come up short and lack the necessary interpersonal skills required of good coaches and mentors.

## No Actors Need Apply

Granted, there are a lot of great actors on the business stage. There are men and women who can fool us all for a time by achieving positive results in their managerial roles. But in the long run, their acts invariably wear thin, and the real personalities must, sooner or later, show their faces. And when those faces resemble the gruesome Freddie Krueger, their managerial gigs are up.

The aforementioned character traits of dysfunctional managers make the case that respect and trust in workplace environments are absolutely crucial if employee satisfaction and company profits are to be maximized. And this cannot be stressed enough. The ethical standards that you establish as a coach—by both your words and deeds—set the overall tone for your employees. In the common parlance, it's known as leadership by example.

## The Managers from Hell

At some point, some of you may have worked for the dreaded "Manager from Hell." (And if you haven't yet, your day may well come.) Here's an illuminating case study of one such manager named Andy:

*Andy was a marketing whiz with an undeniable creative streak. He was charming and quite ambitious—a man destined to "go places," people said. And he did indeed go places. Andy was a very successful salesperson, a high-paid consultant, and finally a manager of a sales division with a large staff in a very big company. He fancied himself the right man for the job, properly schooled and highly experienced, who knew by heart all those managerial textbook bullets on how to get the most out of people. Andy could recite backwards and forwards all the conventional techniques to motivate people. And merely increasing his team's productivity wasn't Andy's only goal. Are you kidding? He desired increasing sales by leaps and bounds and smashing all kinds of company records. Andy viewed his managerial moment as a chance to get the biggest feather yet in his career cap.*

*Aside from his inflated opinion about himself and runaway hubris, the trouble with Andy was that his personal life was in total shambles. Andy conducted himself as the quintessential swinging bachelor, but was married with an infant son. His frenzied lifestyle dazzled his subordinates at first, most of whom were young and more or less in sync with him in letting the good times roll in the after hours. Gradually, though, Andy's personal indulgence severed the cord of trust between him and his staff. Ultimately, his employees perceived him as a man who looked out for number one only. On the occasions that his wife and child would come to the office, Andy would play the part of doting husband and father, while his staff looked on aghast, knowing full well their leader was insincere and downright disreputable.*

Your immediate reaction may be to condemn Andy for his personal life. However, the particulars of Andy's personal life are not a business concern. What is a business concern in this scenario is Andy's utter lack of discretion. His personal behavior led directly to a breakdown of respect and trust at the office, the two cornerstones of a manager-employee relationship, and predictably shattered his ability to effectively lead and get the positive outcomes that he so desperately wanted from his people. And when he didn't get all that he wanted, Andy lashed out at his team, blaming them entirely for their less-than-brilliant performances.

Maybe you've had the displeasure of working for an Andy type. If you have, it's a safe bet that the office atmosphere was absent of the respect and trust that is critical in any productive and healthy working environment. Without respect and trust emanating from the manager's office, you can, rest assured, predict there will be day-to-day bedlam with fast and furious turnover in the staff, until the day comes when the Andys themselves are turned over.

## Working Within an Ethical Framework

There is a flip side to this ethical coin. How do you as a coach confront the ethical conundrums that arise from the employee side of the office? And where exactly do you fix these moral and ethical boundaries? What can you, as a coach and a leader of men and women in a business setting, legitimately expect from your staff's on-the-job behaviors? What follows is a guiding framework for you to operate within, which should assist you in establishing such boundaries, and in walking that sometimes very fine line between respecting people for who and what they are and demanding that your employees respect what you are trying to accomplish in job performance.

As a coach, you are not required to manage as some sort of equalizer. You are not expected to parcel out your time on an equal basis. Some employees need more counsel and more of your time than do others. Recognizing who needs a little extra attention—and when it is needed—is an important part of a coach's job.

## The Three Ps and Values Versus Virtue

First and foremost, never lose sight of the three Ps of coaching and mentoring: people, performance, and positive outcomes. Give your employees as much latitude—responsibilities and challenges—as possible, but never cut them adrift. Pay careful attention to their every move! Keep a watchful eye on their individual progress in all job roles and office projects, while wholly accepting that specific talents and temperament vary widely from person to person.

Also, scrupulously differentiate between values and virtue. Very often these two words are used interchangeably, but they do not mean the same thing! You may have a completely different set of values than one of your employees. Respect that this gulf exists and that there's nothing you can do about it. But don't ever confuse values with virtue, which is something you must possess and insist that all of your employees likewise uphold. Virtue is integrity; it's honesty. Virtue on the job means, among many things, reliability. And employee reliability is what you need—always—to achieve positive outcomes. For instance, you may disapprove of how an employee on your staff disciplines her children away from the job. (You heard it in the gossip mill.) That's a completely different situation than the same employee covering up her mistakes in her job role with lies and distortions, or shifting the blame onto others.

## Make Your Expectations Realistic

Be certain you have realistic expectations for your employees on a personal basis. John may thrive in a pressure cooker. Melanie, on the other hand, may be productive in a more sanguine setting. Recognize and reward progress, not just results. By offering positive feedback along the way, you will ensure positive results.

As a coach, you've been given the imposing responsibility to shape a work environment to a great extent in your own image. And so it's your job—and duty—to forge a workplace with high morale and a highly motivated staff of people. This doesn't mean that you are a people pleaser come hell or high water. It's not part of your job description to give the office the feel and flavor of a Madonna concert. It is, however, your obligation as a coach to construct a work setting that's most conducive to heightened productivity.

### *Make Adjustments—But Never to Ethical Standards*

Impressive results more often than not come out of a contented, galvanized group of people. A bunch of malcontents is not ordinarily a very productive group (unless they're in a band or are comedy writers). So this may require that you, from time to time, make adjustments to various employee performance plans, and even some concessions on occasion to the disparate idiosyncrasies in your employees' personalities.

However—and this is a biggie—no adjustments or concessions should ever be made to the core ethical standards that you lay down. You must insist that each and every member of your team respect these ethical boundaries. And, of course, you yourself must painstakingly abide and live within them.

## *Your Place in the Observation Tower*

As a coach, you are cognizant of everything that goes on in the office environs. You both set the work agenda and challenge your team of employees to achieve lofty but realistic goals. You expect a lot out of them and you let them know precisely what it is. But you also expect a lot from yourself, and your employees appreciate this.

Coaching and mentoring are art forms because they are firmly rooted in something known as "enlightened scrutiny." That is, coaching in management is continually surveying and evaluating people and the results they can deliver when working in optimum environments.

As a coach, you let your workers know when they're doing things right. On the other hand, when things go awry, you take the culpable individuals aside and, in positive terms, show them the errors of their ways and how to avoid similar snafus down the road. This is managerial art in action.

# Chapter 3

# Motivating Employees: Easier Said Than Done

Like all other managerial approaches, coaching and mentoring must produce results. But as you may already know, working with people can be highly unpredictable. It is your job to make sure your employees stay motivated, and this task could mean a number of different things. This chapter explores the ways and means that coaching and mentoring employ to motivate employees. It reveals exactly how you can unleash members of your team to accomplish great things in an enlightened work setting.

## Being All That You and Your Employees Can Be

Motivation is a fashionable word today. In fact, it's a whole lot more than just a word; it's an industry unto itself. Turn on your TV set at any hour of day and you are sure to see someone peddling motivational books, cassettes, and DVDs. There are legions of people making serious profits "motivating" you to reach for the stars, or whatever you're supposed to be reaching for. But what are these self-proclaimed motivators actually doing?

First of all, what they are offering is a brand of "inspiration," not "motivation." There's a difference. They are endeavoring to inspire people to motivate themselves to do this, that, and the other thing. And the reality is that some folks are motivated to do things at the drop of a hat, while others are immovable objects rooted in one place. What this means is that it's entirely up to you to get motivated or not get motivated. You are the one who motivates you, not a coach or mentor at the office, or Tony Robbins on QVC.

In your own coaching efforts, you are not on the job to motivate your employees *per se*, but hopefully, to inspire them to motivate themselves. Essentially, your job as a coach is to apply a cattle prod—metaphorically speaking, that is—to the dormant motivation percolating in the hearts and souls of your people. What is this metaphorical cattle prod? What is it exactly that motivates workers to motivate themselves? Personal gain, such as improved financial circumstances, or better relationships, is the ultimate motivator. In other words, the possibility of an overall richer and more superior life will motivate men and women to do certain things to get there. These are the same broad reasons why so many people buy Tony Robbins's paraphernalia; and this is the all-important starting point for your coaching efforts to begin in inspiring your employees to motivate themselves.

**FACT**

Renowned football coach Lou Holz had an interesting view of self-motivation. He once said: "My task is not to motivate people to play great football. They are already motivated when they come to me. My challenge is simply not to de-motivate them."

Employees must accept the notion that their productivity on the job benefits them in uniquely personal ways; that their job performances—up to the hilt—will make their lives better on numerous fronts and in myriad ways. That is, in ways beyond the confines of the workplace and beyond, too, those weekly paychecks. Sure, many employees' self-motivation revolve around the Almighty Dollar. And this isn't some greedy capitalistic compulsion. It's merely the reality that money translates into so many wonderful things, not the least of which is the freedom to pursue interests and hobbies outside of work and career. Freedom from worry about mortgage payments, credit card bills, and health insurance premiums is a liberating sensation. Money makes the world go around.

## Inspiring Commitment

Before you aim that aforementioned cattle prod, pause and take a deep breath. You must aim it carefully or it will do more harm than good. You want to inspire your employees to bona fide commitment. And the only way to successfully realize this is by clearly enumerating the many personal benefits that will accrue to them when they do their jobs and do them well. You've got to make your team understand that these benefits are very real and immediate, and not some pie-in-the-sky-when-you-die mumbo jumbo. By shaping a work environment that fully taps into this natural human desire called self-interest, you've completed a very important first step. People want to better themselves. It's in their self-interest to do so. And remember that self-interest is not the same thing as selfishness. Rather, it's an integral slice of humanity, and it's what drives all of us to some extent (albeit some of us more than others).

### Put Yourself in Their Shoes

Foremost, you can inspire commitment to the job at hand by empathizing with your employees' self-interest. By closely working with them—as coaches must do—you effectively make the case that their personal goals (present and future) are in complete sync with the company's current goals and needs. As you might imagine, this is not always an easy case to make. Most men and women are justifiably skeptical of the notion that laboring in the salt mines to sweeten the profits of a big company is somehow essential to their personal and professional growth and development as human beings. And what about toiling for a bureaucracy? Obviously, this natural cynicism makes going all out for the company or government agency difficult and sometimes nearly impossible.

Coaches do not motivate their staff; they inspire them to motivate themselves. This is best accomplished by allowing employees to see clearly where they stand in the organization versus where they want to be in their careers. That is, what are their self-interests versus what the company can offer them?

If, however, you paint an honest picture of the reality—with no hype and false promises—you can nicely illustrate just how and why your employees personally benefit by motivating themselves to deliver the goods in the here and now. And when you as a coach succeed in this admittedly thorny area by inspiring your team to give it their all, you've accomplished something that you can take a great deal of pride in. You've succeeded in moving people to move themselves—and that's the most intricate and difficult task facing any manager, regardless of the managerial playbook being utilized. It is, however, a task that coaching welcomes with open arms.

Knowing the difference between being assertive and being aggressive is fundamental to good coaching. You should be assertive in dealing with your staff. This means confronting problems at the source and continually communicating with those in your employ. On the other hand, aggressive, in-your-face managing is highly counterproductive.

Creating a work climate that's both enlightening and employee friendly inspires commitment on your part. You need not promote a "don't worry, be happy" office climate. Coaching and mentoring requires only that you make your individual employees feel they are part of a team effort. Simultaneously, you want to make your people feel that what they're doing in the here and now is important in the long-term scheme of things, including to each and every one of their individual futures.

## Remember What Motivates Employees

There are many motivational tools at your disposal that you can use to encourage your employees to self-motivate. As a coach and a manager of men and women, you are afforded countless ways to reward your people for jobs well done and spur them on to further productivity. Here are just some of the available possibilities:

- Pay raises
- Bonuses
- Stock options
- Promotions
- Positive performance reviews
- Positive feedback
- Paid holiday or added vacation time
- Opportunities to travel (for the company)
- Increases in job responsibilities and challenges
- Equipment upgrade (laptop computer, cell phone, and so on)
- Gifts (for personal pleasure ranging from dinner to a timepiece)
- Educational training (advanced degree)
- Mentoring
- Telecommuting (work from home options)
- Public commendation (via company newsletter, award, and so on)

When you make yourself aware of what drives employees you can work with them to achieve your common goals.

## The Importance of Performance Planning

Coaches work with performance plans or work plans to keep their employees motivated. They operate with such plans in place for each and every one of their team members. Performance planning is often what separates successful coaches from their less fortunate brethren, the dinosaur managers living in the corporate equivalents of Jurassic Park.

**How much time should performance plans cover?**
A performance plan can span one, two, even ten years. But realistically, it's best to keep such plans under six months. Longer periods of time tend to make such plans lose their precision and focus. Metaphorically speaking, performance plans should be lean, mean, and deliver the green.

## Goal Posts

The first phase of a performance plan consists of goals, sometimes referred to as objectives. It's important that you work closely with your employees in getting their input into the various performance-related goals that get performance plans off and running. Next, in concert with your people again, you fix target dates for reaching these goals and establish the time parameters of the plans. Throughout the unfolding of any and all performance plans, your staff should be fully in the loop. Under your careful supervision, they should co-author their individual performance plans and, of course, be largely responsible for seeing them through to successful conclusions.

**FACT**

The goals or objectives in a performance plan are very simply what you—the coach—expect your employees to accomplish. As a coach, you arrive at these goals in one-on-one consultations with your staff members. The goals should be both clear and realistic.

Each member of your team can simultaneously work with several performance plans (no more than six at a time is a good rule of thumb), covering the full range of his or her jobs and responsibilities. And individual performance plans, inaugurated with reasonable goals, should span time periods that don't take you and your employee into the world of *The Jetsons*. Intricate planning too far into the future often results in fuzziness and a loss of clarity, something all coaches want to avoid like the plague.

## Standards of Performance

The standards of performance—the quality bars that you set—are your next consideration to insert in performance plans. Standards, for short, are essentially the meat on the bone of the goals, establishing expectations for the quality of the results and overall performance in achieving each goal. Depending on the nature of the job or project, this could mean upgrading customer service to a particular level, meeting specified sales targets, product upgrades, and so on.

Performance plans are part of the arsenal of every good coach. You work with these plans, which are comprehensive road maps designed for each one of your employees, specifically detailing what they are expected to do. Performance plans are collaborative efforts made by you in concert with your individual team members.

This brand of thorough planning stands in unmistakable contrast to the management methods that operate one day at a time without an eye on tomorrow, let alone 30, 90, or 180 days into the future. "One day at a time" works wonders in self-help programs, but it amounts to poor business planning, especially where foresight is an essential ingredient, and particularly in this fast-paced, technologically advanced world.

## *Seeing the Plans Through*

Setting goals and standards are merely the first pieces of the performance plan puzzle. Once you've fixed the goals and a standard of performance that you expect each and every one of your employees to execute in reaching the goals, it's time for you to get down to the specifics of how exactly all of this is going to come to pass.

### *Action Plans*

Action plans are the next hurdle that you, along with your staff, must leap over. Think of action plans as akin to gasoline in a car. Let's say, for example, that you've built a snappy-looking, powerful automobile with all the necessities and extras to not only "burn rubber," but to do so in stylish comfort. Even the best-quality and fanciest cars in existence are useless (other than as museum pieces) without the fuel to put them in motion. And so it is with goals and the standards to reach them. As a coach, you could have the most laudable and far-reaching goals in place for your employees. You could couple them with the most rigorous of standards. But that and two bucks will get you a ride on the New York City subway these days. So, what you need to do next, in close concert with your employees, is develop action plans to grease the skids of the goals and standards in each performance plan. These are, in essence, the plans within the plans—the energy source of performance plans.

**FACT**

Action plans are the meat and potatoes of performance plans, and document the specific ways that tasks and jobs get done. If a goal in a performance plan is to cut costs in a particular area, action plans specify the step-by-step methods on just how and when this is going to be accomplished.

Essentially, action plans are crisp and clearly defined directions—A to Z—detailing precisely how the desired goals are going to be reached, and what physical efforts (actions) are expected from team members in getting there. Action plans, in effect, summarize why employees are hired in the first place. They indicate what people do on the job. Nobody is left in the dark with action plans. Everybody knows what they are expected to accomplish, in what time frame, and how they are going to execute their prescribed duties. There's no room for guesswork.

## Measuring Sticks

Lastly, in a thorough performance plan replete with clear goals, standards, and precise action plans (there could be several for each goal), there must be measures in place to check the quality of the results. It's one thing to cast your fate to the wind. It's quite another thing to cast your employees' performance plans to the wind and hope that everything comes out exactly as planned. Plans without regular checkups are like English muffins without toasting. They just don't happen. Appropriate measures must be in place from the beginning to the end of all performance plans. While affording your staff great autonomy, you must nevertheless monitor the progress of each one of your employees' performance plans.

When President Ronald Reagan signed historic arms control accords with Russian President Mikhail Gorbachev in the late 1980s, he was asked how he—a staunch anti-Communist—could sign on to a deal of such breathtaking proportions and importance with an undemocratic nation and totalitarian form of government. Reagan quoted the Russian proverb, "Trust but verify." Translation: Show good faith and accept at face value that a former foe (in this instance) could be trusted. But continually verify that the agreed-upon arms control reductions are actually taking place when they are scheduled to take place.

You must likewise show trust in your employees, but you must also, on a recurring basis, verify that they are doing exactly what was mutually agreed upon at the onset of their performance plans. You must verify that all concerned are in fact reaching their targets—in terms of time and quality—on the way to achieving their ultimate goals. Measures inserted in performance plans as checkpoints are not the equivalent of showing a lack of faith in your team. On the contrary. As professionals in the private or public sectors, men and women must come to expect continual measurement of their performances and be held strictly accountable for their work efforts.

# Measuring Performance

What are some of the performance plan measuring tools available to you? There are many, so feel free to use any and all of these measures as appropriate. What follows are some of the popular ones:

- Numbers
- Timelines
- Physical products
- Reports
- Audits
- Feedback

## Money and Time

There are no better measures than unvarnished numbers. Sales figures, cost reductions, and the like are prime examples of data that can be easily measured at any point in a maturing performance plan to assist you in getting a fix on how things are going and whether or not targets are being met, and so on. Follow the money.

Another measure utilized in many performance plans revolves around timelines. Because these types of plans are generally conceived within defined time parameters and specific performance goals, it is imperative to regularly measure results at agreed-upon junctures to see whether or not the plan is meeting expectations or coming up short. Time waits for no man or woman—especially in the workplace.

## The Five Senses and Paper Trail

In some performance plans, depending on the industry or particular department in the company, there are physical byproducts, i.e., samples, which can be regularly measured. For instance, a product developmental performance plan will showcase something that you can see and maybe even hear, smell, touch, and taste. An ice cream flavor under development would be something worthy of a taste or two along the way.

Old reliable paperwork on the status of the performance plan is always a plus. Written records—even though they are mostly on computers today—haven't lost their importance. A coach needs to be fully apprised of what's happening every step of the way, and written records of all that's going on provide a beneficial paper trail as the plan unfolds. In particular areas of business operation, such as finance, audits are practical measures. Audits are also used to perform quality checks.

### The People Have Spoken

What are people saying? Many performance plans involve directly servicing customers. So who better than the customers to talk to in these instances! They are the ultimate fonts of information on the success or failure of plans involving their satisfaction. And just as with old reliable reports and the written word, there's another measure that can't be beat—observation. Depending on the exact nature of the performance plans, there may be an opportunity to watch employees in action (selling, communicating, and so on). There's really no substitute for seeing with your own eyes and hearing with your own ears whether they are meeting their goals and living up to the agreed-upon quality standards.

## By the Employee, for the Employee

A successful performance plan is a thing of beauty. In order for a plan to reach this awe-inspiring level, however, it has to be a blueprint in large part drafted by the employee for the employee—with, of course, your wise and overseeing counsel and final imprimatur. The traditional manager-employee doctrine more or less says that the manager is the boss—end of story. And that the boss is the one who tells employees what to do—period. Employees do what they are told to do, or they are shown the door. Performance planning is the province of the bosses, and the "little people," mere employees, are never "in on" this fundamental decision making. Coaching torpedoes this anachronistic way of conducting business by fully bringing employees into the important decisions that will most affect their jobs.

To a great extent, employees are asked to craft their own performance plans. And courtesy of this forward-thinking approach to managing, employees, in reality, "own" their performance plans. They own their jobs. After all, who knows better what you can do than you? The dinosaur managers, who dole out orders from their imperious pedestals, and permit little if any employee input into their planning and decision making, naturally foster more resentment than commitment from their staff. Employees who aren't consulted on their jobs and project assignments often feel that expectations for their performance are unreasonable or even far-fetched. And this sometimes means too little work and too few responsibilities. Because commitment is so primary to winning coaching efforts, you cannot bypass your employees in any planning process that involves their participation. A coach understands completely that in order to expect employees to share in a sense of accomplishment on the job, they must be more than mere pawns on a chessboard.

A key tenet in coaching is collaboration between the coach and the employee. Successful coaching includes showing confidence in your employees by delegating responsibilities and challenging them to be self-sufficient. However, this doesn't mean—by any stretch of the imagination—that you make important decisions by consensus.

Keep in mind, too, that performance plan preparation should always be consummated in one-on-one meetings with your employees. Employees should be given advance notice of when these meetings will occur, and what will be expected of them. This gives them ample opportunity to come ready and armed to author their own performance plans. Performance plans are contracts with clearly defined goals, and so they should be written down and not treated like handshakes. Performance objectives should be verbalized in only a sentence or two because they need to be readily understood. Leave nothing to chance and the results will be positive.

You must feel comfortable that your employees know their specific job responsibilities, as well as the deadlines in their performance plans. This meeting of the minds between coaches and team members inevitably leads to more focus by all the players involved. Everybody understands their roles, feels part of the entire process, and works in a genuine team effort. Focus is the forerunner of success.

## Chapter 4

# Mentoring 101

Although people repeatedly pair the words "coaching" and "mentoring" to describe a particular managerial methodology, coaches and mentors are not one and the same. This chapter differentiates between the two and then takes an especially close look at mentors and the valuable roles they play in countless environments and situations in both the private and public sectors.

4

# The Difference: Coaching Versus Mentoring

Some words in our lexicon are overused, misused, and applied to this, that, and the other thing. After a while, the words get so muddled that they lose their original meaning and preciseness. And this has happened to the term "coach," and likewise to the term "mentor," which are often confused in some circles as identical twins. However, these descriptive appellations do not mean one and the same thing, even though they are often used interchangeably. And to make matters worse, the words "coach" and "coaching" have been bandied about with such frequency of late that the significance of the title "coach," and the practices of "coaching," have gotten twisted beyond recognition, too. So what exactly is the difference between the words "coach" and "mentor"? This is the gray area where the greatest confusion exists. Explaining the difference between "coaching" and "mentoring" is the most appropriate place to get started in sorting out this mess. Throughout this book, coaches are regularly referred to as managers on the business frontlines. Indeed, there are increasing numbers of men and women who manage people not as "managers" anymore but "coaches." But there are also many independent "coaching consultants," or external coaches, brought into companies from the outside. Chapter 5 will arm you with a mother lode of details on this valuable auxiliary aspect of coaching.

**QUESTION?**

**Is coaching the same as mentoring?**
Although there are many similarities and intersecting methodologies, they are not identical. Actually, one of the skill sets within coaching is mentoring. Many coaches are also mentors to their employees. Generally speaking, mentoring is a more informal and open-ended relationship than is coaching.

Coaches in managerial roles employ coaching applications that revolve around setting goals and establishing comprehensive performance plans for their employees—with, and this is key, their individual staff members an integral part of the whole enchilada. This process was covered in detail in Chapter 3. In other words, coaches work in close cooperation with their people—on a one-on-one basis—to cultivate healthy and productive work environments. They endeavor to forge breeding grounds for the expansion of knowledge and multiplying of skills. By venturing down this constructive route, coaches strive to increase employee job satisfaction, overall efficiency in the office, and—of course—the company's bottom line. Coaching is nothing if not results-oriented.

A coach can also be a mentor—and often is. This is why the duo of coaching and mentoring often stand side by side in book titles (like this one), in management seminars, and in training video workshops. This is also why there is so much confusion. The terms are inextricably linked and for very good reasons. Both coaches and mentors are bound by a common desire to enlarge human possibilities by judiciously guiding people and encouraging them to better themselves in atmospheres of ongoing learning. Both coaches and mentors work intimately with individuals. Dinosaur managers do no such things.

There are many differences between coaches and mentors. The most overt distinction is that, in most instances, coaching is a paying job—be it internal or external—whereas mentoring is a voluntary setup. Mentoring relationships regularly exist informally on the business scene, and are not specific, full-time job roles.

If, however, you delve a little deeper, you see that mentoring is quite distinct from coaching in some of its practices. And when mentoring stands on its own two legs, as it often does, it is hardly a carbon copy of coaching. The rest of this chapter discusses mentoring as a distinct entity and furnishes you with indispensable tips on how to mentor like a—well—proficient mentor.

## *Mentors: Powers of Example*

What's the first thing that springs to mind when the subject of mentoring is broached? What kinds of images careen through your cranium? An Ancient

Greek pontificating in the Parthenon? Perhaps a fortunate adult offering hope and succor to an at-risk young person? A wise elder passing on his learned lessons to a wide-eyed understudy, maybe? Or possibly, a trusted and experienced senior executive in the corporate world sitting down with a young and ambitious cub manager? These images of mentors and mentees (those who are mentored) are all accurate portrayals and attest to mentoring's vaunted history, as well as potent present. Mentoring is part of the human condition and always will be. In the modern-day corporate realm, the mentoring tradition is not only alive but well and welcomed. Mentoring complements coaching with an informality that works like a charm in the more formal business atmosphere of goals, plans, measures, performance reviews, and the like.

A mentor performs the role of prudent counselor, dispensing advice on career paths, and offers beneficial problem-solving hints on the more immediate matters of the work at hand. Mentors base their instruction on their real-life experiences. Essentially, the mentor points the mentee, a.k.a. protégé, in the right direction regarding opportunities within the company. Ideally, a mentor is one level (or two or three) above the mentee in the organizational hierarchy.

Encourage brainstorming in all your coaching and mentoring efforts. Brainstorming sessions between coach-employee and mentor-mentee are often quite productive. Nothing should be held back when brainstorming, because there are no bad ideas in these informal settings, only great possibilities.

## *Mentors Can Boost You Up the Corporate Ladder*

Foremost, a mentor must be in a solid position to offer direction on the ways and means of getting ahead in the company and in the corporate world in general. "Movin' on up!" in the fine tradition of sitcom character George Jefferson is often what a mentor means to a mentee. Moving on up not only in job title, or pay and perks, but in personal growth and human development as well. Mentors aim to broaden their mentees' job skills, overall worldviews, and understanding of human nature.

Learning how to overcome obstacles is the most important lesson mentors can pass on to their mentees. Mentors withdraw from their own experience banks examples of how they confronted similar obstacles in their career paths. Thus, they show their mentees what worked and what didn't work for them. And these very real situations carry far greater weight than do theoretical textbook accounts of comparable subject matter.

When you succeed in overcoming obstacles in your path, and learn to deal with the predictable bumps in the managerial road, you've learned the most valuable lesson in the workplace—and in life itself for that matter. Successfully attacking the obstacles in your way with ever-increasing self-assurance puts you on the career fast track. For there are few managerial skills more valued than levelheaded problem solving. Getting a handle on tough situations—without flying off the handle—is what separates the men from the boys—and women from the girls—on the managerial scales. By showcasing your ability to beat back obstacles in a professional manner, you reward the faith the company placed in you by giving you a mentor, or making you a mentor, in the first place.

## Mentors Have Impeccable Credibility

Needless to say, mentors must be individuals of impeccable credibility and their advice must always ring true. Mentees have to be able to implicitly trust their mentors. Mentors cannot be perceived as hot-air balloons who love the sound of their own voices more than anything else in the world.

When you're mentoring someone, understand that you'll be looked upon as a vast treasury of knowledge with keen insight on the ways of the business world and maybe even the world in general. A veritable Wizard of Oz. Don't let it go to your head. The best mentors in the business world understand their limitations and accept their need to always learn and improve their skills. And if you're always learning, you can't possibly know it all—can you?

Let's return to the Wizard of Oz analogy for a moment. As a mentor, do you want to be perceived as a person with heart, brains, and courage to spare? Of course you do. But just remember who the Wizard of Oz was.

He was something of a fraud, cloaking himself behind a curtain and creating a big-screen illusion of power, fear, and all-knowing wisdom. And that's precisely what you don't want to do. Because, as in *The Wizard of Oz*, your act will eventually be uncovered, just as Dorothy, with the help of tiny Toto, unmasked the ersatz wizard, who, it turned out, was a rather pathetic, mousy old man.

As a mentor, you must always be grounded in reality and carry yourself with some semblance of humility. An overbearing manner in any mentoring relationship is a surefire ticket to failure.

**FACT**

There are many best-selling books (often anthologies of inspirational stories) that are meant to inspire their readership in some way, shape, or form. Likewise, mentors' successes in the business environs can be appreciated if they have inspired others to reach bigger and brighter plateaus. A good mentor is a good teacher.

You have to establish a mutual respect and trust with your mentee. Your tutelage will be welcomed and listened to by your mentee, without any hesitation or dispute whatsoever, if you cultivate an easy rapport, which is essential in any mentor-mentee alliance, just as it is in any other positive human relationship.

Mentors must, of course, back up all their sage counsel with resumes of past achievements. They must showcase rich and diverse work experiences. Also, they must be capable of recounting their stories of, say, having made the move from a claustrophobic mail room to a sprawling office on the forty-first floor with windows overlooking lush Central Park (something a little less dramatic will suffice).

And you never know—you could well find yourself mentoring someone a peg or two below you, while simultaneously receiving guidance from a higher-up (that senior executive in that dreamy office). After all, many mentors are also mentees.

# *The Mentee: A Star Is Born*

The mentoring role is generally conferred upon the rising stars in a company, and not every Joe or Jane who comes down the personnel pike. Senior management chums the office high seas for the senior managers of tomorrow. Middle managers perpetually hunt for tomorrow's middle managers. And so it goes. For the wisest managers acknowledge that nobody lives forever, not even the biggest of big-shot executives in the business world. In fact, part of all good managers' job responsibilities is locating diamonds in the rough. Finding and keeping (for as long as is feasible) good men and women with solid skills and a desire to learn and better themselves is what makes coaching run smoothly and effectively over the long haul. A good coach is always on the lookout for employees willing to take on new responsibilities and bigger challenges—i.e, for individuals who exhibit a penchant for self-motivation and self-sufficiency. And mentoring fits neatly into this picture of preparing good people today for tomorrow's new and imposing challenges.

Rising stars in business always need an objective ear. Mentors are those objective ears. They are not meant to be obsequious cheerleaders for their mentees, telling them only what they want to hear. There's no such thing as a sycophantic mentor.

Utilize your life story and myriad experiences as a backdrop in your mentoring activities, but don't ever ask that your mentee be a carbon copy of you. Your mentee is a unique individual with unique talents who needs to follow a unique course in life. Remember that you're not out to create a Mini-Me.

Mentors fully grasp the fundamentals of the company they work for, as well as the overall business picture because they've "been there and done that." They assist their mentees in wading through all of those thorny job-related situations and transforming the inevitable work lemons into the most refreshing pitchers of opportunity lemonade imaginable. Mentors enrich their mentees' knowledge base by always answering their questions and giving them feedback on their job performance. Mentors are readily available to their mentees, to help them solve the unavoidable problems encountered while working with real people with real personalities in a real work environment. Mentoring is the real thing and not a detached textbook lesson or lifeless lecture delivered to sleepy eyes.

## Mentoring Do's and Don'ts

Whether you have or haven't had a mentor to assist you in your rise to your present position is not the decisive factor in determining whether you can mentor another person effectively. Obviously, having had a trusted mentor who helped you grow and develop as manager material and as a human being is a net plus. You then have a role model to pattern your style of mentoring after. But, regardless, there are certain approaches to mentoring that all successful mentors practice and, equally important, don't practice.

### A Mentor Is Not a Greyhound Bus

The longstanding Greyhound Bus advertising slogan is "Leave the Driving to Us." A mentor's slogan must never be "Leave the Decision Making to Me." You should never make decisions for your mentee.

A mentor always exercises the power of suggestion. That is, wise mentors offer up platefuls of suggestions to their mentees. They pose alternatives; but they refrain, as much as humanly possible, from telling their mentees exactly what to do.

Your counsel to the mentee is designed to fill in the blanks—to provide the mentee with options and more options—but the mentee must always make his or her own decisions. Mentors strive to make their mentees' ultimate decisions as informed and reasoned as possible. One of the overriding themes in all coaching and mentoring applications is the watertight objective to help people help themselves.

## Know When to Say When

As a mentor, you must recognize that your guidance is most appreciated when it's specifically requested. This is not to suggest that you, as mentor, sit idly by like Marcel Marceau or Dr. Evil's pint-sized clone. No, your role is not to sit in silence or to utter a grunt of acknowledgement every now and then.

Nevertheless, dispensing specific advice to your mentee vis-à-vis his job responsibilities should be held back until he asks you for said advice. As much as possible, refrain from "let me tell you what to do" kinds of instructions. People are funny that way. In many self-help programs, for instance, it is practically written in stone that continually imploring—nagging, as it were—an abuser to shed an addiction is counterproductive. Overcoming an addiction is a very personal journey. It's a difficult pathway to start down, but it always begins with recognition and acceptance by the individual that his or her life is spiraling out of control. The same reasoning applies to the mentor-mentee relationship. Unsolicited advice on an unremitting basis will inevitably clog the ear of the mentee, who will eventually come to automatically disregard everything that you've got to say.

## The Dialogue

In every successful mentor-mentee relationship, there is a dialogue. Leave the monologues to Leno, Letterman, and Stewart. This dialogue should be the rule. It should be relaxed, candid, and unconfrontational.

Mentoring is all about sharing experiences. Mentors impart the multiple lessons that they've learned to their mentees and help them better navigate the rough seas of their own careers. By absorbing these lessons—including both the mentors' mistakes and successes—mentees are better prepared to move forward with knowledge and confidence.

As a mentor, you are not a college professor delivering a lecture in an auditorium-sized classroom, with your mentee sitting around taking notes that she will have to memorize for a final exam. This is meant to be a one-on-one relationship with a robust give-and-take. It's a two-way street from start to finish.

### Timesharing

To further expand on the importance of real dialogue in a mentor-mentee relationship, let's touch upon the notion of intimacy. It's been said that the mentor-mentee relationship is an "intimate" one. And it is.

But please get your mind out of the gutter—it's not that degree of intimacy. A firm handshake should be the extent of physical contact between the mentor and mentee. More to the point, an intimate mentor-mentee relationship necessitates genuine sharing of insights, observations, and suggestions. This give-and-take dialogue should be entirely uninhibited.

## The Mentoring Model

If you fancy yourself a gourmet chef and know your way around the kitchen, then you know that cooking is an art form—not too far removed from coaching and mentoring. Okay, that's a bit of a stretch. But you guessed it: An analogy (yes, another one!) is on its way. This is an analogy between preparing a succulent repast and laying the groundwork for a scrumptious model of successful mentoring.

Unless you use cult inventor Ron Popeil's "Set it and forget it" Showtime Rotisserie Oven, cooking is more involved and demands that you pay close attention to what you are doing at all times. It matters what kinds of ingredients you use, how much of them you use, and when you use them. It matters what you cook in and what you cook on. It matters how high a heat you use, when you choose to stir, flip things over, and so on. Get the picture? True gourmets, just like mentors, have a lot more in their pots than mere ingredients. Figuratively speaking, they put themselves in their pots. Give the same recipe to two people and look at the final product. Oftentimes the differences are startling. And the same applies to mentoring basics. This book, and others on the subject, can provide all sorts of direction on the particulars of proper mentoring, but it all boils down to the individual players and what they do with the materials.

**ALERT!**

A solid mentor-mentee relationship is rooted in trust. A mentor is aware of this important bond and is constantly on guard to maintain this trust. A mentor knows that the foundation of trust can take many months to build, but only a nano-second to destroy. Ditto for coaches.

That said, this section gives you a simple recipe for mentoring—a model. And as with all recipes, it's what you do with these ingredients that will govern the results. Your character and approach to mentoring will determine whether you get a moist and mouthwatering pineapple upside-down cake (a mentee who is better for having had your tutoring), or a gooey pool of flour, milk, and eggs (a mentee who is no better off than when he or she first met you).

The four chief mentor-mentee ingredients are:

- Trust
- Time
- Dialogue
- Sharing

Trust has to be established from the beginning of the relationship. Once this firm bond is secured, the mentor must be freely available to the mentee. None of this "Don't call us, we'll call you" kind of stuff. The relationship must then be rooted in a rich dialogue between the mentor and the mentee. The overall atmosphere should be one of sharing—and caring, too. Information should be freely and regularly exchanged. When these four elements are put in the mix and properly executed, both parties reap the benefits of a lively, insightful relationship. Most important, mentees are stimulated to grow and develop their knowledge and skills so they can overcome obstacles, make deliberate and more informed decisions, and improve their understanding of and empathy for coworkers and people in general.

## From Mentee to Mentor

If you've been among the select few who've been assigned a mentor at some point in your career development, you've been, in effect, groomed for bigger and better things. You then may have been asked—or will be asked in the future—to mentor an employee below you in the organizational hierarchy. Mentoring at various levels in an organization is a forward-thinking approach to managing and increasingly commonplace in the corporate world. The benefits of furnishing such tutors throughout an organization—from top to bottom—are demonstrably positive. Because of the knowledge transfer and perpetual sharing of ideas and observations, mentees are positioned to adapt more readily to the fast-paced changes in the organization and the overall business environment. It's a win-win situation for all involved.

# Chapter 5

# Using External Coaches to Your Advantage

This chapter examines the increasingly important roles that coaches hired from the outside world play in today's work environments. Running the gamut from experienced trainers who conduct seminars to hands-on consultants who troubleshoot specific problems, improve particular skills, and adapt personnel to new roles, a wide variety of external coaching options will be explored here.

# Why Some Companies Look Outside for Coaching

You might need a little outside help? It's nothing to be embarrassed or ashamed about. There are very sound reasons why, on occasion, businesses venture outside for assistance in the area of coaching and mentoring. They include:

- Skills upgrading
- Lessons in professionalism
- Career development
- Trust issues
- Managerial sea changes

## Technology and Its Demanding Nature

Courtesy of advances in technology, altogether new and improved skills are needed to fill countless jobs in the workplace. The skills demanded yesterday are not the same as the skills demanded today. And, guaranteed, tomorrow's technology will require a whole new level of work-related skills to get the job done and to optimally run the show. What this all means is that companies are sometimes compelled to hire external coaches who can acclimate their workforce to the essential skills needed to remain competitive.

**QUESTION?**

**Can anybody be a coaching consultant?**
Today, anybody can place an ad in the yellow pages advertising his or her services as a "coach." No special education or accrediting is necessary. However, calling oneself a coach and being a competent one are two entirely different animals. Before getting any work, you are going to have to show prospective clients what you can deliver.

External coaches also play significant roles in tutoring managers and employees alike on the right and proper behaviors in the workplace. Among many things, knowing how to behave is indispensable for career advancement. This may sound like third-grade stuff, but it's a monumental problem in the labor force as a whole. That is, the modern-day educational system is graduating a lot of students who, besides not being able to read and write up to snuff, do not know how to deport themselves as professionals in work settings. (For a full discussion on the ABCs of workplace professionalism, see Chapter 10.)

The retail and service sectors of the economy expose this reality for all to see. For instance, you walk into some stores and are treated like the Invisible Man or the Invisible Woman. You're ignored and viewed as a veritable intruder. Where are the managers in these noxious work environments, you ask? The managers are right there, actively participating in the inappropriate behaviors. Indeed, coaching and mentoring's next conquest is the retail and service sectors of the economy. (A complete overview of this groundbreaking subject matter can be found in Chapter 19.)

External coaches are regularly brought into companies to deal with complex relationship problems. An example of one such multilayered people problem revolves around the challenges facing newly promoted employees in managerial roles. That is, fledgling managers now lording over subordinates who were, only a snapshot in time ago, their peers and pals.

## Career Paths and Matters of Trust

External coaches sometimes serve as sounding boards and advisors for career development, providing help to the manager or employee being groomed for a new job and new set of challenges. An example of this is a coach hired to counsel and train a promoted employee who finds himself in the role of boss presiding over a coven of his *former* coworkers. This is not always an easy adjustment to make.

"Our people are our greatest asset." So that's the cause of all that laughter emanating from the lunchroom of Company XYZ. The employees there have just been handed the company's Mission Statement. In your career travels, you may have encountered this rather cloying sentiment in an annual report or company newsletter. It has become something of a corporate cliché. And, because it's not intended to get laughs, it's not very funny. A company that makes use of this "our people are our greatest asset" motto and doesn't really mean it has a serious problem on its hands.

**FACT**

In 1964, Yogi Berra took the helm as New York Yankees manager. He simultaneously retired from the game, finding himself boss of a roster of former teammates. Despite Berra winning the American League pennant that year, he was unceremoniously dumped after the season. He was not, it seems, accepted and respected in his new job role.

The best and brightest in the labor pool gravitate to the companies that genuinely believe in providing their employees with more on-the-job responsibilities, challenges, and opportunities for genuine advancement. In other words, places that truly view employees as their "greatest assets." On the other hand, companies that spout empty platitudes and offer vague promises won't attract the best and brightest to their doors. There's nothing more depressing than a work environment where employees know beyond a shadow of a doubt that they're being used and abused for one purpose only—to get the most work out of them for the least amount of compensation. People don't want to feel that they are as expendable as yesterday's news.

Coaching and mentoring embody the antithesis of this dog-eat-dog management philosophy. This managerial methodology aims to build commitment in employees from the ground up. It seeks to enhance employees' skills by furnishing them atmospheres of perpetual learning that are replete with responsibilities and challenges worthy of their personalities and unique talents. But the reality is that companies who sincerely desire such enlightened workplaces may, in fact, require outside help in letting employees know that they're serious about making people their greatest assets.

## Managerial Changes

External coaches are also brought into companies that are in dire need of a change in managerial attitudes and approaches in leadership. Often these outside coaches work with line managers, team leaders, supervisors, and fresh managerial talents, to tutor them in the ways of coaching and mentoring—ways that are both satisfying to employees and pleasing to the company's bottom line.

If you, in any managerial position, require assistance in making the transition from directive-style managing to coaching, an external coach is something worth considering. Keep your eyes and ears open at seminars and conferences for these outside coaching specialists. Look for the right fit. Not all external consultants are created equal. These professionals have different specialties and methods, and get different results, too.

The typical manager of today, as well as the manager of tomorrow, does not possess coaching and mentoring DNA. It's not something you are born with. Nevertheless, a one-on-one coaching education can perform miracles in schooling self-motivated managers and others on the procedures of coaching and mentoring. And what this means is on-the-job training—not sterile classroom lessons—where real results can be observed, discussed, and fine-tuned.

If you need an external coach to supplement your own coaching efforts, check out the human resources department in your own company for possible leads. Look into seminars, professional organizations that are dedicated to training coaches, and the various publications in the field of coaching and mentoring.

There are plenty of conferences, seminars, and workshops that teach coaching and mentoring tools and techniques, including the "secrets" to managing as a coach and behaving as a trusted mentor. In addition, there are comprehensive training videos readily available that offer up hours upon hours of instruction, which you can watch at your leisure in the comfort of your home, if that's what your heart desires.

No matter how you look at it, though, coaching and mentoring, whether internal or external in nature, are all about uplifting employee performance. In whatever guise, the mission is to overhaul the structure and culture of the workplace. Coaching and mentoring ask always for positive and consistent communication between managers and employees. As a matter of fact—and you may have personally experienced this in performance planning—coaching and mentoring bring employees into the heart of the business operation by making them an essential part of it. Employees are coached not to be mere clock punchers, but, rather, to fly metaphorical missions—missions that improve their lives by making their job roles both meaningful and satisfying. Linking today's job with tomorrow's job, and the job after that, is what rock-solid coaching and mentoring accomplish. Linking job satisfaction with life satisfaction is also what rock-solid coaching and mentoring accomplish.

## Are You Secure Enough to Ask for Help?

Are you ready to bring a coach in from the outside? External coaches brought into companies to rectify particular shortcomings, or teach new skills, are increasingly working alongside internal coaches these days. That is, coaches themselves are going outside their own companies and looking for specialist help. Even the best coaches sometimes find themselves confronted with particular problems that are beyond their expertise, or, perhaps, they don't have the time to address. There are only so many hours in a day and so many days in a week. And depending on the size of the staff and the results that are expected, even a coach may, on occasion, need a helping hand. A supplementary coach from the outside world—an expert at a task desperately needed—might be just what the doctor ordered.

As a manager and coach, you may be a bit hesitant in bringing in help from an outside source. This is understandable. It's human nature for managers to desire control of their staffs and their job responsibilities.

Managers—even those wearing the coveted "coaching" label—are, after all, judged by the results their employees deliver, just as all other managers.

**FACT**

External coaches charge their corporate clients $200 to $300 per hour for their services. Some charge as much as $500 per hour! There are some business coaches earning more than psychologists and psychiatrists. In other words, coaching is a highly valued service. And good coaches are worth their weight in gold.

Well, fear not, coaches! There are a few things that you can do to make this arrangement work like a charm. First, the more self-assured you become in your managerial odyssey, the less trepidation you'll feel about bringing in an outsider to assist you in getting the most out of your employees' abilities. The only thing you have to fear is fear itself.

## Maximizing External Coaching Effectiveness

When you bring in a coach from the outside to assist your own coaching efforts, you must first make absolutely certain that you have a very specific, clearly defined reason for doing so. The objectives that you want the external coach to achieve must be clearly spelled out to him or her. Likewise, the employee or employees who will be working with this adjunct coach should also be fully briefed.

### Preparing Your Employees

Don't ever dump an external coach on an employee or entire staff without explaining to them precisely what you have in mind. These kinds of surprises are not appreciated by team members and violate some basic tenets of coaching and mentoring—open communication, employee involvement, and so on. Such a unilateral path reduces the chances of a fruitful relationship ever developing between an outside coach and your people.

On the other hand, fully apprising employees of just what these ancillary relationships will entail increases the possibility that any added coaching they receive will bear fruit. Prepare, prepare, prepare. And do keep work-related surprises to a minimum.

## Getting Your Employees on Board

Listen, too, to what your employees have to say about a prospective relationship with an external coach. If your employees are dead set against the setup, you might want to reconsider going through with it. External coaches, remember, aren't philanthropists working free of charge. If you feel that your employees' resistance to this brand of tutorship is as hard as a diamond, then you are confronted with three choices:

- No external coaching.
- Convince employees to give the relationship the "old college try."
- Tell your employees that they are getting the extra coaching—end of story (not a coach thing to do, by the way).

# Setting Parameters for the External Coach

Let's assume for argument's sake that after deliberating with your employees, you settle this matter in the affirmative. The next step is to bring the external coach into the fold and lay down—clearly—the parameters of the job you want done.

When you bring in an external coach to work with a member of your staff, be sure to keep tabs on the relationship by regularly meeting with both the coach and the employee. But, if it is to work as planned, also recognize and respect the importance of confidentiality in such a relationship.

The time frame that you establish is essential here. Never give external coaches a blank check and an open-ended invitation to linger until they feel the job is done. This often leads to the Unwanted Relative Syndrome making its way into the office. You know, the cousin who came for a weekend visit, liked your hospitality (or more likely, the free room and board), and hung around for two months.

You must have unambiguous objectives that you want the external coaching to accomplish. And you must also have a precisely defined time frame in mind for this external coaching to realize those objectives.

## *Staying Fully Apprised*

Just as with the performance plans of your employees, you must stay fully apprised of the external coach-employee relationship from beginning to end. You are still the head honcho, and you are responsible for your employees' performances in all areas. You can't step away from this sidebar relationship just because it will be over in short order. You've got to know what gains (if any) your people are making, and how those gains will impact your relationship with them, and all future projects on which you will be working together.

Seek and ye shall find help. Liberally use outside resources to supplement your coaching and the special training efforts that come with the territory. Potential sources of help include professional associations, books and periodicals, public workshops, college courses, technical seminars, and so on.

Throughout this entire process, it's imperative that you consult frequently with the external coach and share your thoughts on the progress of the tutelage and whether it's getting the results that are desired. And likewise, you need to talk to your employees about how they feel the special instruction is going. That said, this doesn't mean that you impose yourself on the relationship. As a coach yourself, you know that the coaching process is about giving employees latitude and as much freedom as is possible and sensible. This same latitude has got to be extended to an external coach. Outsiders, in particular, need to feel comfortable right from the start. They need to work in an environment of relative independence, performing their specialty without interference and unnecessary roadblocks. Coaches-for-hire are ordinarily specialists at what they do, with track records of accomplishment, and shouldn't be treated as upstart employees. They are working for you, yes, but they are also independent.

So you've got another fine line to walk. That's part of the life of a coach in business. You need to be fully aware of what's going on within the confines of your office space, taking measure of everything from time to time, but you also need to respect others' abilities in doing their jobs with minimal amounts of interference and nitpicking on your part. This certainly extends to external coaches, who need to maintain a certain level of autonomy in working with employees, while simultaneously being on the same page as you, the coach who brought them in to fix a problem or teach a skill.

## Putting Internal Employees to Work as Mini-Mentors

As a coach, have you thought about calling on help from the inside? Yes, the inside! That is, have you considered asking a member of your staff to work with another one of your employees? Think about it. You have a wealth of resources at your fingertips—the people who work for you. As already seen in the examination of the ways and means of coaching and mentoring, people and their unique personalities, talents, and possibilities are what make this birdie fly.

It stands to reason then that your employee Pam may well possess certain competencies that are eluding her colleague, and also your employee,

Matt. If this is indeed the case, why not permit Pam to tutor Matt on his shortcomings? You can, in effect, allow Pam to take Matt under her wing in an informal setup within the perimeters of the workplace. By implementing such a relationship within your team or department, you're exercising a very prominent coaching and mentoring technique. You are maximizing your talent base by filling in the gaps of knowledge and skills that invariably exist in one employee with the expertise of another member of your team. It's no different than high school or college tutors who help out their classmates.

**FACT**

Advancing employees' skill levels and abilities to assume greater responsibilities and challenges is the surest way to keep employees in your fold. Employees whose job interest remains high are more likely to want to stay put than are bored or disgruntled employees.

We'll call these in-house "taking under the wing" efforts mini-mentoring. From one person to another, the passing on of know-how is at the foundation of what is called mentoring. Tutoring and upgrading the knowledge base and skills of another is mentoring doing its job and doing it right.

## *Understand What You Want to Accomplish*

Now, just how do you make this setup work? Aren't there a lot of egos just cruising for a bruising here? Again, just as with bringing in external coaches, you have to know precisely what you want accomplished. Before you apprise your employees of your mini-mentoring idea, make sure you yourself can clearly verbalize just what you have in mind, and just what you want to achieve by initiating a mini-mentoring relationship.

Next, you've got to establish a time parameter for this mini-mentoring, too. Open-ended relationships of this kind often set in motion the Law of Diminishing Returns. You've seen it happen time and again in so many teacher-student learning relationships, and in comparable learning environments.

## Monitor Progress

They start out fresh and with a sense of grand purpose. The bright-eyed and bushy-tailed students are, at the onset, sponges for learning. Real sponges eventually become waterlogged and require a squeeze or two, or the absorption ceases. Ditto for the students absorbing their lessons.

So, carefully consider your objectives and time frame, and, of course, monitor the progress of the relationship from both sides of the employee aisle. That is, periodically talk to the employee recruited to assist her coworker—Pam, in this example.

Ask how things are going, and if she feels she is making headway in the education of Matt. And then reverse the process and query Matt about how he feels the relationship is working. Keep the communication lines open—always.

Chapter 6

# A Coaching Blueprint

There are critical skills that come with the territory of enlightened coaching, including listening approaches and delivering feedback on a consistent basis. Coaching efforts can easily get caught in office quicksand unless the coach follows a blueprint. This chapter unfurls that all-important coaching blueprint and discourses on the key tools and techniques that augment this managerial art.

## What Dinosaur Managers Lack: Empathy for Employees

Coaching and mentoring require a multilayered knowledge that dinosaur managers don't need to call their own. They ask of those who coach and mentor to get to know the people they work with as real people with unique talents. A coach is therefore required to be an empathetic individual. That is, you've got to grasp fundamental human psychology and recognize the importance of elevating both body and soul to get the job done, and done right.

And showing empathy for a fellow human being is not something that can be readily gleaned by reading a book or attending a seminar. Empathy is rooted in life experiences. "I can understand how he's feeling right now." "I can see she needs a word of encouragement, because I've been there." "That happened to me once."

A lot is expected of coaches. They are expected to raise employees' self-awareness, self-confidence, and self-development. And when these three come together synergistically, the results are stronger employee performances and a more healthy work environment.

A solid analogy can be drawn between parenting and the art of coaching and mentoring. Can anybody be a father? A mother? Well, most adults at some point in their lives have the biological tools to answer in the affirmative. But, as you can plainly see all around you, some people do a better job of parenting than others. Some mothers and fathers totally abrogate their parental responsibilities and lack even the most rudimentary of skills—and yes, the empathy—to undertake what parenting entails.

## The Coaching Blueprint for Success

If you want to wear the veritable black belts that a good coach and mentor earns, carefully consider the following points and incorporate them into your day-to-day interactions with your employees. It amounts to a blueprint for success.

- **Embrace the philosophy.** The primary purpose of coaching and mentoring is to unlock human potential on the job (and elsewhere, where applied) by fashioning a work environment that is most conducive to helping employees reach their utmost potential.
- **Appreciate the individual.** Appreciate that each and every employee is a unique person who needs to be recognized as such, if the true coaching and mentoring philosophy is to be lived and realized.
- **Encourage self-motivation.** Bridge the gap between an employee's self-interests and the organization's self-interests and make them one and the same.
- **Establish goals.** Assist in establishing on-the-job goals for employees on a personal basis based on each individual's level of skills and desire to advance and grow—and, of course, on the organization's needs.
- **Commitment.** Forge a firm commitment from employees to simultaneously work for the organization, for you—the coach—and for themselves and their respective futures.
- **Communicate.** Keep open lines of communication between coach and employee at all times. Give recurring feedback on job performance, employing your talent to listen, hear, and value your staff.
- **Resolve conflict.** Practice immediate and assertive on-the-spot problem solving. Address today's problems today, not tomorrow or next week.
- **Be solution-oriented.** Always seek positive solutions that will engender positive outcomes. View every obstacle and crisis as an opportunity to remedy problems and move forward.
- **Delegate responsibilities.** Acknowledge your duty to provide your team with weighty job responsibilities, challenging tasks, and opportunities for career advancement. Appreciate that this is the surest way to keep productive employees in the organization and to attract the best and the brightest people from the outside.

- **Show appreciation.** Reward progress and positive results on a person-to-person basis. Acknowledging a job well done today increases the chances of a job well done tomorrow.
- **Never stop learning.** Create a work atmosphere of uninterrupted learning, where augmentation of knowledge and growth in skills are always encouraged and never capped. Offer workshops or lectures to assist employees in staying up-to-date with their respective job responsibilities and industry trends.

## Listening Skills

You may think that it's incredibly obvious to suggest that you be a good listener to successfully coach people. But good listening, as it were, is often taken for granted. Coaching and mentoring skills are built upon a foundation of dialogue between coaches and employees and mentors and mentees. Unfortunately, there are some souls that consider a dialogue anything that permits another person to utter a word or two edgewise. That is, 98 percent of the conversation comes out of their mouths versus 2 percent everybody else's. That's not a dialogue!

Coaches and mentors should finely hone their listening skills, because employees should be listened to and heard from on a regular basis. This entire managerial methodology revolves around raising the level of employee participation in defining their own jobs, so it stands to reason that team members should have some say—a literal say—in what's going on. This means that they need to say a few words on occasion—to hear and to be heard. This isn't to suggest you must always like and take to heart what your employees are saying. Nor does it mean you have to implement their suggestions or grant their requests. Coaches are still managers and are the final arbiters in all decision making, unless the responsibilities for the decisions have been specifically delegated to others. The listening tool of coaching is richly beneficial in dealing with employees in matters ranging from performance planning to problems of professionalism. It's akin to brainstorming in the sense that it can't hurt to listen. Listening opens up doors. You can discover so much by merely hearing what your employees have to say and connecting with them in a decidedly confidential way.

Employees who are not performing up to speed have to be listened to all the more. What's causing their slumps in performance or hostile attitudes? What do they consider their roles on your team? Where do they see themselves in a year's time in the company? Do they think they've got a future in the company? Ask—and listen very carefully and respectfully—and ye shall find out. The decisions that you ultimately make after these listening tours will be fairer and sounder than they otherwise would be if you managed with cotton in your ears.

As a coach, you must be an active listener, which means that you must make certain at all times that you are both hearing and understanding your employees. You accomplish this by clarifying important points in discussions with the techniques of paraphrasing and the frequent posing of probing, open-ended questions that can't be answered with just one word.

Okay, you've got it. You listen to your staff. You talk to them on a one-on-one basis and let them all speak their pieces. That's the first step. But now it's time you absorb the precise skills of being a good listener. Yes, there are genuine skills involved in listening, and it is important for a coach to possess them. But listening to your employees without hearing what they're saying is not listening at all. Some managers fancy themselves employee-friendly with a so-called "open door policy." And, yes, they'll let you come in and sound off when something's on your mind. But in the end, nothing ever seems to come out of all this "listening." That is, you lodge a complaint, ask for a new job role, request a raise in pay, a time extension on a project, and so on—and nothing is ever done about it. Eventually, you come to realize that talking to your manager is about as fruitful as talking to the plaster-board wall in your office cubicle.

As a coach, you want to scrupulously avoid being this kind of "open door policy" manager. You must both listen *and hear*. This is one of many key aspects that distinguish coaching from the more traditional management styles. Employees should know beyond a shadow of a doubt that when they are talking with their coach, they are being heard. They should feel confident that what they ask of their coach will be considered—either acted on affirmatively or rejected. The employees must, in turn, accept the facts of work life that maybe—just maybe—they won't get what they want. But at least they know their manager—their coach—will always take what they have to say under careful consideration and not completely disregard it. That's really all employees can ask for: a fair hearing.

## Paraphrasing Skills

You've got to be able to paraphrase what's being said to you to show your employees that you're indeed listening to and hearing them. During any confabs with your employees, periodically paraphrase what they're revealing in the discussions. "So what you're saying is, you'd like more challenging tasks in your next assignment." Punctuating your listening with such paraphrasing reassures your employees that you're not a brass monkey—not a department store mannequin—but a real person listening, hearing, and understanding what they're saying.

If your employee unhesitatingly accepts that you are doing these three things (listening, hearing, and understanding), you've passed the coach's listening test. Remember, though, that you aren't the judge on whether you are an accomplished listener. You may sincerely feel you fully give your employees a fair hearing when they come to you with their various concerns. But what's key in these scenarios is not what you think, it's what your employees think.

## Checkup

Sometimes our perceptions of ourselves are not quite the perceptions that others have of us. This is precisely why you need to find out how you are perceived and whether you are in fact connecting with your employees in the way that you would like. After each and every coaching encounter and "listening time" with your staff, you need to do a checkup—on yourself. You accomplish this by soliciting feedback from your employees on whether they feel that you are listening to and hearing what they have to say. You ask them point-blank whether they feel that you are grasping their concerns and reacting to them appropriately. If you think that you are in complete sync with the feelings, hopes, and desires of your team—well, that's peachy keen, if in fact it matches the true feelings, hopes, and desires of your people.

Consider this checkup your reality check. You owe it to yourself, your employees, and the company that signs your paychecks to know where your people are coming from and where they are going, too. You are, after all, endeavoring to create a choice work environment. And you know that this pathway to positive outcomes and pleasing results all around cannot be traveled alone or with a deaf ear.

## Open-Ended Questions

To further enhance your listening skills, there's yet another verbal device that can be added to your coaching toolbox. To categorically connect with your employees, you must make sure that you are in sync with their points of view and perspectives. In addition to paraphrasing their responses, the intelligent use of questions will ensure that your listening encounters remain on track. That is, if you intermittently question your employees throughout discussions, you will not lose your way. So, pepper your people with questions. Not in an aggressive manner designed to put them on the spot, but to clarify points along the way and assist you in "understanding" them.

Questions can be classified as either close-ended (requiring an answer of just a word or two) or open-ended (requiring an explanation). Which do you think should be a considerable part of a coach's querying arsenal? (Open-ended questions, of course.)

Close-ended questions are posed for definitive and short responses:

- "Where is the cafeteria?"
- "How long has Michelle been supervisor?"
- "What time does the meeting begin?"
- "Is that Mr. Roach's real hair?"

As you can see, these questions are not posed to elicit elaborate answers. A couple of words in response to them will suffice. Close-ended questions have their place for closed answers—for information purposes. But they are not the driving forces in a dialogue.

Open-ended questions, on the other hand, are very powerful weapons in a coach's arsenal. These types of questions are calculated to produce more thoughtful rejoinders. They are posed with an "open end," so to speak, and have no right or wrong answers attached to them. Open-ended questions go hand in glove with proper listening. They afford you golden opportunities to extract more from your employees. For instance, you can question them on any cloudy points that they make, or ask them to flesh out some of their opinions, suggestions, or requests. Here are several examples of open-ended questions:

- "How do you feel about your coworker John leaving in the middle of the project?"
- "Can you further explain this idea of yours?"
- "Is your performance plan unfolding as originally anticipated?
- "What's your opinion on the change in bonus policy?"
- "Do you have any thoughts on why sales are down in your department from last year?"

All of these questions are meant to elicit honest and thinking responses. Coaching and mentoring methods frequently utilize open-ended questions because they, in essence, "open up" the sometimes-intimidating workplace environment. Employees are afforded opportunities to more freely express themselves in response to them. They are given chances to discuss the progress of their work assignments, their feelings about their status in the organization, their relationships with their coach and coworkers, and just about anything else.

Of course, not all open-ended questions are positive in nature. Questions leading with "Why," for instance, are in fact open-ended, but often put the employee on the defensive. "Why did you make that decision?" "Why did you choose this new approach instead of the one that worked so well last time?" These open-ended questions are somewhat loaded and accusatory in nature. Try the alternatives: "What was the thinking process that went into your decision?" or "Please explain the reasons you chose this new approach to solving the problem instead of the previous one."

## *Mirroring Feelings*

A final listening skill worth noting gets to the heart of your employees' "feelings." Yes, coaches need to be sensitive in ascertaining the emotional states of their team members during day-to-day encounters with them. Granted, this isn't always easy. Some people are poker faces by nature and carefully rein in their emotions. On any given day, they could just as easily have won $50 million in a Powerball lottery or been diagnosed with a terminal illness, and you couldn't tell the difference. Most people, however, are not so accomplished at completely concealing their true feelings. And so emotions—in varying ways and degrees—are visible at all times, with the office environs being no exception. Thus, you can unearth so much just by gleaning the moods of your employees when you speak with them. How they are feeling when they are in your presence cannot be discounted as immaterial and unrelated to the work at hand.

If an individual is visibly upset when he speaks with you, it's important that you listen and respond with this reality in mind because feelings run deep—very deep. And just because they're revealed in the workplace, feelings cannot be cast aside as irrelevant. A person's feelings directly translate into job performance. Coaches and mentors know this and don't shy away from it. Coaching and mentoring—rooted so deeply in people, performance, and positive outcomes—equate feelings and mindset with productivity. Coaches never ignore employees' feelings because they recognize and appreciate that these feelings are not separate from the productive individuals behind them.

Receptivity to others' feelings adds a powerfully empathetic dimension to the art of listening and, indeed, the art of coaching and mentoring. It enables coaches to venture beyond the words being expressed by their employees. Feelings properly gauged put mere words into a meaningful perspective.

So, what you've got to do is incorporate into your listening skills, and overall coaching methods, the ability to mirror the feelings of your employees in your responses to them. Use open-ended questions to more fully comprehend why your employees are feeling this way or that way. Get to the heart of the discontent if you have to. Understand where anger is coming from and at whom it is directed.

The more traditional managers of the world are apt to equalize the emotions of their employees. Come to work with a tear in your eye and you are advised to go to the bathroom and pull yourself together. Coaches don't pack their employees off to the bathroom in lieu of forthrightly dealing with genuine human emotion and real feelings. They conscientiously link their employees' emotional states with their ultimate job performances, and are right to take this approach.

## Lots of Feedback, Not Criticism

Soliciting feedback from your employees, querying them on their perceptions of you, is very important. It enables you to make adjustments in your coaching methods and helps cement rapport between you and your staff. But you also have to dispense constructive feedback quite liberally in all your coaching undertakings. It's a valuable communication technique that you should wield wisely because it is the greatest information dispenser in town. Feedback focuses its lenses on employee performance issues—good and bad—and other workplace concerns. Feedback amounts to your observations and is not based on personal feelings and subjective judgments. Employees clamor all the time for information concerning their work performances and what they need to know to improve themselves on the job. Feedback from their coach provides them with just that.

### Keeping Feedback Objective

The feedback that you offer your employees, however, needs to be as objective as is humanly possible. It needs to be honest, succinct, and lucid. "Beating around the bush" feedback is bad coaching. That is, don't start an important meeting with your employee with a discussion about the weather, football, or your preference for boxers over briefs.

Be up-front and get to the point. If the feedback is negative in nature, don't leave your employee squirming in her seat for what seems like an eternity. Explain very precisely where you see the problem and what you believe is the root cause or causes of it. Discuss openly possible solutions to correcting the problem, and, of course, solicit return feedback from the employee and an assessment of your feedback. In other words, make the feedback process positive, even when it is initiated to correct something negative.

## Distinguishing Feedback from Criticism

Remember that feedback and its objective nature differ from outright praise or criticism. When feedback is offered up like, "You really screwed up on this project," it is subjective and critical. Overt criticism is *not* a self-motivating tool. It immediately puts the person on the receiving end on the defensive. It often leads to anger, humiliation, or both, and thus warps any helpful, give-and-take dialogue. It makes finding positive and forward-looking solutions that much more difficult.

Sure, there are many managers who use praise and criticism like a policeman's billy club. They attempt to build up or bash their employees into greater productivity. Fear of getting hit over the head with the boss's cudgel is sometimes a temporary impetus for an employee to perform at a higher level. Fear of losing one's job also works on occasion—that cannot be denied. But these are short-term solutions at best and unprincipled on top of that. Traditional managers who practice these heavy-handed approaches don't create an optimum work atmosphere—that's for sure. Anything but!

**QUESTION?**

**How do you test your trust quotient?**
Just ask and answer these four questions. Am I consistent? Do my employees believe what I say? Do they perceive me as competent to execute what I say? Do they perceive me as looking out for them? Answer all four in the affirmative and you pass the test.

What, then, is the difference between negative feedback and criticism? Negative feedback is open-ended; it is not condemnatory. It is dispensed with good intentions, in hopes that the bad performance or behavior can be corrected. It seeks a solution with a positive outcome. Negative feedback is intended to point out just where and why mistakes were made and how logically they can be corrected in the future. Criticism is close-ended and usually personal in nature. It is not solution-oriented. Solutions and suggestions intermingled with criticism are often ignored because they tend to get buried beneath the vitriol or harshness of tone. "Ed, you've been dragging your feet on this project for weeks now. Your group is near mutiny. You'd better fix this problem, or you are in serious trouble, my friend." "My friend" suffixes are often giveaways of criticism, by the way. Let's try it this way. "Ed, you're running behind schedule on your project. You're going to have to come up with solutions—and fast—because your group is very unhappy with the progress and your leadership. This is unacceptable. Do you have any ideas how you can right this situation?"

Negative feedback. You've made it very plain that you are dissatisfied with Ed's performance. He's been told that his group is displeased with him, and that he needs to make changes in the way he is doing his job or suffer the consequences that come with prolonged bad performance. Of course, depending on the severity of the problem, negative feedback comes in many forms. Some of it is light and lean, with subtle references to particular problems that need to be corrected or improved upon. On the other end of the scale, negative feedback could entail placing it all on the line. "Your performance of late has been unacceptable. You're going to have to make some serious changes in your attitude and work ethic, or we are going to have to let you go. Are you prepared to do what it takes?"

## Positive Feedback Versus Praise

What's the difference between positive feedback and praise? Again, positive feedback focuses on the specifics of job performance. You bolster your employees with a critique of all the things that they are doing that please you. "Sandra, your communication skills have dramatically improved over the last couple of months. The report that you just prepared for me on your project status was thorough and concise. I appreciate all the work you've put into it, as do your team members, who have informed me that you are always there for them in answering their questions." Praise on the same subject might go something like this, "Full speed ahead. Keep up the good work!" Obviously, the positive feedback received by the employee carries greater weight. It's more uplifting to her because it goes to the heart of her job performance and what she actually does.

You may have worked for a boss who offered praise in lieu of substantive positive feedback. And the workplace atmosphere was probably a distant one. Managers who dispense one- or two-sentence praiseworthy comments to their employees, and never any positive feedback, inevitably leave their staffs with empty feelings in their guts. In these kinds of situations, employees feel that they are there for one reason and one reason only—to work for the bottom line. They feel no sense that they are appreciated as individual talents with specific desires to learn and grow on the job. Constructive feedback—positive or negative—is a coach's way of letting employees know where they stand. Feedback is forward-looking and not intended to either launch or sink any boats. Rather, it promotes dialogue and is solution-oriented without personal judgments and opinions getting in the way.

## Always Keep Your Cool

As a coach, you may be justifiably enraged at certain employees from time to time and feel like dressing them down. Take a deep breath on these occasions. It's best to avoid such turbulent encounters. This may entail that you put off a meeting until you can temper your temper and look at things less emotionally and more objectively.

In all verbal encounters with your employees, you should be cognizant of your tone of voice and bearing. That is, avoid sarcasm, haughtiness, and the attack mode. Be objective and consistent in your demeanor at all times. This will maximize the employee-employer relationship and performance results.

Avoid, "Ed, get in my office right now!" Instead, tell Ed in a controlled tone of voice, "I'd like to have a discussion with you on the progress of Project Mindshift. In my office at ten o'clock tomorrow morning, okay?" This will give you time to cool off and think through the feedback that you'll be imparting to Ed about his project performance and overall behavior on the job. It will also give Ed, with twenty-four hours to mull things over, a fairer chance to state his side of things.

## Where Predictability Is Trust

"Oh, he's so predictable." How often have you heard this sentiment expressed about somebody? And when it is applied to a person, it's usually not meant as a compliment, but is said pejoratively. In other words, being "predictable" is a put-down. Ironically, predictability is a trait that employees value very dearly in their managers. Not predictability in innovation and delegation, which is really a contradiction in terms, but predictability in managerial style and temperament.

You've read a lot in this chapter about listening, hearing, and understanding—in other words, communicating with your employees and connecting with them. And it all comes back to that little matter of trust. Trust and predictability go together like peanut butter and jelly. You need to be predictable in countless ways, so that your staff will know what to expect from you at all times and on any given day. There are no big surprises in predictability. Employees feel more secure in workplaces that are stable and run by coaches who are predictable in their methods and routines (for example, what meetings are like, consistency in follow-ups, overall competency, dependability, and so on).

Trust blossoms from this general predictability. Don't say one thing and do another. Because the next time you say that you are going to do something, your employees will be less inclined to believe you. Negative snowball effects wreak havoc in office environments. You don't want a member of your staff saying, "Why should I do X, based on the coach's saying that he's going to do Y, when I don't believe that he's going to do Y?" Yes, there's much to be said for predictability in coaching. It's an essential part of a workplace atmosphere that is both stable and serene. It's a matter of trust.

# Chapter 7

# Overcoming Workplace Obstacles

Workplace obstacles and problems are a part of every coach's daily grind. Whether it's hiring new personnel, addressing less than stellar job performances, or raising skill levels, the work frontlines are not for the faint of heart or less than completely dedicated. In this chapter, you will be alerted to the telltale signs of trouble. But, more importantly, you will be armed with the necessary ammunition to overcome every imaginable workplace conundrum.

# High-Octane Coaching

There are certain situations in the workplace that require extra special attention. It's during these critical moments when you need to pull out your metaphorical coach's whistle, briskly blow into it, and concentrate on the considerable job at hand. Let's examine some of the workplace circumstances that are ripe for this brand of high-octane coaching.

## The New Kid on the Block

The most obvious moment that calls for special training is the introduction of new employees onto your team. Young, inexperienced employees are wont to feel ill at ease in their new surroundings. And that rings equally true for your existing staff, who are being asked to absorb outsiders into their tight-knit fraternity. People who work together for extended periods of time are often clannish, and they reflexively view strangers with unease and as a threat to their way of doing things. More times than not, the new employees gain the confidence of the group. Sometimes this acceptance is immediate; on other occasions, it may take a while, depending on the personalities involved.

High-octane coaching merely asks that you pay special heed to your new hires. It is your cleanest opportunity to instruct and orient them. You fill them in on the ways of the organization as a whole and the peculiar customs of your office. This is the right and proper time to let your new employees know exactly what is expected of them and the procedures that they must follow if they are to work for you and on your team. By taking this immediate and up-front approach, you avoid the on-the-job training method comparable to a father teaching his son to swim by hurling him headfirst into a six-foot pool of water.

## Improving Skills

You now know that the coaching and mentoring methodology is firmly committed to growing employee skill levels. And the reason for this is quite simple. Skills, self-motivation, and professional work habits are what translate into productive workers. And, this bears repeating again and again:

New and upgraded skills are needed all the time to keep pace with rapid technological advances.

**FACT**

Coaching and mentoring are dedicated to advancing employee skills, every day and always. Skills can be categorized as either hard skills or soft skills. Soft skills refer to communication abilities, interpersonal relations, and so on. Hard skills cover the more technical, hands-on skills required to do a job.

So, part of your coaching responsibilities involve training, or setting the training in motion (via external coaching, employee mini-mentoring, mentoring, and so on) to raise your employees' skill levels, or perhaps teach them an entirely new set of skills. Technology and the razor sharp competitiveness in today's business world make retraining of employees more often a necessity rather than a luxury. Thus, your job as a coach requires that you be keenly aware of what's happening all around you. You've got to know what's going on in your own office, of course, but also in the organization as a whole, and indeed in the entire industry that you work in. It is also imperative that you keep one eye on the overall health of the economy and understand how the business cycle impacts on your industry, company, and the employee skills needed to compete and survive.

## No More Repeats

The philosopher George Santayana once remarked, "Those who ignore history are condemned to repeat it." And, of course, he was referring to the mistakes made time and again by societies that lead to wars, oppression, appeasement, and just about everything else that's deleterious to humankind. As a coach, you need to take special heed of Santayana's advice. When your employees err, you need to be right there to correct their missteps and offer them instruction on what exactly went wrong and why.

By working closely with your team members on a personal basis from day one of your relationship, you are more apt to spot performance slip-ups and other problems, and catch them early on, too. When you give them on-the-spot tutorials, you are disciplining members of your staff not to travel down those same roads again. In going down this road, repetitions of the same mistakes, errors in judgment, and interpersonal conflicts leading to poor performance are less likely to occur a second time. Learning from one's mistakes is a time-honored cliché, but it is also very true. A good coach is conscious of this fact of human nature from check in to check out.

## Grooming

No, this is not something that you ask your employees to do each morning when they look into their bathroom mirrors. This is what you do when you find employees who stand out from the pack—who show that they are clearly at the head of the class in skills, professionalism, and self-motivation.

Grooming these bright lights for bigger and better things is what allows coaching and mentoring managerial practices to not only keep pace with swift technological advances, unavoidable employee turnover, and intense competition, but also to thrive and come out on top. Good grooming is an important part of a coach's arsenal. It is another example of coaches working in the present with eyes looking to a bright future.

## Corrective Coaching

Corrective coaching springs into action when certain attitudes and behaviors point to serious problems in their development stages. Performance problems and dissension inevitably arise in workplaces and must be dealt with promptly and intelligently. These kinds of workplace issues are a given. What you want to accomplish via corrective coaching, then, is problem solving at the source. You want to tackle problems in their infancy and dispatch them in short order. Your grand aim, with corrective coaching actions, is to reduce both the quantity and severity of problems that come your way.

In every work environment with two or more employees, there are inevitably going to be squabbles; there are going to be performances adversely affected by interpersonal relationships not being what they should be. In Chapter 13, we'll look closely at troublesome employee relationships and attitude problems and how coaching handles them. Meanwhile, as we get increasingly enmeshed in the fast-paced, fluid corporate world of today—where the stakes are higher and the salaries are, too—the obstacles and variable pitfalls loom larger and more complex. It stands to reason, then, that these more layered problems need to be more thoroughly understood. And nobody is better qualified to manage in this new-fashioned age than an insightful coach.

**FACT**

Corrective coaching specifically refers to coaching applications that address explicit problems ranging from incompetence in job roles, to performance dips caused by declining interest in work responsibilities, to personal matters affecting job performance, to behavior-related issues that cut across a wide swath.

Now that we've established beyond a doubt that an office led by a coach is a better-managed place than one run by a traditional manager, the table may be set with the specific problems and obstacles that invariably are found in every imaginable workplace. Foremost, coaching and mentoring don't claim to be problem-solving panaceas—there are no such things. However, they embody a managerial approach that attends to root causes of problems and gets at them fast and furiously.

Coaching and mentoring are active styles of managing that attempt to cut problems of any kind off at the pass and stop their spread. How exactly is this done? In consultation with your employees, you set high but attainable expectations for them. In addition, you expect each and every one of them to be responsible and accountable for their ultimate performances. It is with this solid foundation in place that you address and dispense with the problems that arise on your watch.

## The Seeds of Common Workplace Problems

Now let's look at the more common workplace problems. These are the kinds of hurdles you will be required to leap over during your coaching career. Foremost, it's important to identify the symptoms of problems in the making, because a full-blown problem is often so far along that finding a positive solution is a tougher undertaking. For example, if terminating an employee is your first resort in ridding yourself of a problem, then you've more than likely let the problem fester for far too long, or didn't detect it early enough. Your job is to unearth solutions leading to positive outcomes, and that means you're going to have to tackle problems in stage one of their development and not in stage two, six, or fourteen. This highly aware and very aggressive posture affords you more options in your decision making. The more room you have to maneuver in problem bailiwicks, the more circumspect and productive your ultimate decisions will be.

## Employee Incompetence

Let's start with one of the most obvious workplace problems—obvious, but not always easy to solve. These are performance problems directly related to employee competence or motivation. The question you've got to ask yourself in these situations is whether or not you've made a mistake in evaluating the skill level of an underperforming employee or, perhaps, whether the performance deficit is rooted in a lack of motivation and commitment to the job.

If the performance problem rests in competence, then you are presented with two unmistakable choices. The first is further training of the employee, to raise his or her skill level to what is required to do the job. The second, if you determine that the employee is the wrong fit for what you need and not likely to pick up the necessary skills, is to bite the bullet and let the employee go. Teamwork in the workplace today is dependent on each and every employee understanding his or her individual job responsibilities and being highly competent in fulfilling them.

It is your assessment of the precise reasons for the poor performance that matters most. If you feel that this employee can be brought up to the productivity level that you need, then you've got to act fast and impart the necessary job-related skills to this underachiever. You could personally offer the employee a little extra of your own time and expertise. Or you could have a coworker take this underachieving employee under his or her wing for mini-mentoring. You could even find someone from another department in the organization to help out, or go outside for external coaching if need be.

Letting employees go is the single most difficult act of a manager, and it's even more so for you, a coach, who keeps people and their unique talents and possibilities foremost in your thoughts. But the productivity of employees cannot ever be glossed over if it is below the bar you've established. And this bar is the company's bottom line. Hopefully your empathetic tendencies will make the parting of the ways as painless as possible under the unfortunate circumstances. A person's lack of key skills in one work environment doesn't preclude another environment proving a better fit, where the skills more appropriately complement the work that needs to be done.

## Performance Dips

And then there are those mystifying performance dips. No, these aren't the things you plunge your potato chips into. They're what you are up against when employees under your direction demonstrate a noticeable slip in productivity. Your corrective coaching skills must spring into action when you discern that a formerly productive employee is no longer as productive as in the past. It's your job to find out exactly why.

Is there a personal problem behind the performance about face? Is it boredom with the job role itself? Is the employee overworked and burned out? Having difficulty working with a new teammate, perhaps? Whatever the root causes of the problem, it's your responsibility to uncover them and address them in a very timely fashion.

In stark contrast to the more traditional managerial approaches, coaching is tailor-made for comprehending the reasons behind performance dips. By establishing and building relationships with employees on a one-on-one basis, you're in the unique position of genuinely knowing and understanding the people behind the performance problems. Since you have fully rounded profiles of all of your employees, as well as substantive work histories to refer to, the skids of your detective work are greased.

Poor performance based on a dearth of necessary skills is one thing. And, as we've indicated, this problem can be dealt with in a straightforward manner, i.e., bring the skill level up to snuff or not. Employees, however, who have proven that they can do the job—and do it well—present a much more complex dilemma for a coach when their performances regress. Dinosaur managers who encounter performance drops in their employees are inclined to address these problems in their usual coarse ways. You know, the age-old ultimatum: Raise that productivity level or suffer the consequences—demotion or termination. With this approach, there's no serious attempt to understand why there are the performance problems in the first place; no serious attempt to getting to the root causes. Meanwhile, back in Coach Town, you reach into your skills arsenal and pull out your communication tools. It's precisely in situations like performance dips where your listening skills (open-ended questioning, paraphrasing, mirroring feelings, and so on) play vital parts in getting to the heart of the problem.

A continuous and dynamic learning atmosphere in the workplace—which includes opportunity for advancement—is the key to staving off employee boredom. Boredom on the job inevitably leads to drop-offs in performance and the desire to look elsewhere for employment.

As a matter of fact, there are no more opportune circumstances to employ open-ended questioning than when confronting slumping employees. There are no better times to mirror their feelings. These are not moments to come on strong and to bully. Common sense tells you that performance slips are not camouflaging happy times—on the job or off—except, perhaps, if an employee won $50 million in the lottery and is sticking around until the first check arrives. Proceeding on the assumption that the performance reversals of your employees are not lottery-induced, you must then attempt to unearth the reasons for the problems without leaving scars in the process. You don't want to put your employees on the defensive. Instead, you want to carefully engage them in dialogue, while bringing to the surface what's bothering them. You need to know precisely what's behind the performance decline.

Here are some examples of open-ended and probing questions that are appropriate in delicate situations like these:

- "Your performance has dropped off of late; you're missing your deadlines and coming up short in reaching your goals. Do you see where there's a problem? Are there any reasons that you can think of for this decline in your productivity?"
- "Do you feel comfortable working with your team? Are there any problems with any of your coworkers that you feel are impeding your own job in any way?"
- "Any ideas as to why your performance has been slipping these past couple of months? Are you unhappy with your work assignments or role?"

Again, you must be persistent but always understanding. You also must be candid and encourage your employees to behave similarly by reaching into themselves for the reasons why their performances are heading south.

## The Boredom Bomb

A dip in employee performance is sometimes the result of sheer boredom. Work that's all too familiar—not challenging anymore, intellectually unfulfilling, or not the least bit interesting—is a boredom bomb waiting to detonate. To ensure that your employees don't get bored, you must create a work environment that is a perpetually bubbling and stirring brew of learning. If it's anything but this spicy mixture, employees will rightly feel that they are treading water. And it's then that boredom and declining productivity takes root.

What can you do to make certain that you coach in a dynamic learning environment? For starters, keep a watchful eye on your people. Periodically evaluate whether or not each one of them is being sufficiently challenged in his or her individual job, and whether or not individual employees are genuinely afforded opportunities to advance and grow under your leadership.

Alas, it must be conceded that even a coach's little world doesn't always run as planned. Boredom on the job front requires healthy doses of corrective coaching. If you believe you've got a bored employee who has shown potential and sports a solid knowledge and skill base, plus an insatiable desire to learn, then you need to act, and act fast. You've got to alter the circumstances of this particular employee's job responsibilities and role in a positive way before it's too late. A bored employee is an employee poised to fly away from your nest.

# Strive for True Delegating of Responsibilities

Delegating important responsibilities is a big part of what coaches do—it's an important responsibility, as it were. But these important responsibilities are *important responsibilities*, not trivial tasks. True delegating entails showing confidence in your employees' special talents and abilities to do big things. It means giving them important jobs and increasing their overall roles in the larger picture. By doing this, you are entrusting your employees to perform not only for you, but for their teammates as well, not to mention the company's bottom line. Real delegating is the ultimate office yawn buster. You can set a fire under your wilting employees by plying them with significant job responsibilities. You can show confidence in your most lethargic employees by putting them in roles that matter, not only to them but to other people as well. So, sit down with your dispirited team members and pull out your finely honed listening skills—yet again. Initiate dialogues with probing, open-ended questions that get to the heart of exactly why your employees are bored and not performing as in the past.

It's important to keep in mind that "bored with the job" is not a one-size-fits-all description with a one-size-fits-all solution. One employee's lackluster performance and discontent with the job may be quite different in nature from another's. And you should fully grasp these differences. It boils down to individual personalities and self-motivation.

**FACT**

Opinion polls suggest that more than 50 percent of workers name a "sense of accomplishment" as the chief ingredient they desire in a job, over and above even compensation. Coaching and mentoring aim to furnish employees with freedom, challenges, and opportunity for advancement, affording them that coveted sense of accomplishment.

You might assume, with all of the talk about coaching and mentoring as the people-approach to managing, that coaches, by nature, have to be sentimental softies who bow to their employees' every wish. This is not the case. The art of coaching and mentoring is not about being nice, *per se*. It's certainly not about being nasty. Rather, it's about getting the best results possible and understanding how best to get them. Major Frank Burns of the TV classic *M\*A\*S\*H* once eloquently uttered how "it's nice to be nice to the nice." And it is. But "niceness" is not a business mantra. Business decisions are rooted in the dollars and cents reality of what's best for the company. So, if your employees are out of bounds with their requests, you've got to set them straight and offer objective feedback on their performances, overall abilities, and immediate futures in the company. Above all else, you must strive to be fair, not necessarily nice. Hopefully, you can be both fair and nice.

## Coach Certification: The Skills You Need

If you're a coach, you're a teacher. Okay, so you didn't necessarily get a degree in education or get certified by the state, but you are a teacher nonetheless. You've been entrusted with the job of managing people who produce results for you—or you're walking the unemployment line. Let's explore some of the specific skills that you might be asked to teach at some in time in your coaching tenure.

### Technical Skills

Technical skills refer to the indispensable knowledge and precise skills that are required to perform a given job. If you hope to maximize employee performance in today's ultra-competitive business environment, you've got to make certain that these skills remain razor sharp and cutting edge.

This is definitely the most intricate and diverse area of teaching that you'll be responsible for. Technical, job-related skills run the gamut from engineering to human resources, whatever the job requires. If you work in a financial area, the skills, obviously, will revolve around interpreting and processing numbers. If customer relations are what the job entails, then people skills are the most important skills required for the job.

Whatever the necessary job skills, you've got to know your stuff inside and out. You've got to be eminently prepared to impart your wisdom to others. You've got to know how to pass on your know-how, too.

## Computer Skills

This, of course, is tied in with technical skills. Today's job reality is that there are very few white-collar jobs that don't use computers in their daily grind. Computers are not luxuries anymore, but a necessity in conducting business. And regardless of what position an employee holds, use of computers, even if it's merely inputting data, is more likely than not likely. As a coach, you're responsible for making certain that all your employees are not only computer literate, but also competent in exactly the computer applications you need to get the job done. This could entail lessons in word processing, data entry, graphics, and so on. It seems that software advancements are making new demands on employees with each tick of the clock.

## Reading and Writing Skills

Bet you never thought that you'd have to concern yourself with teaching reading and writing in a corporate setting. Well, surprise—you do. Courtesy of a sometimes wanting educational system, many students wind their way through higher education without mastering some of the most rudimentary reading and writing skills. If you have any doubt about this, check out some of the financial discussion boards on the Web. Presumably, most of these investors are college graduates. Read some of their posts. It's downright scary.

**ALERT!**

Teaching new skills to your employees should always be accomplished incrementally. Crash courses usually don't cut it. Paced learning is required to master a skill. Step A must be fully absorbed before moving on to Step B.

Believe it or not, written communication is a must in business circles. There are constant memos bandied back and forth and lots of reports that have to be written. Because communication is one of the pillars of coaching and mentoring, you cannot ignore this aspect of the job. An employee of yours who cannot read and write at the level of an adult in the business world will be unable to communicate with the clarity necessary to perform at a peak level. And—we've said it before—so much of business today is teamwork. This makes each individual's performance, or lack thereof, all the more important to others.

**ALERT!**

Teaching soft skills is often more difficult than imparting hard skills, such as computer applications and so forth. For instance, teaching employees utterly lacking in people skills how to behave in a professional manner on the job is one of a coach's greatest challenges.

## Behavior Skills

You've no doubt heard the stories of infants raised by wolves who grew up to behave like wolves and not human beings. And so it is with many people in today's workforce who were, in effect, raised by MTV, Jerry Springer, and crude sitcoms. Couple all that with minimum educational standards and you've got men and women in the workplace who, in some instances, do not know how to behave in such a setting. They lack even the most basic skills to deal with coworkers and customers in a professional manner. (Check out Chapter 10 for a full discussion on what constitutes professionalism in the workplace.)

## Setting the Right Tone

You achieve respect and acquire the trust of your staff, not by flaunting an authoritative title and throwing your weight around, but by earning it with your words and deeds. You must always be approachable and frank, delegate real responsibilities to the responsible, and listen to and hear your employees' concerns. You've got to be consistent in your methods and—above all else—competent at your own job. All of this amounts to positive tone setting by you at the managerial level, which filters on down to all of your staff members and makes coaching—high-octane, corrective, and so on—successful.

## Chapter 8

# The Power of Positive Thinking

In 1952, Norman Vincent Peale penned the best selling book, *The Power of Positive Thinking*. More than a half-century later, its abiding message resonates stronger than ever. This chapter surveys the positive focus of the coaching and mentoring managerial philosophy, zeroing in on its indefatigable desire to realize positive outcomes in every imaginable workplace situation.

# Judgment: There Is a Place for It

There is a trend nowadays to avoid exhibiting judgment so as not to be branded "a judgmental person." While certain forms of judgment can be harmful and offensive, others serve us well in the many varied areas of our lives. The key for a coach or mentor is appreciating the difference between good judgment and bad judgment—and knowing when to exercise this aspect of human behavior.

## Good Judgment

The good brand of judgment is a vital part of everyday living. People make judgments all the time—it can't be helped. Judgment and rules allow a free society to both exist and thrive. Judgment and rules are an essential part of every business, too. We choose our friends, whom our kids should play with, where to send them to school, whether or not to give money to a particular charity, whose phone calls to ignore, whom to leave our money to when we die, and the list goes on and on. And there are all sorts of reasons for making these kinds of decisions that require judgments on all of our parts. And some of these judgments are quite personal and pointed.

As a coach, you must be judgmental in situations that call for it. You must, however, appreciate the differences between the good brand of judgment and the bad brand of judgment. A coach's job demands both making firm judgments and knowing when to eschew the role of judge, jury, and executioner.

As a coach, you cannot be stripped of your capacity to judge. When you preside over a staff of diverse people and personalities, decisions are made all the time that call for swift and effective judgment on your part. Of course, it's wise judgment that you must demonstrate—and that's the good brand of judgment. We'll differentiate between the good brand and the bad brand in a moment. For now, just heave a big sigh of relief. You can freely embrace the fact that you not only can judge, but also must judge on many occasions. It may initially surprise some of your friends, but they'll understand it all when you explain the differences between the good and the bad brands of judgment.

## Bad Judgment

What, then, is the bad brand of judgment? It's clear that a coach has a critical role in sometimes playing both judge and jury. As a solutions-driven, results-oriented coach, you are always aiming to find solutions and achieve positive outcomes to any and all problems that come your way. Searching for negative outcomes to problems would certainly make you unique in the annals of coaching and mentoring, but you'd soon be savoring that singular distinction on an unemployment line. You are in place to solve problems and overcome obstacles, from performance snafus to interpersonal conflicts to, yes, even poor employee hygiene. And the reality is that you don't achieve positive outcomes by managing with the disposition and manner of Judge Judy. You don't say to an underperforming employee: "Boy, you are really stinking up this office! What the heck is wrong with you? Do you have half a brain?"

Now those statements are harshly judgmental and stark examples of the bad brand of judgment in action. If you go down this route in your problem-solving efforts, you aren't about to see positive outcomes. You don't solve the problem of underperforming employees by branding them as "nincompoops." If your goal is to chase employees away (by hurling invective at them until they quit), then you are not worthy of being a coach.

## Using the Power of Judgment in Your Coaching

Because you are a coach in good standing, you must utilize the tools and techniques outlined in Chapter 6. You must establish healthy dialogues with your underperforming employees that crisply focus on finding solutions (positive outcomes) to poor performances. Instead of delivering judgmental broadsides (such as "Boy, you are really stinking up the place"), you lay the groundwork for civil, productive dialogues with your employees. You make it clear to them that you're seeking to correct their performance problems, and that you're not there to pass judgment in any way on their personalities, but to make things right on the job, which is, of course, your job. "Can you think of any ways to get your project back on track? Are there any changes that you feel can be implemented to put you back on schedule?"

**ALERT!**

Your job as a coach is to effect positive outcomes in all areas of your managing. You accomplish this by examining every problem in the office—big or small—and finding optimum solutions for them. In other words, you address every problem from the angle of its best possible solution.

Remember, also, in this positive outcome posture of yours, to avoid discussions with employees that become debates. Leave the debating to the forensic club in high school, or aspiring politicians promising their way into office. Coaches never debate members of their staff. And, really, there's no quicker way to snuff out positive outcomes to problems than by engaging employees in contentious disputes. Civilized dialogues are the best breeding grounds for real solutions to tough, even seemingly intractable problems. And very often, this give-and-take, free-flowing exchange of ideas leads to people owning up to their mistakes or performance slips.

The coaching and mentoring methodology seeks to mold employees who can think for themselves and take initiative. This encompasses an ability to solve problems on their own, even righting their own wrongs and seeing where they've messed up, or why they are not performing as in the past. Positive outcomes are more often the result of employees figuring out how to rectify their own problems, than of a coach dictating solutions to them. Dictated solutions to problems are often received with resentment. And resentment doesn't inspire self-motivation, nor enhance job satisfaction.

## Keeping Negative Feedback Positive

Has it fully sunk in yet? You have to walk on the positive side of the street when coaching your employees. But wait just a minute, what about this thing known as negative feedback? It's discussed in detail in Chapter 6, and it's an important part of a coach's job to dispense it when appropriate. How does negative feedback work with all of this power of positive thinking stuff?

First, you may recall that negative feedback lies under the beach-sized umbrella of constructive feedback, which means its aim is just that—to be constructive and advance positive outcomes. It's not meant as criticism. It's not personal in nature. It's not intended to be judgmental in the negative sense.

Part of your job as a coach is to offer constructive feedback—positive or negative—as warranted. You must also make it clear to your employees that negative feedback is dispensed with the purpose of achieving positive results, i.e., helping them correct their negative behaviors, and not as personal attacks.

Negative feedback should be parceled out to an employee if he or she exhibits a performance or behavioral problem. When things go awry at the office, you're not expected to put your head in the sand in the interest of somehow being positive. There's nothing positive about ignoring problems and hoping they go away. This is real life we're living in. Dealing with problems fast and firmly—even if it means dispensing negative feedback—is positive, because the end game is to uncover the best possible solutions.

Yeah, right! Tell that to employees who are the recipients of negative feedback! Not everybody takes negative feedback in the spirit in which it is intended. Some employees feel that the negative feedback given to them is—well—negative. And they don't see it as delivered with their best interests at heart. So, guess what your job is in these circumstances? You guessed it—convincing your skeptical employees that you're not being critical of them, but merely seeking solutions to problems (yours and theirs), of course.

## *Adaptability on the Coaching Frontier*

A coach's life is never dull. Employees now and then are going to take things personally, even if your feedback is calculated to help them in the

Honest Abe tradition of "with malice toward none—with charity for all." Accept this as part of the reality of dealing with so many temperamentally unique employees. Some people are very sensitive souls and are prone to be defensive. Hence, they may have a tough time with any kind of negative feedback.

Still, you have no choice but to work with these personalities. They can't be avoided, nor can they be treated just like everybody else. That said, you've got to treat sensitive and defensive employees with extra special care. We're not talking about TLC or anything so syrupy. It's more about you understanding that individual personalities will react to your coaching methods in distinctive ways. The advantage of being a coach, in contrast to the more traditional manager, is your adaptability to a variety of situations and a variety of temperaments.

**ALERT!**

With employees who are hypersensitive and apt to be on the defensive, it's imperative you practice sensitivity-plus with them when problems arise. That is, make a concerted effort to modulate your tone and overall presentation, and make them free from anger and any hint of personal judgment.

The important first step in this adaptability mode requires that you accept that not everybody in your employ will fully appreciate what you're trying to accomplish in your role as a coach. It's just the nature of the beast—insecurity lives on Main Street and on Wall Street. Okay, you accept that negative feedback given to Ellen impacts her in a positive way, which is what you want. But the same negative feedback given to Kenny impacts him in a decidedly negative way, which is what you don't want. When your employees accept your feedback, run with it, and make the necessary adjustments in performance or behavior to better themselves, you've achieved your objective. On the other hand, if your employees receive the feedback and react defensively and angrily, this is liable to engender negative outcomes to already negative situations. And this compounding of the negative with a negative is unacceptable to a coach.

# The Sensitivity-Plus Approach

Is there an alternative to giving negative feedback? The answer is yes and no. No, negative feedback is an important part of coaching. But yes, there's a way to tweak negative feedback a bit to make it more palatable to the sensitive sorts in your employ. Get out your communication tool kit and add sensitivity-plus to your already sensitive managerial methods.

Sensitivity and mirroring your employees' feelings is something we've previously touched upon. You employ this perceptive approach in all your coaching encounters with your employees. It is an important technique that cements a bond between you and the members of your team. Courtesy of your sensitivity antennae, you learn to decipher who among your employees requires this extra special treatment—this sensitivity-plus. You learn to separate the thin skins from the thick skins who work for you.

Sensitivity-plus, for the thin-skinned, entails you being thoroughly cognizant of your tone and overall manner of presentation when you sit down with a sensitive employee to discuss a problem. For starters, always keep in mind that you are functioning in a business environment—sensitivity-plus or not. Negative feedback, when justified, must be passed on to its deserving recipients—or undeserving, as the case may be. But even negative feedback can be delivered in a variety of positive ways.

## Keeping Anger at Bay

Foremost, anger must never be permitted to rule the roost in a dialogue between you and a member of your staff. Even when you're trying to keep it at arm's length, sometimes anger works its way in there. Hey, you're only human. Yes, a coach is permitted to be human.

Nevertheless, with the ultrasensitive members in your work tribe, you've got to be on special guard to remain even-tempered and matter-of-fact in your presentation at all times. This exacting control is an important personality technique of coaching. That is, coaches must maintain complete control of themselves (from their choice of words to tone of voice) when confronting particular personalities, or they risk negative reactions to their negative feedback, which inevitably leads to negative outcomes. (A negative plus a negative equals a negative every time.) Exacting control also asks that you be on guard to leave the bad brand of judgment (personality-related opinions) out of your feedback. Defensive personalities often react to perceived negative judgments—even if strictly related to their job performances—as personal attacks. It is essential that you deal gingerly with these delicate men and women.

**FACT**

Coaching and mentoring, from top to bottom, asks both managers and employees alike to be solution-oriented at all times. Engaged in finding solutions to problems, instead of affixing blame on one another, fosters collaborative efforts that lead to creativity and positive outcomes.

## Buttering Up Belongs on the Breakfast Table

Conversely, avoid the buttering-up, soft pose in dealing with touchy employees. This is a common mistake managers make all the time. Employees who are hypersensitive to any kind of negative feedback are also highly sensitive to diversionary tactics. So any hesitancy in delivering your punch only compounds an already awkward situation—with more apprehension the byproduct. Needless to say, a sensitive and defensive employee does not thrive in an extremely apprehensive environment! Who does?

Yes, you need to mollycoddle these easily upset employees and accept their quirks of temperament. If you desire finding lasting and positive solutions to their problems on the job, you've got to impart negative feedback in a manner they can easily digest. So serve your feedback to them as if it were pabulum. You don't want any of your employees getting irritated, pulling back, and ultimately shutting down completely, when you most need them to do just the opposite.

## Don't Avoid the Inevitable

The bottom line is that you must never avoid the dispensation of negative feedback to employees who have earned it. Some managers live on the street called the Path of Least Resistance. That is, they avoid confronting particular employees with negative feedback for fear of their predictably hostile reactions. All employees, regardless of their personalities, have to produce results and be held solely accountable for their performances, attitudes, and behaviors. And when employees are not performing up to speed, they have to be informed of it. When the appraisal is negative, individuals have to be able to accept it and make every effort to turn the negative into a positive.

It's your job responsibility as a coach to communicate with all of your employees, and this entails dispensing with good as well as bad tidings. Thus, you've got to work your magic in delivering your message—be it positive feedback or negative feedback—to each individual, sensitive and defensive personality or not. Yes to adapting your methods when called for—no to capitulation!

## The Importance of Giving Regular Feedback

You want all your employees to fully understand that feedback is a technique you will wield, and wield very frequently at that. You want your employees to be comfortable receiving it, and to expect it as a matter of course. When your employees anticipate feedback as the rule, and not the exception, they are less likely to be intimidated by it, and more apt to see it as a beneficial summary of exactly how they are performing at their jobs.

Nobody likes operating in the darkness of night. Even when things are running smoothly, employees should be acknowledged. Positive feedback is a recognition tool that is just as important to dispense when things are going well, as is negative feedback when things aren't running as planned. Don't overlook the most productive people on your staff. There's a tendency sometimes to take for granted the biggest achievers on your team, simply because they do their jobs and do them well. Sure, it is tempting to say to yourself: "Why should I worry about Lisa? She runs ahead of schedule on all her projects, and the quality checks always check out. She never utters a negative word or a complaint. If she's got a problem, she'll find her own solution. So I'll concentrate my time and efforts on Fred, who doesn't always seem to be too sure of himself and rarely meets his goals."

When you must deliver negative feedback to employees, consider the big picture. Address their performance or behavioral problems head-on, but readily acknowledge the positive aspects of their work, too. This enables your employees to view the negative feedback as opportunities in bettering themselves and correcting their wayward job courses.

Yes, Fred does indeed need to be watched more closely and consulted with more frequently than Lisa (high-octane coaching in action). But this doesn't mean you cut Lisa out of the feedback loop just because she's doing her job with such alacrity and aplomb. Positive performances need to always be recognized and rewarded. There are a lot of Lisa types who move on in jobs, not only to greener pastures, but also to pastures where the feedback is more generous and flowing. These are the people, remember, who are the coaches of tomorrow, the ones being groomed for greater responsibilities and bigger challenges. These are the very persons you want to keep in the organization and working for you.

## A Positive-Thinking Case Study

Here's a genuine case study from the coaching files. It deals with an employee who exhibited a serious behavioral problem that negatively impacted an entire team. His name was Larry, a highly competent computer systems analyst—as good as they come:

> *Whenever a technical problem arose in programming or working with the newest software, Larry was the man who had the answers. And he was willing to help anyone at any time, even if his bluff manner was sometimes supercilious. Chuck, the manager and coach, appreciated Larry for his abilities and didn't dwell on Larry's personality excesses. Specifically, Larry's problem was that he liked his female coworkers a little too much. In other words, he occasionally made inappropriate comments and leered at them time and again.*

*Melissa, a coworker, found working closely with Larry very uncomfortable. And there was no avoiding him, because her job required that she be in constant contact with him. She actually admired Larry's skills at tackling difficult problems and squashing all those awful job-related bugs. But even though she learned a lot about the job from Larry, which she knew would benefit her immensely in the future, she could not ignore the fact that he crossed the line with his unprofessional behavior.*

*Fed up one day, Melissa approached her coach, Chuck, and told him all about Larry's improper side. She was hesitant at first, knowing that Chuck was a fan of Larry and his technical expertise. Nevertheless, it had to be done. She remembered Chuck's initial orientation to her about the importance of communication between the employee and the coach. Chuck had advised her on day one to come to him with any problems or concerns that she might have, and that he would do his best to help her find the solutions to remedy any wrongs. So she told Chuck the whole story, not holding back the fact that other female members of the staff didn't appreciate these same aspects of Larry's personality, either. She made clear that while she admired Larry's supreme competence in his job role, as well as his willingness to help others, she nevertheless couldn't tolerate any more of his shenanigans.*

*Chuck listened like a good coach should, asked questions, and promised immediate action. And true to coaching methods, Chuck called Larry into his office the following day. He gave great thought to what he was going to say to him and how he was going to say it. When Larry sat down before him, Chuck informed him that a serious problem had been brought to his attention. He proceeded to tell Larry of the complaint lodged against him. He intermingled his negative feedback—about the unacceptability of Larry's professional behavior—with positive feedback on his consistently solid job performance. Chuck told Larry, "Your knowledge and skills are an asset to the company. You wouldn't want to see your future impeded by behavior unbecoming a man of your talents." Larry was quite surprised at what he was told. Like so many people with such behavioral excesses, they often don't get it. They don't see their antics as in any way a problem, and they can't understand why anybody would be offended. So Chuck had the additional burden of communicating to his employee not only the problem itself, but also why it was a problem in the first place.*

*Finally, with persistence and tact, Chuck got his point across with the help of the sensitivity-plus approach. He allowed Larry his ample say in response, and ultimately the two reached solutions to a positive outcome. Larry agreed to be strictly business from that moment forward. He also set out to apologize to all the injured parties. His idea, too! He told Chuck that his job was extremely important to him, and that he didn't want to hinder, in any way, his climbing up the organizational ladder. Chuck then offered to give Larry follow-up feedback in the ensuing weeks. Melissa also agreed to wipe the slate clean, and graciously accepted Larry's apology and promise to rectify his behavior.*

This was a positive outcome to a very difficult, negative situation. Performance-related problems are usually clearer cut than are these dicey interpersonal situations. Now, if Larry's apology subsequently proved insincere, Chuck would have another problem to confront, and his search for a positive outcome would inevitably lead him to very different solutions the second time around.

# Chapter 9

# Communicating Vision and Goals

The most successful business enterprises know exactly where they want to go and how they're going to get there. In other words, they visualize their futures. This chapter underscores the importance of visions and goals for coaches, employees, and the companies at large, showing exactly how coaching and mentoring in management build bridges that span to the future.

## The Role of Coaches in Vision and Goals

The coaching and mentoring managerial philosophy is the ideal fit for forward-looking companies with a vision. All the tools and techniques described in the first eight chapters of this book are future-oriented. From performance planning to problem solving to trust building, the emphasis of coaching and mentoring is on doing the job today with a 20/20 pair of eyes peeled on tomorrow and the tomorrow after that. Simply understood, coaching and mentoring in management endeavor to make today's workplace a better place and ensure better futures in the process. Coaching and mentoring comprise a results-oriented managerial methodology that views every business situation and every personality through a prism of positive light and forward movement. This is why it's the perfect brand of leadership to meet and greet the unique demands of running a business in the twenty-first century.

**FACT**

Your mini-vision of the future as it pertains to both you and your employees is more significant than the company's mission statement. This is because you, as coach and mentor, can translate your company's broad, long-range goals into meaningful and doable personal goals that your employees can achieve in the here and now.

The role of senior leaders in any company is, among many things, to articulate a vision for the entire organization. But it's your job as a coach and manager of a particular niche in a company to take that grander vision and transpose it into a mini-vision of your own that channels all of your coaching decisions. A big company can espouse a lofty vision with noble, aggressive goals for its future growth. But, realistically, for the average employee in such an organization, a vision from on high doesn't amount to a hill of beans. The lower-echelon persons in a business enterprise are far too removed from the so-called big picture to get overly excited about it. This is precisely why the vision you articulate and apply as a coach has a whole lot more impact on your employees than the company's glowing and general goals for the future.

# Why Long-Term Planning Is So Important

An organization's vision often stretches out over years—ten and twenty years into the future are not unusual, and sometimes even longer than that. And that's fine and dandy for a company's long-range hopes and aspirations, but it's far too theoretical for the job you have to do. Let's face it: Neither you nor your employees are thinking much about the company in the year 2030. All of you, however, are focused on what you've got to accomplish in your current job roles. Foremost, as a coach and leader of men and women, you have to fret over the immediate future. You need to persuade your employees that what they do right now, and over the next six months, is relevant to both their present job situations *and* their long-term job futures. The coaching and mentoring mindset always links today's job with tomorrow's job.

Not to scare you, but you're actually charting many futures in your role as a coach—your own, your employees', and the company's to some extent. This is why you must remain vigilant and keep your coaching objectives sharp and measurable. What do you have to accomplish? What would you like to accomplish? What kinds of people do you have on your team to get the job done? How will you utilize this talent pool to maximize their productivity? How will you deal with the different personalities on your staff when problems arise?

Goal setting is at the heart of good coaching. Not only do employees need to work with goals, but you, as a coach, also need to be guided by them. Goals should always be realistic and reachable. Don't hesitate to make goals aggressive and bold, but keep the pie-in-the-sky where it belongs.

Spread out your objectives over a maximum six-month time frame—and no longer than that if you can help it. After that time span, begin the process all over again with new objectives that are equally as sharp and equally as measurable. Throughout this vision-building process, make certain that your employees understand that the building blocks for their long-term careers are taking shape in their present job roles while working for you.

## Goals Provide Direction

In order for any company's vision to unfold as planned over a period of years and decades, people like you—in coaching positions throughout organizations—have to see your own mini-visions through to successful conclusions. Your vision is, of course, derivative of the company's way of doing things. It has to be. You can't entertain a competing vision with the company that employs you. However, you need to extrapolate from your company's vision goals for yourself. You then embark, with your employees, in the mutual establishment of their individual goals.

**ALERT!**

Constant innovation is indispensable for companies that desire growth in the twenty-first century. And that includes employee innovation at all levels of the company. Coaching and mentoring invite employee innovation by both respecting human resources and constantly challenging individuals to find ways to do their jobs better and more efficiently.

### Above All Else: Goals Are Realistic

This notion of goal setting sounds a lot simpler than it actually is. You don't just sit around and, off the top of your head, blurt out goals for this and for that. If you want them to be taken seriously, goals must be serious business. The office scene isn't like the third grade, when Mrs. Victory asked you what you wanted to be when you grew up. Your life goal may be to build a raft, cross the ocean in it, and forge the next *Kon-Tiki* adventure. That's a nice dream. But the reality is that most people won't take your audacious goal very seriously.

Your goals—and the goals of your employees—should be realistic and attainable. If you espouse goals that are grandiose by nature, you'll promptly destroy your capacity to lead. You'll probably find yourself pounding the pavement, too, looking for another line of work. The discussion of employee performance plans in Chapter 3 included the job-specific goals that are the key starting points of all plans. These goals essentially summarize what each employee is expected to achieve (via action plans) within an agreed-upon time frame. And they are realistic and attainable.

## Individual Goals Are in Concert with Company Goals

Setting goals in all areas of a company is indispensable in today's cutthroat business climate. Goal setting transcends employee performance plans. They establish direction all across the board, and when realized, make the whole organization better in fundamental and demonstrable ways, not to mention the individuals responsible for seeing them through.

We've talked at length about performance goals and, of course, monetary goals, the quintessence of business achievement. But there are goals that revolve around attitudes and behaviors on the job, too. There are goals that focus on overall job satisfaction and others that concentrate on learning new skills. The list of goal-setting possibilities is infinite in scope.

## Career Development

As a coach, you care about your employees. This personal touch in a business environment is what most distinguishes you from your dinosaur manager doppelgangers. You care about your employees' futures, too. In fact, this is one area where you have no choice. You must concern yourself with your people's career development because of the nature of today's job market. That is, you must lord over an enriching work environment, where your employees can augment their skills and not fall behind the times—or you're going to lose the bulk of them to the competition. If you box in your employees, and cut off all learning opportunities, many of them will leave your employ for bigger and better things. It's that simple! This is yet another reason why conscientious goal setting is so critical. The goals you set with your employees are, in actuality, their growth and development potentials verbalized and then acted upon.

## Boldly Go

Contemplate this: When you set goals for yourself, you anticipate being more adept at something when they are realized. Think it through. If, for example, one of your goals is to see your entire department increase total sales by 20 percent in a six-month period—over and above the previous year's same time period—and you achieve that goal, you are a highly prized managerial commodity. By reaching your bold—but obtainable—goal, you've positively charted your future. You've immediately afforded yourself more choices in where you can venture next in your career.

**FACT**

Career development is a personal journey, unique to individuals. As a coach, it's not your job to make career decisions for others. However, it is an important part of your job description to cultivate and maintain a learning environment in the workplace.

As for goal setting in concert with your staff, the same logical reasoning applies. Your employees are naturally thinking about their careers—their futures—and not yours. Don't feel too bad about this! Just work closely in assisting them in setting their uniquely personal goals in the framework of the business goals you need to accomplish. Be always cognizant of how their present on-the-job goals can positively impact their futures. By making this enlightened long-range connection with your people, you will bond with them like crazy glue, and they in turn will work their arms and legs off for you.

## Let Your Employees Structure Their Goals

Both you and your staff should always view goals in the larger context of what all of you will have gained when they're met. This is precisely why your employees' job-related goals must be made *with* your employees and not *for* your employees. When individuals are largely responsible for charting their own courses, they more fully appreciate what goal setting means for their futures.

You know what's best for your own career development. But it would be presumptuous of you to assume that you know what's best for any one of your employees' careers. Remember that coaching is a support system first and foremost. Support doesn't mean dictating jobs, goals, or career moves.

## Advising Employees in Their Careers

What follows are some valuable career-development pointers that you should drive home to your employees. It's based on the experiences of successful men and women in business, their many lessons learned, and an overall understanding of the way things work and, of course, the way things are going to work tomorrow. The tips are designed to empower individuals to chart their own career courses.

### Establish Credentials

No matter what kind of work you do, keep on doing it, and doing it well. A successful track record of accomplishments gives you the vaunted credentials that so many jobs demand. Whether you want to write a book on botany, or hope to manage an office staff of sixty people, you're going to be asked, "What are your credentials?" If you've majored in accounting in college, and worked as an investment banker, and have nothing else on your resume, you're probably not the best-qualified person to write a book on botany. Similarly, if your job history is that of a night watchman at a milk-bottling plant, you're not the best candidate for managing an office crammed with people in the light of day. So, always give it your best in Job A, for it will help you get Job B. And Job C will be largely based on Jobs A and B. That's the way the cookie usually crumbles. A solid job track record adds up to solid job credentials. And with solid job credentials, you can write your own career ticket.

### Strengthen Strengths

Coaching and mentoring deem individuals to be unique beings with special talents and unique abilities all their own. Coaches labor valiantly to maximize individual performance by carefully tending to people, and understanding what they're all about, on a one-on-one basis. You know best what you excel in and what you most enjoy doing. These are the areas you should concentrate on and rely on to fulfill your career objectives and long-term ambitions. There's nothing more deflating than individuals in careers that bring them little joy and satisfaction, even when the money fields are green. Develop your special qualities to their fullest. Strengthen your strengths and know your weaknesses. Don't end up a square peg in a round-hole job.

**FACT**

Career development is something coaching and mentoring management practices are cognizant of at all times. Both you, as the coach, and your employees are in an environment where achieving on-the-job goals places you all on higher planes as worker commodities. In other words, there are more positive options available to you along the highways and byways of your individual career journeys.

### Be a People Person

Don't ever look upon your coworkers as if they are invisible, or worse, as obstacles in your career path. The most successful businesspersons are the ones who work alongside people and produce results in harmonious team settings. These men and women view their peers as extraordinary individuals—each with something to teach them. And they know that someday, one of these people may be in a position to help—perhaps in getting a job or supplying the name of somebody who can provide an important lead. The bottom line is: Establish amicable, professional relationships throughout your whole working career. Do this and you'll have plenty of useful contacts to tap into as your career unfolds and takes those inevitable twists and turns. It helps to know people. People, that is, who both know and respect you.

### Instill a Sense of Destiny

A crucial role of a coach is to instill in workers a sense of destiny. If you manage with the realistic goals we've talked about, for both you and your employees, and you all realize them, you are on to something big— really big. Your employees' success here will convince them, like nothing else could, that they're the prime movers in charting their career courses.

By seeing goals through, individuals in all positions are better for having set out to do big things, succeeded in doing them, and emerged from the whole goal-setting process more valuable worker commodities and better human beings, with greater knowledge, skills, and self-esteem.

### Conduct a Reality Check

All of this focus on the importance of goals in the workplace sometimes confuses people unfamiliar with the purposes of coaching and mentoring in business circles. They think that coaching gives rise to a workplace more on the entertainment side of the ledger than the work side. These misguided souls envision the work climate under the leadership of a coach as something akin to visiting a theme park with cotton candy melting in their mouths and big red balloons in their hands. It's time to burst those balloons.

Please your staff and the company that pays your salary, and you've accomplished what you were hired to do. This one-two punch always leads to success on numerous fronts. That is, you've improved your immediate lot and the lots of those who work alongside you. You've also brightened your future, as well as the futures of hardworking employees.

Coaching and mentoring have nothing to do with employees having a grand old time, nor are they about satisfying workers' delusions of grandeur. Coaching and mentoring methodologies are nothing if not firmly planted in reality. It's a reality of what people can do, and what makes them want to do it and do it well.

So, it's an absolute necessity that you always keep your employees rooted in the possible, because impractical goals are more than just pointless; they are disruptive in a business setting and harmful to job satisfaction and the overall bottom line of the company. On a person-to-person analysis, you've got to assess what each member of your team is truly capable of, and in what time parameters they can produce the results you need.

## Enhancing Self-Awareness in Employees

A key tenet of coaching and mentoring involves the coach getting to know his or her employees. The reason for this valuable connection is not so they become best friends with one another. As a coach, you want to identify your staff's real talents and abilities—i.e., their job skills, be they technical, interpersonal, leadership qualities, and so on. It's one thing to know that your employee Albert just became a father for the first time, but it's far more important to know what Albert can do for you as an employee of the company. Nevertheless, congratulate him on the new addition to his family.

When you know your people inside and out—know exactly what their specific job roles are and how they are performing in them—you are best prepared to stave off any debilitating disruptions in performance. This deep-rooted knowledge helps you maximize positive results and productivity at the same time.

### Help Employees Become Self-Aware

Some people, let's face facts, are not particularly self-aware. You know their kind. They often have perceptions of their talents and possibilities that don't jibe with reality. It's very often the case that these men and women believe they can do things that they plainly cannot. And vice versa. Some folks are capable of doing many things that they don't think they can do.

Most people know all too well from their own experiences that perceptions and reality are not always one and the same. An important part of your job is to make perceptions equal reality in the office. You can't have it any other way in a business setting. You can't allow employees to lead important projects just because they want to do it. There must be compelling evidence that they are qualified and up to the task. If you, and/or members of your team, don't feel that these ambitious employees are ready for such key job roles, then you know what you have to do. Just say "no."

Yes, a coach has got to say "no" on occasion. When perceptions do not measure up to reality, this is one such time. This doesn't ever mean that you condemn employees to their current level of skills or job roles. Not at all. Among your many roles as a coach, you are a matchmaker, too. But it's compatible jobs—not soul mates—that you are finding for your employees. But then, the right job is something of a soul mate, isn't it?

Often you will be confronted with employees who have perceptions of their talents and abilities that don't correspond with reality. An important part of your coaching job is to place people in job roles they can fulfill. Employees believing they can do particular jobs is not enough—they've got to be able to do them.

## Matching Employees' Goals with Their Skills

So much of coaching involves evaluating employee abilities and matching those abilities with specific jobs and tasks. Mismatching employees' abilities with their jobs—not uncommon in the business realm, sad to say—leads to lackluster performances, overall disarray, and widespread dissension. You're not in a coaching role to act as the blue fairy granting your employees' every wish and satisfying their every desire.

As a coach, you're charged with putting the right people in the right jobs and inspiring them to perform at their highest levels. If your employees are overrating or underrating themselves, it's your job to set them straight. People with strong people skills should be in jobs where people skills count most. People with top-notch skills in financial management should be showcasing their stuff in this area. And so on and so forth.

## A Coach's Performance Plan

There's no time like the present to organize all of your coaching efforts. Chapter 3 laid out the key elements of performance planning and discussed how each employee is guided by the minutia of such plans. However, not much mention was made of a coach's own performance plans. Yes, you read it right. A coach's performance plans! These are not formal contracts, as are employees' performance plans. They are, nevertheless, essential. Work with several performance plans of your own and evaluate your progress every step of the way.

A coach sits atop a coaching triangle with communication and coordination at its two bottom angles. Regular and consistent communication leads to solid coordination of job efforts. These highly choreographed endeavors ensure positive outcomes to performance plans and achievement of goals.

Your acute supervisory role in the office makes it imperative that you be a model of probity and consistency in all of your coaching actions. That is, design your own performance plans based on the coaching standard known as principled coherence. Principled coherence merely asks that you do exactly what you tell your employees you are going to do, and when you tell them you are going to do it.

For example, the safety checks inserted into your employees' performance plans are put there for sound business reasons. If you neglect follow-up evaluations on the progression of these plans, you will quickly lose your credibility as a coach. Similarly, when your employees set goals of any kind, you've got to always be aware of what they are, and whether or not they're on course to meet them. Your own performance plans must thus record when any employee evaluations are to take place and what measures you'll be using in doing the evaluating. Don't expect your employees to come to you and say, "It's time for my evaluation!" You always need to be one step ahead—and fully prepared for each new step you take.

# Chapter 10

# Measuring Your Coaching Effectiveness

There will come a time in your coaching career when you will need to conduct a thorough inventory of your myriad coaching and mentoring efforts. This chapter will show you how to properly evaluate your coaching and mentoring managerial moves and determine if you are realizing the best possible results. It'll furnish you with all the right tools to measure your overall effectiveness at achieving the positive outcomes that you need as a leader in a highly competitive, results-oriented business environment.

## *Evaluating Your Coaching Job*

Unlike more traditional managers, coaches anticipate and welcome fine-tuning in managerial thinking when necessary. Coaching and mentoring is nothing if not a very resilient style of managing. When the situation calls for it, coaching is prepared to change course at the drop of a hat.

You must regularly evaluate your employees' performances, but also your performance as a leader of men and women. Taking stock of the effectiveness of your coaching is something you should do on a frequent basis if you hope to keep your managerial tools and techniques sharp and employee output maximized.

This is precisely why thorough, but not smothering, supervision of your employees' overall performances is so vital. Based on these periodic evaluations, coaching facilitates smooth changes and shifts in planning, without upsetting the office apple cart. By now you appreciate that goal setting, performance planning, and checkpoint measures play critical roles in good coaching. But regularly taking stock of your successes and failures as a coach is equally important. Ascertaining whether your coaching efforts are at the level they should be will help you maximize your performance, which in turn maximizes your employees' performances.

## *Your Unique Coaching Style*

Coaching asks that you manage and work with employees on an individual and very intimate basis. It stands to reason, then, that your coaching style will be quite distinct from the style of another coach working in an entirely different setting, with a totally different gaggle of personalities. Coaches are people, too. You are a unique fish in a pond who will interpret the many tools and techniques of coaching in a way that complements your personality.

Coaching formulas are pliable and open to a great deal of interpretation as to how they should be applied. Coaching is always a work in progress.

Chapter 9 addressed the problem of perceptions versus reality and how you must recognize the discrepancies that exist between one and the other with regard to your employees' talents and performance possibilities. But before you can make any of these critical judgments about your staff, you have to make absolutely certain that you're on solid ground yourself. That is, you have to know how your coaching style is playing in Peoria, as it were—among your people. You must know how your employees perceive your leadership and how they are reacting to it. You must know if you are truly getting the most out of their performances, while simultaneously fashioning a satisfying and healthy work environment conducive to maximum productivity.

## Coaching Treasure Hunt

How exactly can you ascertain if you're maximizing your own job performance? There are many telltale indicators that can clue you in as to whether or not your decision making is engendering maximum employee performance and the positive outcomes that are at the foundations of all successful coaching efforts. Let's say, for example, that you go out on a limb and tap high-performing employee Kelly as an ideal candidate for mentoring. You see her as ripe for advancement in the company because of her growth in skills, her insatiable appetite for learning, and strong self-motivation. In your estimation, she's done everything you've asked of her and more. You've in effect taken her under your wing, and you believe now is the appropriate time to give her a mentor—a higher-up in the organization to groom her for advancement into the managerial hierarchy.

In taking proper stock of your performance as a coach, pay extra close attention to your enthusiasm and passion for the work at hand. It has been established that leaders who exhibit passion for their job duties inevitably induce the trickle-down effect, with their employees following in their fervent footsteps.

So, you speak to Kelly about the idea. And not surprisingly, she exhibits excitement and expresses her gratitude for the confidence that you're showing in her abilities and potential. Soon after your chat, however, with the wheels set in motion, you notice that Kelly is neglecting her immediate job responsibilities, with a noticeable drop-off in her performance. And as if that's not bad enough, you hear she's been telling a few coworkers that she's interviewing for jobs with competitors. Hey, you've got a huge problem here. You've also got a warning bell sounding that your overall coaching, decision making, and evaluation apparatus has a few bugs in it.

Your employees are going to make a lot of mistakes and behave unprofessionally on occasion. And even you, a noble coach, are going to make your fair share of misjudgments, too. You've always got to manage with this reality in mind. You've got to learn from your mistakes and move forward, not wallow in them and backtrack.

## QUESTION?

**Is "work ethic" another term for "hard work"?**
The work ethic encompasses more than mere dedication to hard labor. It entails conscientiousness in doing a job—any job. There are some very hard workers in the corridors of business who are unprofessional to the core in their attitudes and behaviors. You want to instill a true work ethic in your employees.

This example of your mentee Kelly reveals an evaluation error on your part. It's incumbent upon you to fully grasp the many ingredients that impact your decision making. What were the variables that went into your tapping of Kelly as a rising star in the organization? Why did you place your complete trust in her? Why did she rebuff the loyalty that you showered on her? Was it something in your coaching approach that caused this apparent breach in faith? Was there something in your coaching ways that caused you to misread Kelly's intentions? You've got to uncover the root causes of a predicament like this—and, indeed, every other problem in the office that involves your decisions and judgment calls.

# Professionalism: The ABCs

This book presumes that you know, without a lengthy explanation, the difference between professional and unprofessional behavior on the job. In trying to define pornography and what constituted it in a legal sense, Supreme Court Justice William Brennan once said, "I know it when I see it." Most coaches say the same thing about professional and unprofessional behavior; they know it when they see it. Nevertheless, in this era of a general coarsening of our lives, the line between professional and unprofessional behavior in business has been blurred, just as it has everywhere else.

**FACT**

The professionalism that you insist on as a coach, and as a leader of men and women, defines the overall work habits that reign in the office, and hence, the end results. When your employees function in their jobs as true professionals, a positive and productive work environment is the inevitable byproduct.

## Understanding What Is and Isn't Professional

Professionalism gets to the heart of right and wrong; what's ethical and what's unethical. It can't be easily measured because it often involves attitude and certain behaviors, and not hard, quantifiable results. For instance, monetary objectives produce quantifiable results—they're either met or they're not met. But how one achieves these monetary results—and all other results in business—is just as important as the results themselves.

This statement might come as a big shock to some businesspersons. However, the ends do not justify the means in any organization that puts a premium on fairness and on the integrity of its personnel.

For example, Ed, in sales, may be a wizard in finding new customers and pumping up orders. But if his selling tactics involve deceit, or browbeating his coworkers to generate more of this business, then his inflated results are not something to laud or reward. Professionalism on the job encompasses how the job is done. It's about the methods that employees use to go from point A to point Z and accomplish what they were hired to do. It's also about their interactions with others, be they on the inside (coworkers) or the outside (customers). The corporate world is awash in overambitious men and women, some of them seemingly successful if measured by their 401(k) plans. But this measurement of their success is meaningless if the road to their ever-increasing riches is littered with unprofessional actions.

## How Your Team Mirrors Your Professionalism

You need to measure the professionalism of your team because it is the ultimate reflection on your leadership. Problems, and the importance of addressing them early and at the source, often mean confronting the unprofessional attitudes and behaviors of some of your employees. And although unprofessionalism covers a wide array of poor attitudes and behaviors, it is nevertheless important to stress that no manifestations of them should be permitted to take root.

Negative outlooks, actions, and work habits disseminate more easily and freely than do positive outlooks, actions, and work habits—another unfortunate but important fact of life that coaches need always remember. There are the people who think, "John uses a lot of people for his own ends and cuts a lot of corners—and nobody notices or seems to care. So why am I being conscientious in my work and doing all these little extra things, when it doesn't seem to matter?"

You may have the most knowledgeable and skilled employees in the world, but if they don't exhibit the professional work habits to match their get up and go and know-how, you might not get the results you expect and desire from them. Solid work habits fuel talent and permit genuine expertise to shine.

This kind of chain reaction mentality is commonplace. Poor attitudes and bad behavior spread like a cancer if the unprofessionalism of one employee is ignored or in any way tolerated or condoned. This is why the ethical boundaries and work ethic that you establish at the core of your coaching must be defended as well as declared. You must insist that the proper ethical attitudes and behavior be adhered to faithfully on the job. By requiring anything less, you render such behavioral standards frivolous.

Your employees must never be permitted to regard professional behavior as some vague or nebulous textbook stuff. They've got to see ethics on the job as something living and real, as something that matters, and as something that is faithfully guarded by you, the coach, without exception.

## The Minutia of Professional Behavior

The movie classic *Love Story* gave us a haunting melancholic theme and the oft-repeated platitude, "Love means never having to say you're sorry." Well, coaching means never taking anything for granted—anything at all. So don't fall into the trap of taking on-the-job professionalism for granted. Don't assume that all the men and women who work for you fully grasp the ABCs of professionalism. This is a roundabout way of saying that you are going to have to teach some of your employees these essential ABCs. Some of them will need more help in this area than others. A few unrefined employees may even fall into the Ernest T. Bass (boorish to the core) category, but most will be reachable and teachable.

In your initial orientation and training of new employees—high-octane coaching—your job is to make known and abundantly clear the basic ways the office functions, including the specific expectations you have for each one of your staff members. Don't neglect to mention here that a professional demeanor is something that every employee of yours, regardless of job description or role, is expected to maintain at all times—without exception. Some managers inculcate their employees with performance expectations ad infinitum, and focus on bold goals and growth opportunities, while giving short shrift, or ignoring completely, the professional attitudes and behavior behind these performances, which are equally, if not more essential.

Can you impart professionalism to the uncouth employee? In the classic sitcom *The Andy Griffith Show*, Sheriff Taylor failed to impart refinement to Ernest T. Bass, but Bass was as crass as they come. As with so many lessons, learning is entirely up to the student. A receptive student can readily absorb the important tenets that characterize professionalism. But just as in the earlier discourse on motivation, it all boils down to the particular individual's willingness to move forward and better him- or herself. Nevertheless, you've still got to unequivocally define for all of your employees what professional behavior means in the workplace. And you've got to hold them to the standards of this exacting definition. And if any of your employees repudiate professional behavior, and refuse to make the necessary adjustments in their work habits, then you don't want them on your team. Period.

## Working with Professionalism

There are five points of professionalism that you can work with and insist your employees both understand and abide by at all times:

- Integrity
- Initiative
- Resilience
- Positive Attitude
- Teamwork

### Integrity

If you can't trust your employees to be truthful—open and up front with you and their coworkers—you won't maximize their performances, nor will you preside over a robust, positive work environment. In addition, the further points of professionalism will be rendered meaningless if integrity is not firmly entrenched. Integrity is the bedrock of professionalism.

What happens when honesty and integrity aren't King and Queen in the office? You get workplaces that are rife with backstabbing, deceit, and slothful performances—unprofessional environments in which to conduct any kind of business. So it is incumbent upon you to closely monitor whether you are always getting the straight facts from your people, variations of the truth, or—in the worst-case scenarios—bald-faced lies.

You've got to be eternally vigilant in this all-important area and fully appreciate that in today's business world the sharing of information is vital. This means that one person's veracity or lack thereof will have a negative impact on countless other people and their job performances.

No workplace, or any other place for that matter, exists in a state of chastity. But this is one of the big reasons why coaching and mentoring in corporate management was born. Its tools and techniques confront and correct imperfections that run a wide gamut. Unprofessional behaviors (imperfections) need to be nipped in the bud before they become the dominant way of life in the office. And when they win the day, you lose your job.

> An employee attribute that you must always insist on is reliability. Each and every member of your team has to be reliable—someone that you can trust come hell or high water. The bottom line is that you need the men and women who work for you to deliver both timely and quality results on a consistent basis.

There is indeed a societal paradox that powerfully impacts on business life. And that's the enduring conflict between what we know is right and just, and our embracing and even endorsing proven liars in our culture at large. Still, we need to not only expect and demand professionalism in the workplace—where again, honesty and integrity are at the apex—but to insist upon it, too, in our families, friendships, and political leaders.

## Initiative

The second point of professionalism is initiative. A professional employee exhibits a perpetual openness to initiative and the creativity that springs from it. In the rapidly changing world of business, nobody can sit back and watch these changes pass them by. Professional behavior involves a desire to acquire knowledge and develop new skills, coupled with a willingness to take these advanced skills and knowledge to a higher level.

As a coach, you are a teacher and trainer in a continuous learning environment. Your aim is to be the proverbial magnet for talent. You want to attract people to join your team and the organization you work for. You want men and women working for you who exhibit an insatiable appetite for learning and forward movement.

## Resilience

The third point of professionalism is resilience. Professional people can take a few punches and they don't fall down. Professionals bounce back and acclimate to new circumstances. They aren't averse to change, but instead welcome it as a challenge and as an inevitable part of working in the modern business world.

Resiliency, in fact, is more than ever necessary in these technologically driven times. If you aren't resilient in today's workplace, you are sentenced to a life of dead-end jobs in low-skilled occupations. As a coach, you have a perpetual bounce in your step and should expect your employees to bounce along with you.

## Positive Attitude

The fourth point of professionalism is a positive attitude. Employees with negative attitudes, sad to say, are roaming the business landscape like Bigfoot in the wilds of the forest. One of the greatest challenges in all of coaching is sorting out exactly why a particular employee is so negative, so unprofessional. In these cases, you've got to determine if the poor attitude stems from the job itself, a personality quirk, a personal problem, or a combination of all three (which is often the case).

The truth is, even one employee's negative attitude can prove a very toxic thing in the close confines of an office. And there will always be employees who harbor negative attitudes and spread discontent to one and all who will listen to their displeasure. Keep a watchful eye out for these kinds of people.

## Teamwork

The fifth and final point of professionalism is teamwork. So much of corporate life today revolves around work getting done in teams or groups. And, because of this strong reliance on others, you've got to make sure all of your people work together in perfect harmony—or something close to it. You've got to make certain your staff gets along with one another as professional men and women pulling toward the same positive result. That every single person who works for you must be "on the same page" is truer now more than ever.

The need to share information to get the job done makes it imperative that you have team players working as individuals but also in unison. If you permit a lone wolf to run around howling to the office ceilings, when coordination of efforts is an absolute necessity, you're going to encounter disruptions and other serious problems. Professional behavior and the capacity to work well with others are inextricably linked.

## *The Work Ethic*

Most people agree that smoking is a bad habit. Even if you're a smoker, you will probably concede that point. Most likely a similar consensus could be forged that a Twinkie and six cups of coffee is not a healthy breakfast. But these kinds of bad habits can be tolerated in the work environment provided they don't adversely impact on job performance. The bad habits of particular interest to coaches are work-specific and need to be meticulously weeded out and corrected.

The work habits, i.e., the work ethic, of your employees are what will make or break you as a coach. This chapter talks about taking stock—making self-evaluations—of how you are doing. And many of these evaluations are not so easily measured because they are abstract in nature. That is, they are subject to a great deal of interpretation on your part—interpretations, often, on your own conduct, decision making, and overall leadership abilities. The work ethic in your office, and on your team, covers the vast spectrum of what we've addressed in this chapter. Professional behavior on the job means that work habits are solid and consistent. If you don't see to it that both you and your people maintain a work ethic that is solution- and positive-results-oriented, you will not thrive in the role of coach.

There are many treasuries of knowledge out there who sport exceptional technical skills. In other words, there are individuals you want on your team because they bring with them mother lodes of impressive credentials. But they've also got to perform their imposing skills in a professional manner. Those who lack the professionalism to get the most out of their know-how do more harm than good in the workplace. Voters don't elect a resume as president. Nor do companies hire a resume as an employee. The person most qualified to do the job may not be the one with the best credentials on paper. Education, experience, and technical skills are obviously very important, and that's where your employee search begins. But it's people with the best work ethics and desires to improve themselves who often emerge victorious when the final hiring decisions are made.

Chapter 11

# Time Management

There are only twenty-four hours in a single day, and the workday is considerably shorter. In the business trenches, coaches are expected to master the challenges that time management consistently presents. Whether they are in the private or public sectors—it doesn't matter—coaches battle the enemies of time management with everything at their disposal. This chapter surveys the vital role of coaching and mentoring methodologies in maximizing productivity by properly managing the finite constraints of time.

## *Prioritizing Is Job One*

If the role of the coach in the workplace had to be spelled out in several words, it might read: *setting the right priorities*. So much of business and business success is rooted in the prioritization of tasks and making certain that they get done in a reasonable period of time. The expression, "Time waits for no one," assumes a higher meaning in the often pressure-filled environs of business, where every boss wants things done right and right away.

### *Today Is the Day*

As a coach, you are charged with making every day *the day*. Essentially, your job is to motivate a team of people into believing that they are working on the most important tasks and in the most important roles *today*. Even though you operate with long-term plans and goals stretching into the future, you've got to remain grounded in the here and now. You've got to make certain that those working alongside you are likewise concentrating their efforts on today's priorities—not tomorrow's or next year's.

**FACT**

There are twenty-four hours in a day. The workday is typically eight to ten hours. These facts of nature and societal mores underscore that time itself cannot *literally* be managed. What can be managed are individuals and what they do with their finite time. This is the truest definition of time management.

It all sounds so simple. But getting your employees to consider each working day as somehow vital to the big picture isn't always a stroll in the park, particularly when they are working on so many ongoing projects that stretch months and even years into the future. This acute slice of business reality is why you should begin each workday with a clear set of priorities for both yourself and for those whom you are responsible for managing. In fact, at the onset of each workday, among *your* own priorities should be a clear enunciation of each one of your employees' priorities. In business environments—just as in life in general—time flies. And you cannot afford to let it fly right by you, even for a single day.

## A Veritable Who's Who

When prioritizing to best manage workplace time constraints, you would be wise to pull out your metaphorical coaching and mentoring "Who's Who?" book and leaf through its pages. When applying coaching and mentoring procedures in the workplace, you are called upon time and again to view your employees as individuals in very unique roles and responsible for very specific job duties. When you look upon those working for you in such a forward-thinking way, you instinctively get a sharper and more realistic feel for *who's who* under your big tent, and you know—precisely—what each individual in your employ is supposed to be doing and accomplishing every single hour of every single day.

Although delegation of important work responsibilities is an essential part of the coaching and mentoring philosophy, a coach, nevertheless, should know what each one of his employees is working on at any given moment. A coach should also know what her employees should accomplish by the end of each workday. Time management always amounts to painstaking people management.

To their ultimate chagrin (and sometimes loss of their jobs), there are managers who put the entire workday—and, in fact, the entire work scene—on automatic pilot. In the process, they neglect their all-important oversight duties. In stark contrast, coaches delegate real responsibilities and job tasks to each member of their staff, but they also regularly measure results. This crucial supervisory role is fundamental to good time management.

## The Enemies of Time Management

As an ever-vigilant coach, it behooves you to recognize time management's most relentless enemies. They are always at the ready, patiently waiting to torpedo your best-laid plans. But then, if everything always went according to plan and all tasks and projects were completed on time and on the money, there would be no need for coaches and coaching skills. Accomplished coaches know how to beat the enemies of time management at their own game.

**FACT**

The most common enemies of time management in the workplace are procrastination, poor planning, unnecessary interruptions, overwork, and good old-fashioned incompetence. Coaching and mentoring methodologies are designed to triumph over these longstanding adversaries. While every workplace is confronted with time management snafus on occasion, properly coached ones have considerably fewer to contend with.

### Procrastination

Procrastination has long been a thorn in the backside of humankind. Generals in war have put off key battles for less propitious times and met with disaster because of it. Individuals have allowed health concerns to fester into major medical problems until, in some unfortunate instances, it was too late. Unsuccessful businesspersons are notorious for *not* taking the bull by the horns and, as a result, falling by the wayside into the dustbin of entrepreneurial failure. Indeed, there are many procrastinators in our midst. And, no surprise here, the workplace is chock full of them.

Because it is such an entrenched shard of human nature, procrastination is always an issue on the job frontier. As both a coach and leader of men and women, you cannot afford to procrastinate. Procrastination from on high is guaranteed to develop into a careening snowball that will roll over every single body—one by one by one.

Let's assume then that you are not a procrastinator. A successful coach cannot be one. How can you ensure that members of your team won't fall victim to the procrastinating virus?

As a team leader, you assign roles and assorted tasks to individuals who are your personal responsibility. You work with persons who are hired, in most instances, to do very explicit things. In other words, your staff has defined responsibilities—i.e., they are expected to accomplish certain things by certain times. This is how business works. By definition then, procrastination on the job is a shirking of one's responsibilities. This is the case you must make—in no uncertain terms—to those who work alongside your patient and guiding hand.

In the workplace, postponing one's prescribed duties for another day is a recipe for disaster—it could even lead to the dreaded firing line. As a coach, you've got to see to it that procrastinating is not part and parcel of your daily work life. You've got to keep close tabs on the work at hand and those who are responsible for doing it. This is the only sure method to overpower this very stubborn enemy of time management.

The reality is that if you know what work has to be done each and every day, you'll always know if it is, in fact, getting done. By consistently evaluating the progress of employee tasks and the overall status of projects-in-motion, you'll know—at any given moment—if procrastination on the job is a problem. Then you'll be empowered with the facts you need to turn the culpable procrastinators into producers (or, regrettably, to turn them loose if they are not amenable to the conversion). The bottom line is that you cannot ever permit procrastinators to erect intractable problems, which they will most certainly do if they are allowed to work at their own paces and in their own ways.

## *Poor Planning*

On the face of it, it's one of the most apparent enemies of time management. It's known as poor planning. Yet, it is anything but obvious in countless work environments—until it's too late.

As a coach, you are obviously expected to plan—to plan today for tomorrow and tomorrow for the tomorrow after that. You set goals and establish important benchmarks for the future. As already emphasized in this chapter, this amounts to keeping a watchful eye on the moment at hand—because you can only build a successful future by what you are accomplishing today.

But because it often goes undetected until it's a fait accompli, poor planning at the starting gate is a monumental problem in workplaces everywhere. If you and members of your staff are working with long-term goals, all kinds of deadlines, and anticipated future results, it's in all of your best interests to be on the right path from the get-go. In other words, your initial coaching road map should be as free of potholes as is humanly possible—i.e., with employees in appropriately assigned job roles and armed with practical output expectations for today, tomorrow, next week, and next month.

**ALERT!**

You can ill afford to discover poor planning well into project development. What you then have on your watch is a mountain of wasted time. Poor planning forces you to alter course. It leaves you with fewer work hours to achieve your ultimate goals and reduces the likelihood of achieving them on deadline.

It may sound incredibly self-evident to suggest that you'd be wise to make sure that your plans are as watertight and well thought out as possible before you implement them. But the reality is that poor planning from up above happens all the time—and it frequently puts both managers and employees in tenuous positions vis-à-vis their jobs and livelihoods. Nevertheless, recovery from mistakes—including poor planning—is always possible. Coaching and mentoring formulas assist in speedy recoveries from all kinds of workplace missteps. But time constraints *always* loom on the work frontlines—and sometimes like heartless leviathans just waiting to gobble up human capital. Plan right—right from the start—and you'll be all right.

## Unnecessary Interruptions

In the time management scheme of things, there's nothing quite like those inevitable but mostly unnecessary interruptions. In the workplace, they cannot be altogether avoided—that's the reality—but they certainly can be kept to a minimum. By establishing certain rules while simultaneously promoting a harmonious work environment, unnecessary interruptions can be tamed in number and, when they do occur, misspent time kept to a bare minimum.

**FACT**

Examples of unnecessary workplace interruptions include personal telephone conversations, frequent trips to coffee machines and the bathroom (when nature isn't calling), and extended conversations with coworkers on matters unrelated to job concerns. These kinds of interruptions appear rather trivial and unimportant in the big picture, but they can rapidly add up to full hourglasses of squandered time.

In practice, tackling unnecessary workplace interruptions frequently asks you to walk a very fine line. That is, you cannot afford to make a name for yourself as the manager who doesn't let his employees visit the lavatory for more than two minutes at a time, or who monitors every word passed between coworkers. This brand of petty managing will surely augur a colossal morale problem, beyond a time management one. In order for coaching and mentoring management to fully take flight, respect has got to be its two wings.

What a coach must do in this decidedly gray area is establish straightforward, but not vindictive, guidelines concerning workplace conduct. The rules shouldn't include timing visits to the bathroom with a stopwatch or counting on an abacus employee trips to the coffee machine. However, they should always insist on a total commitment to the work at hand. So, if Gary drinks a lot of coffee, but does his job—no problem. If Bethany gets an occasional personal phone call, but meets all of her work targets—then okay.

The real problems arise when employees do the very things that Gary and Bethany do, but who don't fulfill their job responsibilities. Herein lies a bona fide coaching task: To treat individual staff members as distinctive persons with singular personalities and work habits. So much of this book's discussion revolves around dealing with individuals on a one-on-one basis in what has long been viewed as the coldest, cruelest, and most impersonal places on the planet—the corporate work environs.

## Overwork

There is an enemy of time management that is idiosyncratic by nature and that often perplexes managers and employees alike. After all, how can too much work be a foe of proper time management? Through the years, many managers in many different industries have fallen prey to the "work them till they drop" credo. In other words, they've asked for more than their employees could realistically deliver.

It's one thing being a marine drill sergeant in front of wet-behind-the-ears recruits. They, after all, are entering a profession that is going to expect a lot out of them, including putting themselves in harm's way on real live battlefronts. But the run-of-the-mill workplace is not quite the same, despite what some tomes would have you believe. There are no bombs detonating nearby or gunfire whizzing by anybody's ears in office places and on retail and service job fronts. And so the typical workplace environments should not be treated as boot camps.

**ALERT!**

Overloading your people with work and job responsibilities that they cannot possibly fulfill are time wasters. Longer and longer hours often create dissension and—in the big picture—poorer results. As a managerial art, coaching and mentoring understands human nature and, thus, how to get the most out of human capital without ever exploiting genuine, breathing human beings.

Sure, overwork amounts to "work" getting done. But, in many instances, it is not the right work—not what you want accomplished. More mistakes are made when people are overworked. In addition, tired and unfocused employees encounter more obstacles in undertaking their regular job tasks. Overwork inevitably leads to more job corrections. That is, finite work hours are expended retracing the tracks of work already done—but not done correctly.

## Incompetence

We know that some people confuse coaching and mentoring managerial strategies with forms of therapeutic counsel. Others think that coaching and mentoring works with a copy of the Declaration of Independence in its proverbial pocket—and that one and all are created equal with no distinctions ever made between or among employees. Well, under civil law, all men and women are seen as equal (or, at least, they should be seen that way). But in the business world, not every individual is of equal competence and equal temperament—far from it. While coaching and mentoring asks managers to scrupulously avoid one-size-fits-all approaches to problem solving, it doesn't ask them to make no distinctions of individual employees' abilities.

Having the right people in the right jobs is essential to good time management. Incompetent job performances inevitably lead to failures in accomplishing goals and meeting crucial deadlines. Just as with poor planning, men and women in roles that they cannot possibly fulfill always portends a breakdown in project development. Incompetent work eats up valuable time.

Sometimes you've got very intelligent and capable people working for you, only they are in the wrong jobs. Coaches are expected to do their necessary homework by not only inhaling people's resumes, but by regularly talking with their employees and assessing their potential. Coaches repeatedly observe what their people do right and wrong and identify areas where improvement is needed. Simply stated: They know their people. This scrupulous brand of people management minimizes the deleterious effects of incompetence.

# Dealing with Problems Head On

Problems that require solving are part of life. In the workplace, problematic circumstances are both plentiful and range far and wide from computer glitches to ineptitude to internecine warfare between and among staff members. But regardless of the type of problem at hand—be it mechanical or personal—it has to be addressed. Workplace problems cannot be ignored in hopes that they work themselves out on their own. (They rarely do.) No, they have to be tackled—*and sooner rather than later.*

## Don't Let Things Fester

While Uncle Fester—the simultaneously beloved and bizarre character from the *Addams Family*—is perhaps the best known "Fester" around town, the workplace knows of another one. That is, the *fester* of festering problems. You know, of all kinds of troubles brewing and not dealt with head on and with a firm purpose of resolving them once and for all. The reality is that festering workplace problems can rapidly become red hot and spread like wildfire, portending more sober problems and, of course, very precious time squandered.

The seemingly painless course that all too many managers take in this dicey area is the pathway of least resistance. Let's say, for example, the workplace predicament is poor morale among the troops. Wouldn't you say that the manager on the scene ought to get to the bottom of the problem—and as soon as possible? Of course you would! And if the manager in question discovers that many in her employ feel that she favors Wendy over Peter, then she's got to do something about that perception—whether she believes it or not.

The most knee-jerk approach to this problem would find the aforementioned manager declaring the perception of favoritism "a bunch of nonsense," and casually dismissing those who might feel otherwise. Many managers function this way. That is, if they don't see what others see—rightly or wrongly—they think the problem or concern is unworthy of their attention.

As a coach, you cannot afford to dismiss anything that even resembles a budding problem—and certainly not anything that will eat up finite time. Good coaches are aware that what may appear inconsequential on the surface—and to the big picture—may, in fact, be a festering situation that will come back to haunt them in considerable time lost—both a productivity and profit hit from which they may not ever recover.

## Heads Up Is Head On

There is an oft-uttered expression heard on sports playing fields and in gym classes everywhere. It goes something like this: "Heads up!" It is bellowed from the mouths of concerned men, women, boys, and girls all across the planet. "Heads up!" serves as an important warning bell for a peer of theirs about to get hit in the head with an airborne baseball, or, in some other body part, by an errant soccer ball.

Coaching and mentoring, and the maximization of time management, can take home a valuable lesson from all of those playing fields and gymnasiums. Maximizing the use of time in the business sphere demands that you are *heads-up* at all times. The business equivalent of those wayward soccer balls and baseballs is a litany of problems dashing toward you while you are completely unaware. If you don't have your head up—bang! This ignorance of what's happening all around you can lead to a whole lot of pain at some point in the future.

# Teaching Employees to Manage Themselves

Fear not! The advice in this section is not a contradiction of what has previously been discussed in this chapter. On the contrary, it is counsel that is perfectly consistent with all that has been said about coaching practices and the maximization of time management. Indeed, a first-class coach educates his employees on the ways and means of managing themselves. Hey, but what about all of the prior talk about a coach's hands-on, heads-up managing and the need to continuously measure results? How then can employees manage themselves? Employee self-management doesn't appear to jibe with a coach's job responsibilities. Ah, but it does.

## The Self-Managing Employee

Under the coaching and mentoring approach of managing, employees are given specific jobs to do. They are assigned very precise roles. And they are expected to meet regular project deadlines. In other words, they are called upon to deliver the goods, as it were, on time and on budget.

The coach—and leader of a team—is responsible for setting the entire worktable. Along the way, he allocates to each one of his employees a job and a very defined role. On an individual basis, he works with members of his team in establishing goals, benchmarks, and—yes—key deadlines, too. When both the coach and the employee sign off on the employee's work responsibilities, it's a covenant of sorts. In the process, the coach is saying that he has confidence in a particular person's ability to get the job done and get it done with minimal interference from him. A coach's normal supervising of progress and regular oversight is not akin to latching a ball and chain to a member of his staff.

Coaches delegate important work responsibilities and job tasks to their employees. Delegation of authority is a fundamental part of the coaching and mentoring philosophy. This empowerment of the workforce is key to proper time management. It maximizes human productivity from top to bottom—from management to a very engaged team of employees.

Coaching and mentoring practices deviate from traditional management in this important area of employee self-management. Coaches are expected to know who's working for them—inside out and upside down. From the moment coaches lay eyes on their prospective team members—in the interview room, for instance—they are, in essence, compiling dossiers on them. While this may sound sinister, it's not. Coaches do not operate clandestinely in a cloak of secrecy. They do not invade people's privacy or anything like that. Rather, these so-called dossiers merely amount to the acquiring of knowledge and understanding of each and every employee on an individual and intimate basis.

The one-two punch of knowledge and understanding of individual employees is a knockout punch. That is, it goes a long way toward the placement of employees in the right jobs and right roles. Acquiring this all-important knowledge and understanding begins with the job interview, and the quest for more of it is ongoing.

It all boils down to a coach knowing more stuff than the traditional manager. That is, before a coach assigns an individual on her staff job duties, she is armed with more knowledge and understanding of him than a traditional manager could possibly have. This thorough due diligence is what distinguishes a coached work environment from the rest. Employees are carefully vetted as human beings, not as mere work automatons. They are looked upon as individuals with unique abilities and personalities, and they are, accordingly, given jobs and tasks that suit them.

In business, time management asks that the right people be in all of the right places. A coach supervises his people, but expects them to fulfill their myriad responsibilities without a heavy managerial hand pressing down on their necks. Good self-management is always a boon to good time management.

## Expectations

Optimally, you want a staff of self-managing men and women. You want your people to know what they have to do and when they have to do it. As a leader, you reinforce the company mission and monitor results and progress every single day. But you have high expectations for those who work for you, because you know them and their capabilities.

In today's highly competitive business circles, managers on the frontlines desperately need people who require minimal handholding. If employees need your assistance every step of the way, you're in trouble. Nevertheless, coaches work very closely with members of their teams. They teach and will, in fact, hold hands when necessary. This markedly helpful relationship between manager and employee contrasts sharply with conventional on-the-job relationships. But handholding cannot be permitted to become a permanent part of daily work life. The coach's instructive methods are designed to get an employee from A to B, so that she can go from B to C on her own two wings. Too much handholding amounts to too much time wasted.

## Keeping Preventable Stoppages to a Minimum

As a coach, you obviously want to keep your ongoing projects running smoothly and on schedule. But the reality is that work stoppages happen on occasion—it's part of life and part of business. What can a coach do to keep these bottlenecks—and squanderers of precious time—to a bare minimum?

## The Solid Lineup

Serious work stoppages most often occur when an employee makes a significant mistake, or when somebody loses sight of his particular role in the framework of the team. When working as a team, it is essential that everybody be on the same page. Individually, team members have got to know what their respective job roles are—or else. Work stoppage! When a group of very unique and diverse personalities are at work on the same project, it is essential that a coach not permit one wayward soul to take the whole team down. In baseball, a team can have the league's most fearsome line-up, but still lose more games than it wins because its pitching staff is short on talent. Likewise, work teams necessitate a solid roster—up and down—to meet their deadlines and achieve their goals. A coach is responsible for putting together the team.

As a philosophy applied to business management, coaching and mentoring works effectively as a molder of men and women. A coach who knows what she's doing gets her people to work in unison and to achieve common goals and reach productivity benchmarks. There are countless work stoppages that efficient coaching can prevent entirely or, at the very least, quickly correct when they happen.

## The Groundwork

Competent coaching always lays a firm groundwork. It is deeply rooted in comprehensive instruction at the onset of jobs and projects. By building solid foundations, the chances of time-gobbling stoppages occurring are much less likely. As a coach, you are expected to educate members of your team on how best to perform their tasks and fulfill their roles.

In other words, a good coach never neglects those important "101" lessons, as it were. An employee shouldn't graduate into advanced work studies until he masters all of the rudimentary stuff. This all-inclusive instruction is fundamental to both proper coaching and mentoring and time management. Employees who thumb their noses at the basics are more apt to find themselves clueless at some point in time. And finding oneself clueless in the workplace is a bad place to be.

# Timesavers

There are innumerable little things that you can do to save time in the workplace. In fact, many of these timesavers are right in front of your nose. You might just want to sniff around for them. Actually, if you function with timesaving always on your brain, you'll uncover the many ways and means that will make your work hours time efficient from punch in to punch out.

## Count the Ways

Think about everything you do while on the job—everything! Then consider how you can make your myriad tasks and commitments a little less time consuming. You'll discover that this small exercise is enlightening on so many levels. Here are several potential on-the-job timesavers for you to contemplate:

- Utilize daily checklists and monthly calendars
- Keep all meetings as succinct and productive as possible
- Work with key benchmarks and deadlines
- Set basic and clear policies
- Do one task at a time
- Delegate authority wherever possible

Timesaving is common sense. The aforementioned timesaving measures are elementary. But the problem is that managers in the workplace don't always see them as such. It's important to view everything that's done in the workplace through the prism of the always-ticking clock.

## Get to the Point

Managers who have a penchant for *not* getting to the point are the biggest time wasters. So, get to the point in one-on-one conversations with employees. Get to the point in staff meetings, too. Say what you have to say and let others say what they have to say—and move on. There is no need to belabor already settled matters.

As needed, correspond in writing. But keep all of this correspondence pithy. All too many managers author business letters and office memos more suited in length for short stories or novellas. Get to the point. You'll save lots of time this way. And your terseness will carry more weight than excessive volubility.

As a coach in good standing, you are also a timesaver in good standing. Find the best people and work with them to produce the results you need. When you've got all of the right pieces in place—and know what to do with these pieces—time is your friend.

# Chapter 12

# Interviewing Prospective Employees

The coach's role in hiring personnel is an essential, although often overlooked, aspect of coaching. Not only can you use the interview process to begin effectively communicating with future employees, you can also properly evaluate job applicants and weed out the bad apples before they worm their way onto your team and cause you untold headaches down the road. This chapter addresses in detail those all-important first impressions.

## Finding the Coachable

In Chapter 10, there were numerous examples of the importance of consistently evaluating your coaching aptitude. Well, you might as well begin at the beginning. That is, by thoroughly examining your hiring practices. What exactly do you look for in new hires? And how exactly do you determine that they have what you want?

### Wise Hiring Decisions Produce Short- and Long-Term Results

American patriot John Adams once said, "Facts are stubborn things." And the facts certainly are, if you're encountering more workplace problems than you had anticipated; if you're confronted with less than stellar employee performances; if you're surprised to see a paucity of skills in certain employees—if, if, if—perhaps you aren't doing a thorough enough job at the onset of your coach-employee relationships. Maybe you aren't making the wisest, most considered decisions in hiring the right individuals at the starting gate.

**FACT**

Billionaire Donald Trump asks prospective job applicants the unusual question, "How brilliant are you?" He hopes to catch them off guard, he says. When applicants answer that they're not very brilliant at all, Trump says he's inclined to take them at their word and doesn't hire them.

The job interview process is as fundamental to coaching and mentoring as it is to every other managerial approach. Why wouldn't it be? But because so much of coaching focuses on individuals and their special talents and possibilities, a coach's hiring procedures are naturally expected to be more enlightened and more meticulous. That is, coaches are supposed to be more adept at not letting all of those important little things slip through the cracks.

## *Not Just Any Tom, Dick, or Harriet Will Do*

The philosophy of coaching and mentoring is frequently misinterpreted. (See Chapters 4 and 22 for a lot more on this subject and the many myths surrounding this increasingly popular managerial art form.) For one, coaching and mentoring are not a managerial methodology that turns water into wine and multiplies fish and loaves of bread. It's not about partying-on in the office. Nor is it some benevolent business boot camp capable of turning "anybody who wants a job" into the next Bill Gates or Warren Buffett.

Nevertheless, coaching and mentoring, and what they personify, offer so much more than traditional management methods because they are supremely dedicated to equipping employees with work environments that are replete with learning, challenges, and career growth opportunities.

Among the most important traits you need to look for in employees are creativity impulses. The people you want in your employ should be men and women with both stamina and free-flowing ideas on how to more efficiently do their jobs.

That said, it's still always up to individuals to display the willingness to work and to grow as worker entities, as well as human beings. Self-motivation wins the day in these instances. The overriding point here is a simple one: Not any Tom, Dick, or Harriet will do as an employee, even in the most enlightened coaching and mentoring environments on the face of the planet.

## *Remember Those Open-Ended Questions*

The interview process can commence with a stream of open-ended questions. You should listen attentively to prospective employee answers and follow-up again and again if necessary. What's the first thing that you want to know about future members of your staff? What their credentials are, of course! Obviously, you want people to fill jobs who can do certain things and who display certain skills. If you're in need of an employee to work intensively and extensively with computer programming, you can't ignore solid computer skills. But, as we've made abundantly clear throughout this book, useful skills are by no means limited to mere technical skills.

Among the areas you should survey in the interview process of prospective employees is their salary requirements. The open-ended question, "Explain why you feel you deserve what you're asking for" allows job applicants to make a case and justify their monetary pleas.

## The Kinds of Questions

Begin the interview process by getting to the meat and potatoes of the talent and ability sitting in front of you. Find out what exactly this wannabe employee has to offer in both hard and soft skills across the spectrum. Here are some examples of open-ended questions you can pose to job applicants in the initial interview:

- Can you describe your greatest strengths? Your greatest weaknesses?
- Are there any skills you have that you'd like to improve?
- What hard decisions have you made in your work career?
- When confronted with problems and obstacles in the workplace, how do you address them?
- If you've been in work situations where you've had to persuade people to follow your lead, how did you accomplish this?
- How well do you work with people? What do you believe are the requirements of a team player?
- How do you handle pressure situations?
- How do you adapt to change?
- How do you deal with performance plans and the deadlines associated with them?
- What knowledge and skills have you acquired in your current job?

Questions like these reveal potential employees' work ethics, which was discussed at length in Chapter 10. Finding people with hard technical skills should be at the top of your agenda, of course, but you need to complement these skills with commendable work habits, and those very important soft skills, too.

In the interview process, don't circumvent prospective employees' educational history. This is an area worth exploring with open-ended questions like, "How did your college experience change your life?" and "What extracurricular activities did you participate in?" And don't forget, "How does your educational background prepare you for the job you're seeking?"

## Examining the Answers—and More!

Most interviewees—and you can count on it ninety-nine out of one hundred times—will give all the anticipated "right" answers to your queries. But scripted answers, remember, are scripted only up to a point. And sooner or later, people go off script, and you've got to be especially attuned to their words and demeanor when this occurs.

In fact, it's your job to get interviewees off their prepared scripts. Consider the interview process an engagement at the Improv. "When confronted with problems and conflicts in the workplace, how do you address them?" This question, for example, is broad and loaded with opportunity—for you, looking to hire a competent employee, and for a job applicant, wanting a chance to exhibit some depth of thought and reasoning.

## How Experience Cuts Both Ways

In your safari to bag talented personnel, you need to aim your hiring bow and arrow at the experience that potential employees can bring to your work Serengeti. When the right experiences match with the right job, great things can and often do happen. So, when you're conducting an interview, make it your mission to gather all the information possible on not only potential employees' work experiences, but also their life experiences and what they say about them.

Keep in mind, however, that experiences can cut both ways. An individual, for instance, who worked alongside a lousy manager is apt to have picked up a few messy work habits in the process. Experience gained—yes. Another person, who worked with a much wiser manager, also acquired a way of doing things. Experience gained, too! Which kind of experienced employee would you prefer laboring in your midst?

**ALERT!**

In the interview process, and indeed in all coaching communications, the anticipated first response of a prospective employee to a question is assigned less weight than the more meaningful exposition responses. That is, answers that are expanded upon are ordinarily worth more than predictable "what I should say" first replies to questions.

## Paying Attention to Experience Particulars

So, naturally, you must pay extra special attention to the kinds of experiences that those looking to work for you have had. If an applicant is used to doing things one way—because that's his or her experience—and you do things a decidedly different way, then that's not the kind of experience you would value in a new employee. When you traverse beyond the resume and deal with an interviewee in the flesh, the questions you ask should take you well beyond the words on that piece of paper.

Experiences chronicled in an impressive list, or grand-sounding words about skills and abilities, must always be put in their proper perspective. Coaches are asked time and again to put things in perspective. There are so many gray areas in managing. Coaches are better suited than dinosaur managers in successfully navigating these various hues of gray.

## *Asking Questions about Experience*

Here are some questions that draw out the substantive experiences of your prospective employees:

- What are some of the work experiences you're most proud of?
- How have your work experiences prepared you for the job you're seeking with us?
- What do you consider some of your biggest achievements? Your biggest failures?
- Do you have any ideas on how to avoid such failures in the future?
- Why do you want to leave your present position? Why did you leave your last job?
- Who was the manager you most enjoyed working for and why? Least enjoyed working for and why?
- Of all your work experiences, what are some of the things that you've learned that make you qualified for the job you're interviewing for?
- What are some of the specific things that you'd like to see in this job that you didn't have in past jobs?

Of course, don't forget to ask, "May I check your references?" Very often the most you get out of checking references these days is confirmation that the person in question did in fact work where he or she claimed to have worked. Don't expect too much information beyond that.

## *Lies and Liars Who Tell Them*

Outright lies on resumes—about employment history, for instance—are bad omens, to put it mildly. It's one thing to inflate job skills and abilities (you know, to overcome obstacles and the like) with all the flowery adjectives in the thesaurus. It's quite another thing to create a phantom job history.

This degree of prevarication brands anyone an unfit candidate for a new job. However, once you confirm the validity of a prospective employee's job history, the open-ended questions previously cataloged afford you the opportunity to determine whether you believe the job experiences of the interviewee are more positive than negative. You've got to determine whether they are in sync with your present needs or way out in left field.

## Finding the Right Fit

Okay, you've gathered all the information that you want about a potential employee's skills and experiences. Is that enough? No, of course that's not enough. Now's the time to build on what you've carefully culled so far and put the finishing brush strokes on the big picture. The next line of open-ended questioning to add to your interview repertoire centers on the open position itself, and specifically what the company's appeal is to the job seeker.

## Focusing on the Position You're Seeking to Fill

This is the prime opportunity for you to get down into the trenches and shift the focus from the interviewee talking about the interviewee, to the interviewee talking about the open position and the company that pays your salary. The job you're seeking to fill, depending on its skill requirements, will attract a diverse group of applicants.

Information elicited from this hungry group about why they want to work for you will be very enlightening indeed. If you're truly concerned about workplace problems down the pike—and you've got to be as a forward-thinking coach—opportunity knocks. The interview process is the time to ask those who want to join your team, and work with you, just why they want to do that.

## Asking Questions about the Job and Your Company

Here are some appropriate interview questions that focus their rhetorical slings and arrows on the open job itself:

- What brought you to this company, seeking this position?
- What special attributes do you offer that make you suitable for the open job?
- What specifically do you look for in an employer?
- Describe your short-term goals? Long-term goals?
- What challenges do you seek in a job?
- What makes you the best-qualified person for the job?

- Is money ultimately more important to you than responsibilities and challenges?
- How do you think the company would benefit if you were hired to fill this position?

**FACT**

The interview moment is your golden opportunity to strike a blow at future workplace problems by thoughtfully questioning job applicants and determining—in addition to finding out if they possess the requisite technical skills—whether they display the right temperaments and character to join your team.

As you can glean from the substance of these various queries, the thrust of the questioning shifts to the job at hand and what the would-be employee could do for you and the company. There is, of course, some overlap in questions about skills, experience, and position, but it's in this last line of questioning where you can get very specific in your follow-ups, and hone in on what you know the job demands in both the short- and long-term.

Your insider information on the various job-related skills needed to perform the everyday tasks and fulfill the roles, and in what time frame, permits you to probe and poke around and determine whether or not an applicant has what it takes—beyond skills and experience—to do the job and do it well. A scrupulous interview process can provide you with a very clear picture as to whether or not the person seeking a job fits into your vision and whether or not he or she can work well with your present team.

## Don't Go There: The Wrong Questions

In a coach's playbook, which seeks to get to the heart of what makes people perform, the interview moment is rife with great possibility. You want to kick off your relationship with an employee the right way. And, for starters, the right way is with the right employee on the job.

Books, magazine articles, and seminars on the subject of interviews abound, from both the employees' and employers' perspectives. These resources have been around for some time now detailing the necessary preparation for both asking the right questions and giving the right answers to those very same questions. Job seekers prepare themselves for interviews, and so do coaches. However, coaches are prepared for the prepared, including both the overprepared and the underprepared.

When you fully prepare yourself for an interview with a potential employee, you approach the get-together with a broad agenda. You view the hiring of a new worker as impacting both your immediate future and indeed your long-term effectiveness as a coach and leader. You accept the fact that a vigilant interview process is critical to your daily managing efforts today, tomorrow, and six months into the future, and that decisions made in hiring are office snowballs in the making. That is, they gather size and strength over time, and can bowl you over if you're not eternally vigilant. A coach's job is to avoid getting buried by these snowballs.

Before closing this important subject of the coach-employee interview process, there are certain questions you need to be aware of that should never be asked of job applicants. There are questions that are inappropriate, some simply because they have no place in a business setting, and some because they're actually against the law. You're a coach, and a human being, and so you may be curious about a whole host of things about a person who wants to work for you. Prurient matters may titillate you. But you must always remember that you aren't the host of a trashy TV talk show interviewing a human curiosity; you are a coach interviewing a person who wants a job. You are managing in a professional business environment and don't need to know what is none of your business. Here are some questions that you have no business asking during an interview:

- What is your age?
- What is your marital status?
- What is your sexual orientation?
- Do you have any physical or mental disabilities?
- Have you ever been convicted of a crime? Arrested for any reason?
- Do you have any serious health problems?

- Are you religious? Do you attend a church? A synagogue? A mosque?
- Do you consume alcohol?
- Are you a Republican? A Democrat? A Green?

And this list could go on and on. In your questioning, just stick with skills, experience, and why the job applicant wants to work for you, and you won't get into any trouble. And as for your curious nature, you'll find out the answers to many of those personal questions in due time anyway, if and when the interviewee makes the cut and joins your ranks. Most people don't conceal their marital status, religion, politics, drinking habits (that's for sure!), and the many other things that have no place in interviews, but are general knowledge in the confines of the office.

We live in a litigious age. You don't want to find yourself the defendant in a lawsuit based on a question you asked a prospective employee. The company that pays your salary wouldn't be too happy about laying out bucks to fight or settle the lawsuit, nor jumping for joy at the negative publicity that comes attached to one.

# Chapter 13

# Conflict Terminators

Even in the most harmonious work environments, conflicts of various kinds will inevitably occur. They might be between members of your staff or between you and an employee. And from time to time, you will have to attend to those omnipresent bad attitudes. This chapter will clue you in on how conscientious coaching can convert these overtly negative circumstances into positive situations by extracting important lessons from them and moving forward.

## Meeting Conflicts Head On

Because your ultimate job responsibility as a coach is to advance a positive and productive workplace, personnel skirmishes, disagreements, and attitude problems can never be brushed under the table.

Don't ever ignore a poor attitude in an employee. Such an attitude is often the first indicator of an overall bad performance to come. It is therefore imperative that you address and correct any attitude problems on your staff before they become full-blown performance problems.

You must not only establish, but also maintain, professional relationships with all the people who work for you. And, aside from making sure that your employees get along swimmingly with you, it behooves you to make certain they can coexist in perfect harmony with one another—or, at the very least, imperfect harmony. Never lose sight of the fact that you're the leader of a team effort. Most of the work that needs to get done in an office setting requires close and continual interaction between and among employees. And that means that persons who have personality clashes with their coworkers or with you, or who flaunt bad attitudes, cannot be ignored.

## Confronting the Combatants

There will come a time when you'll be compelled to confront dissension in your ranks. Even the most meticulous and wise coaching efforts can't altogether avoid such workplace snafus. In fact, it's not whether you're going to see conflict (you will) as a coach; it's how you deal with it that will largely determine your success or lack thereof in bringing home the bacon, as it were. Every now and again, you'll have to address the seamier sides of the human condition in your coaching.

Some people take their squabbling and disagreements to an even higher level, and fight with one another. In an office setting, fighting doesn't mean fisticuffs, or tearing at one another's clothing, although this kind of behavior has been documented. What should most concern you as a coach is verbal hostility. Harsh words bandied back and forth and protracted arguing augur performance breakdowns. The malcontent in your midst with the poisonous attitude should fully engage your attention and light a fire under your corrective coaching side.

## Bad Attitudes

It is every manager's worst nightmare to have a deleterious attitude problem in his or her office. Unfortunately, it comes with the territory of being both human and a businessperson. Bad attitude issues are commonplace in today's work environs.

**FACT**

An employee's attitude refers to his or her overall thinking process, views, and opinions on all things great and small. An employee's behavior refers to his or her physical actions. Negative attitudes frequently manifest themselves in negative behaviors.

### The Way the Workplace Used to Be

Generally speaking, the Depression and World War II generation of workers viewed work and responsibility in a different light than do the majority of people in today's labor force. Most members of that past generation were grateful for just having a job—or jobs, in so many instances. They did what they had to do to support themselves and their families, and it wasn't always easy or pretty work.

As our country became a more and more affluent nation and society— with yesterday's luxuries becoming today's necessities—the expectations of those in the labor market changed. In essence, today's workers want more and more, as do the companies that employ them. The workplace is also more demanding and less forgiving than ever before because of the extremely competitive circumstances that most businesses find themselves in. For sure, some outfits misuse their employees by not respecting them in the least as living and breathing human beings. Fortunately, though, increasing numbers of enterprises—in both the private and public sectors—are giving coaching and mentoring a shot and striving to meld individual needs with business needs.

> If you determine that it's not humanly possible for you, a coach, to convert a troublesome employee attitude from bad to good, you've got to then insist that the employee concentrate solely on doing his or her job, and leave the poor attitude outside the work environs.

## The Bad-Attitude Brigade

But, alas, lurking in the bushes of every business—coached or not—is the bad-attitude brigade. Working alongside an employee with a twisted attitude is something that you will come up against at some point in your coaching career (and probably at many points!). Fear not! You are armed and ready to deal with these personality-related obstructions because you are—and let's all say it together—solution-oriented. Dinosaur managers are less adequately equipped to positively deal with these disconcerting employee attitudes. In stark contrast with coaches, they react to behavior only—physical actions—and oftentimes this is too late for any positive solution to the problem at hand. In other words, the more traditional managerial approaches often permit attitude problems to grow into disruptive performance problems.

## Attitude Adjustment: Is It Really Possible?

Attitude is the precursor of behavior, which is the forerunner of performance. That is, a negative attitude engenders mirror actions, which often lead to poor performance. There is an important distinction between attitude and behavior. Attitude embodies an individual's overall thought process—how he or she relates to things. Behavior, on the other hand, is attitude in action.

## *Attitude Is Viewpoints*

Attitude covers a person's viewpoints and outlook on the world at large. You've no doubt heard the expression that some people see the glass as "half full" and others as "half empty." Well, you've got to insist, as a prerequisite for working for you, that your employees see things as half full, or you'll drown in a sea of discontent for sure. Ignoring completely or giving short shrift to employees' negative attitudes, in many instances, amounts to preordaining unacceptably low performance levels.

You can easily discriminate between negative attitudes and positive ones. Sometimes just a sigh or two emanating from an employee while you are talking to your team clues you in on who is not with you and what you want to accomplish as a coach. Sometimes it's an aside uttered in response to your ideas. Even a snidely delivered remark that's trivial in nature—even unrelated to the job—is not something to overlook.

Attitude comfortably resides in the mind and manifests itself in body language and the flapping tongue. Behavior, in the confines of the workplace, defines specific actions—both visible and assessable—that go far beyond the wagging tongue. And this is, ultimately, what counts regarding your employees. However, you can never isolate attitude from behavior. Attitude may in fact call home the cozy confines of the beautiful mind. But the mind is one powerful instrument. And while you can't be 100 percent certain that a bad attitude will translate into a bad performance, you can be sure that it's an unhealthy thing. You can take to the bank the fact that negativity is the Bubonic Plague of the office world—contagious and ugly.

## *The Bad Attitude Spectrum*

Is trying to overhaul an employee's attitude from bad to good in your powers as a coach? Is it in your bag of tricks? Of course it is.

If it's job-related, it's certainly within your power to turn chicken feathers into chicken soup. After all, sitting down with employees and talking with them is a coach's modus operandi. Employees with attitudes that negatively impact either their own job performances or others' job performances have to be called into your office for candid, no-holds-barred discussions. This much is a given.

Be it an attitude adjustment or reshaping an on-the-job relationship, opportunities abound to better employees as both valued human resources and human beings. A coach is a catalyst who aims to convert all manifestations of discord into positive outcomes.

Naturally, the first item on your agenda is to locate the source of the bad attitude. Let's say, for example, that your employee Paul, who is highly competent in his job, gets passed over for a promotion that he thought he richly deserved based on the merits. This perception (and maybe even a reality) is enough to turn a formerly positive attitude into a negative one. Now, allowing Paul to roam around the office in a bitter, angry frame of mind is an open invitation to increased restlessness in your ranks. If Paul is permitted to convince others that the meritocracy, which ideally should be at the center of all coaching promotions, is not in fact practiced, you've got a major credibility problem on your hands. And credibility is a coach's underpinning. Thus, you've got to make the case to Paul that he was bypassed for reasons that were fair and sound, and based solely on qualifications. You've got to convince him with whatever evidence you have at your disposal. You've also got to recharge Paul's batteries by giving him positive feedback on his overall job performance and offering words of encouragement about his future. By the same token, you must also rebuke him in no uncertain terms for going negative and for not coming to you first to discuss his perceptions and feelings. If you are in reality on solid ground, Paul will have no choice but to accept the fact that he was not the most qualified person for the promotion, or he will have to look elsewhere for a job. A stark but absolutely necessary choice in a positive work environment.

## *Straightforward Communication*

Here's another employee bad-attitude conundrum to consider. Let's say that Meg from Company A comes to work for you in Company B, and immediately starts grumbling about how much better it was working at A than it is working in B. This kind of griping is not unusual but is totally unacceptable in any work setting.

What do you do? That's easy. You call motor mouth Meg into your office and immediately lay it on the line. "Look, Meg, you applied for this job; we were impressed with your credentials and your interview; we offered you the job; and you accepted the terms of employment. So, can you explain what your problem is with us?" Straightforward communication here often turns a problem attitude like this on its head, because many of these purveyors of negativism, like Meg, are unaccustomed to open and frank dialogues with their bosses. And when confronted as such, they're often impressed and regret what they've done in spreading bad cheer. Sometimes they're chagrined and even intimidated by the fact that their unprofessionalism has been called out into the open.

The most intractable of employee attitude problems often revolve around an individual's attitude toward life in general and not to the job *per se*. People who are attitudinally disabled, as it were, carry bad attitudes with them from sunrise to sunset, anywhere and everywhere. Nevertheless, you've got to insist that any bad attitudes remain outside the confines of the workplace.

## Curbing Terminally Bad Attitudes

Let's face it: There are people who wake up and don't smell the coffee. And if by some chance they do, it's burning. Of course, in a business utopia, you would prefer to have weeded out these negative employees—the attitudinally disabled—before hiring them in the first place (see Chapter 12 for helpful advice on doing this). But, as we've said before, this isn't always the way things turn out. Cleverly concealed negative attitudes are a dime a dozen. However, when they finally do rear their ugly heads—and they do—watch out, coaches!

Again, a frank sit-down with any and all violators of your positive attitude edict is in order. Permit the trespassers of your ethical boundaries to explain themselves. All employees get to speak their pieces under a coach's leadership, regardless of the circumstances. Perhaps, through your coaching efforts, you can assist in planting the seeds of a more positive outlook—even in an utterly negative person. Nobody (well, almost nobody) is unredeemable. If it's personal problems and an altogether tumultuous life that are the cause of an employee's incessant negativity, a little succor and understanding on your part can sometimes go a very long way.

If you don't feel that a core change of attitude is humanly possible, you've got no choice but to demand that your negative employees keep their unsettling attitudes at bay. That is, ask them to compartmentalize the problems that are being reflected in their poor attitudes. Some individuals have a remarkable knack for doing this kind of thing, and they don't let their mindsets—their worldviews—impact at all their behaviors on the job.

You should be assertive in all your approaches to managing, but particularly in addressing conflict situations that arise. Assertive communication applied with alacrity is what is required in dealing with the problems of employee discord and bad attitude.

Bad attitudes festering in the workplace shouldn't be tolerated at any time and for any reason. Utilizing all the communication skills at your disposal, you've got to insist on either a bad-attitude makeover or the aforementioned compartmentalization. If neither of these two choices is acceptable to the guilty parties, there's always a third choice.

## When Employees Don't Get Along

In conflict situations between members of your team, consider yourself, in effect, a third party—a very interested third party. "In this corner weighing 175 pounds, from Hoboken, New Jersey—Pat, the financial wizard. And in this corner, weighing 115 pounds, from Duxbury, Massachusetts—Dawn, the marketing maven." What do you do when two (or more) of your employees, who must work closely with one another, like Pat and Dawn, don't like one another?

First of all, whether or not employees like one another is not what is of interest here. A positive, accommodating work environment is not predicated on individuals liking one another. Sure, it helps if your team can give a group hug at the end of a day's labor. But it's not a professional requirement—and a rather implausible one at that. Respecting one another and their job roles is another story. Again, you can apply the concept of compartmentalization. It's the various job functions that have to get done and done well. If employees can do their respective jobs, working along-side coworkers whom they dislike personally, then that's peachy keen, and there's nothing you can or should do about it. If, however, the animus felt between employees filters down into less-than-adequate job performances, you've got to act and act swiftly.

But how do you deal with performance problems that very often stem from something outside the business realm? The first thing that you do is accept the fact that it is now a business problem, i.e., your problem. Also recognize that the problem has to do with performance breakdown, not solving a Hatfield–McCoy feud between two or more people, which may very well be outside your scope.

When people from all over the country and even the world, from different backgrounds and upbringings, with different values and habits, come together in a work setting, there are inevitably going to be conflicts. Some of this discord often stems from the fact that people just plain don't like one another. Your job as a coach is not to harangue employees on celebrating differences or loving one another come what may. These kinds of talks littered with trite bromides invariably do more harm than good. Employees don't ever like feeling that they're being talked down to. Always talk up to your employees. It's more uplifting.

Let's return once more to employees Pat and Dawn and their dislike for one another. Let's take their mutual disdain a step further with their job performances suffering as a result of it. What do you do? Call Pat in on the carpet and talk to him. Tell him precisely what's expected of him as an employee with a specific job to do and performance goals to be met. Ask him what he thinks the solutions to his performance problems are, and what ideas he has to improve his working relationship with Dawn. Then follow the same course with Dawn.

Once you've spoken your piece, and carefully listened to your two quarrelling staff members on an individual basis, your next move is to call Pat into your office for round two, and tell him some of Dawn's ideas for forging a better working relationship. You need to gauge his reaction to her suggestions. Then, bring Dawn in, and tell her some of Pat's ideas on rectifying their mutually destructive performances.

Round two is indispensable, because round three involves you refereeing Pat and Dawn in the same room, and tying together all that you've learned in your one-on-one discussions with them. You've heard their sides of the story; you've gotten their reactions to what each had to say about the others' suggestions about righting things; and now you, Pat, and Dawn are all coming together to agree upon solutions to a positive outcome to a very serious problem.

Traditional managerial ways are apt to skip rounds one and two of this process and call in their battling employees right from the start, telling them point-blank, "Work it out between yourselves . . . or else!" This is not the kind of employee self-sufficiency that we've been promoting throughout this book. Sure, in the end, the battling employees themselves will have to resolve to work out their differences, or nothing positive will happen. That much is certain. But you have a much better chance of securing positive outcomes if you talk with each employee individually, gather what information you can as to the causes of the personal or work-related problems leading to the diminished performances, and then proceed from there.

You must always be mindful of talking up to your employees and never down to them. As a coach, you are not in a role akin to a first-grade teacher. You're a manager of adults in an environment where overall performance matters as much to you as them.

When you simultaneously bring the fighting parties into your office (round three), it is only after you've heard from both sides (round one), and then gotten their reactions to the suggestions and ideas from the other (round two). Round three, then, is as productive as is possible because you completed your homework. This fully informed approach stands in stark contrast to what would be a free-for-all, a highly emotional one, if you chose to immediately call your combative employees into your office and read them the riot act. To emphasize an important point: It's not your job to transform Pat and Dawn into the best of buddies (although that would be nice). It's your job and your responsibility to secure positive results in their performances. And if two employees' personal dislike for one another is getting in the way of achieving this, you've got to put a stop to it—or at the very least the outward manifestations of it that are negatively impacting on work performances.

## Live and Let Learn

At the foundation of just about everything we've said regarding coaching has been strong communication. Employees sitting in your office and talking openly and without fear of saying something that could land them in hot water is a powerful technique that can accomplish remarkable things. Misunderstandings are often cleared up in such give-and-take atmospheres. The better sides of people surface all the time in these aboveboard settings (and, yes, sometimes their ugly sides, too). When you confront problems and put everything on the table—the good and bad—solutions can't help but become clearer, and positive outcomes can't help but be more likely.

In order to more fully understand and appreciate this subject of productive confrontation, you need only revisit situations in your own life, both on and away from the job. Specifically, what were the confrontational moments that made you a better person in one way or another? You are in the unique position as a coach to show your team how they can benefit from the various workplace obstacles that they encounter. And this means making your employees more nimble in rebounding from those inescapable problem moments.

How do you impart to your staff the necessary tools to turn confrontation on the job into productive lessons learned? You do this by communicating from the beginning in a forthright, thorough, and free-flowing manner. You permit your people to clearly see the repercussions of their actions. You're the catalyst, not only in detecting problems, but also in taking the guilty party or parties to task and making them see the error of their ways. Thus, you lead the way in finding the best solutions possible. You effect change and your employees learn valuable lessons in making the necessary changes and moving forward.

Respect and trust are the two features that permit you to effectively deal with disharmony and confrontation within your ranks. Wise intervention is what arms you with the leverage to attack bad attitudes and dissension and come out on top. Firmness of purpose and righteousness define strong leadership. A happy face getting happy results is nice. But a happy face getting unhappy results is detrimental and inappropriate in a business environment.

**ALERT!**

Remember those lessons learned from bad managers! If you've worked for a manager with bad methods and work habits, you're in a position to have witnessed managerial approaches in action that were counterproductive. Naturally, as a coach you don't pattern your style after these men and women.

You absorb many positive lessons from your experiences in the trenches. Coaching and mentoring are grounded in passing on these lessons to others. Profiles in success and failure show people the way to the future. It's not really surprising then that many positive lessons learned are derivatives of bad experiences. That's been the thrust of this chapter. Good coaching on your part imparts beneficial lessons from all kinds of experiences—even the bad ones. And you know what? They're not bad experiences anymore, but good ones, when they are overcome.

# Chapter 14

# Dealing with Employees' Personal Lives

Although you're not expected to chaperone the off-hour lives of members of your staff, you can't ignore the reality that professional and private lives are often bound together in very consequential ways. This chapter will help you sort through the challenges of coaching people on the job with full plates of personal problems and issues.

14

## Coaching Is Not Social Work

Personal problems can effortlessly metastasize into workplace problems. This is a very complicated and dicey area that calls for understanding and empathetic coaching. A good coach can make an enormous and very positive difference in converting personal lemons into professional lemonade. Even if they carry very heavy personal baggage, you can still help your employees realize their on-the-job potentials. You can nobly assist in making their jobs respites from what ails them in their personal lives. But you must always remember that you are a coach in a business setting, not a social worker.

Coaching is not social work, but is keenly aware of the important connection that exists between employees' personal lives and their professional lives. Enlightened coaching fully appreciates that satisfying and healthy work environments can make positive differences in employees' home lives.

The very real personal bond between you and your employees—a proud coaching and mentoring tenet—endeavors to make the work experience a rewarding one. And so, if you create an office climate that taps into people's genuine needs and wants as human beings, you will get what you want—productivity from your team—while simultaneously feeling gratified that you've accomplished this with thoughtful and caring leadership. In other words, you've released human potential like a flock of doves, and not some plague of locusts.

To make the workplace a haven for your employees, there are many things you can do. What follows in the upcoming sections are several positive actions you can take that will make people want to come to work, make their jobs more personally satisfying, and ease some tensions at home by building up self-confidence and self-esteem.

## Encouraging Self-Expression

In all your coaching practices, it's important that you encourage your employees to express themselves in meaningful ways. In building up your employees' capacities for self-sufficiency, you've got to repeatedly encourage them to contribute their ideas and opinions.

You've got to get them over the hurdle of fearing rejection. When you listen to employees' suggestions, respect them, and in some cases implement them, the positive effects of this rebound to all employees, who see themselves as important pieces of a team puzzle. A sense of accomplishment is a very powerful self-motivating tool. When you afford your employees the opportunity to think for themselves and to make substantial, positive contributions to the workplace, you've set the creative juices in motion. Unleash your employees and, more times than not, you'll be surprised at what they can do.

**FACT**

You can make the workplace a haven for your staff, even those with topsy-turvy home lives, by encouraging creativity, problem solving, and mini-mentoring. Jobs that are dynamic in nature encourage employees to tap into their true potentials, and this often spills over into aspects of their lives away from work.

## Provide Greater and Greater Challenges

The last thing you want on the job are employees as complacent as clams snuggled in their beds. Fortunately, most people desire more responsibilities and greater challenges in their job roles. It's human nature. It's human nature for men and women to want intricate jobs with problems to solve and, yes, obstacles to overcome.

This is actually an extension of your promoting creativity in your employees. People look forward to going to jobs that engage their full attention and energy capacities. Let your employees loose and allow them to hammer hard at their various job duties. Challenge them at all times. Employees with less than stable and happy personal lives often seek refuge in the workplace. If they feel appreciated, and are given involved, thinking-intensive jobs, work can, at the very least, partially fulfill what is lacking in their lives outside of work.

## Build Skills

Who wouldn't prefer working in an environment that encourages learning and bolsters skills? A workplace that grows employee skills simultaneously functions as career builders for a group of people. And this coaching double dip is particularly important to those with implacable personal problems at home, who feel that their best chance for upgrading their lives is through work and career.

When you provide your people with genuine opportunities to better themselves, they respond in positive ways. They want to learn more and they also want to impart what they've learned to others. Yes, it's true. Oftentimes employees passionate about their work are eager to pass on their know-how, and they become mini-mentors and assistants to you in your coaching efforts.

## Let Your People Help Your People

Employees who help their coworkers do their jobs better frequently feel better about themselves. Sure, humankind is regularly taken to task for being selfish and greedy above all else—most especially in the business world. This is a regrettable stereotype because, in business settings, many people help others and get a real sense of satisfaction out of doing it, too.

**FACT**

When you lead a staff chock full of high performers, you automatically preside over a dynamic team. And it's much more gratifying for employees to go to work and be part of a team of productive winners than it is to associate with a listless bunch of underachievers and whiners.

Employees with uneven home lives often use their jobs as indispensable balances. They get a sense of genuine gratification out of helping their teammates complete their tasks and fulfill their roles. Team settings permit individuals to make positive differences in other people's lives—on the job or on the sports playing field. A coach advances work atmospheres that put premiums on everybody helping everybody else. An environment where the coach looks out for employees, and employees look out for the coach and one another, is a positive and productive place—a place that people want to come to.

## *Part of the Team*

The people who want to come to work in the morning are more often than not part of a highly productive, dynamic team. An analogy can be drawn here between a professional baseball team that's on the top of the heap versus a team that's on the bottom—a cellar dweller. The number-one team usually features a group of players who are self-motivated with a desire to win. The last-place team is more apt to be a group of apathetic losers, who would rather not show up for work, even if the work is play (baseball).

**ALERT!**

In order for you to have and to maintain moral authority, you must exhibit professionalism at all times in the office environs, and this means maintaining a proper personal detachment from your employees and walking a fine line between caring for them and being their boss.

It's no different in the workplace. Playing a role in a winning team effort is uplifting. It goes back to the sense of accomplishment discussed earlier. Giving a strong performance in a sea of strong performances is personally fulfilling. A similar top-notch performance on a team of underachievers will not be nearly as sweet. You've got it in your power to put a team together that is both attractive and uplifting to employees, particularly those with personal problems at home.

# The Balancing Act: Work Versus Home

The previous section is not meant to imply that the job is in any way on par with home and family. It's not. Sure, there are many people who put work and career at the top of the heap, but they often neglect their spouses and children along the way. They let their interior lives suffer, and permit quality time with their loved ones to pass them by, never to be recaptured. Ideally, a professional life and personal life should be a part of one healthy whole. Because unless you've inherited a fortune, work and career are essential for living. But there's no need for work and career to elbow out a rich home life. There's no reason that you have to choose between one or the other.

It's a popular cliché to say that workers must learn to balance their home and work lives. Your role as a coach is not to do the balancing for them. You've got enough to do in the confines of the workplace itself. However, if you do all the things that elevate your people as worker commodities—encourage creativity, provide challenging job roles, and grow skills—you're helping employees cultivate passion for their jobs.

Passion for work and self-confidence in doing a job can't help but go home with employees. There are no guarantees in life, and you have no magic wand to wave that will make everybody in your employ a happy camper. However, you can make your people productive campers, and in so doing hope that the right stuff on the job filters down to their lives at home.

**ALERT!**

Enhance your employees' private lives by making them want to come to work for you. A productive and satisfying day at work can't help but seep down to life at home. An unhappy and disagreeable work experience will dribble down, too, and that's something you don't want to be responsible for.

# Should Coaches Be Friends with Their Employees?

When discussing the marriage between home life and career, the question of friendships between coaches and employees inevitably arises. Should you, a coach, be buddy-buddy with your staff? It's a timeless argument in business circles. But the argument takes on an added dimension when the coaching principles are thrown into the mix. After all, doesn't coaching preach from its bully pulpit that getting to know employees is so essential? It sure does. Doesn't coaching entail carefully listening to employees and hearing what they have to say? Yes, it does. Doesn't coaching mean mirroring employees' feelings? Certainly. Doesn't coaching ask that employees be treated as individuals with unique personalities? Absolutely. Doesn't coaching mean being personal friends with employees? No…no…no.

## Doesn't Coaching Equal Friendship?

Surprise! The answer is no. This is controversial subject matter for the people who have a difficult time separating the tenets of coaching and mentoring from the buddy system. After all, these folks reason, if coaches really care about their employees, they've got to be their friends and look out for them as only friends can.

Do coaches "look out" for their employees? Of course they do, but in a professional sense. What the "look out for them" principle asks of coaches is that they forge a positive work environment of the kind that we've discussed from the very first page of this book. And that means providing employees with perpetual development opportunities. Coaches want their employees to motivate themselves to do more and be more. That's looking out for them.

Yes, coaches want to be respected, and in turn they want to rely on and respect their employees. Coaches want their employees to trust them, and in turn they want to be able to trust their employees. Coaches want to work in an intimate work environment where open communication and candor are the rule between them and their employees. Ah, but doesn't that sound like friendship? Sure, respect, trust, communication, and candor are the foundations of friendship! But the coaching-employee relationship is not the same thing as a personal friendship.

## Practicing Detachment

It's essential for coaches to maintain a degree of personal detachment between their employees at all times. Your overriding concern as a coach is in achieving strong performance results from your employees. Productivity matters most. That's what you were hired to do. But if you establish close personal relationships with the same employees, how does maximizing their performances fit into this friendship picture? Would your friendships come first and job performances second?

## Nixing Friendships with Your Employees

In life, friendships should come first all the time. That's what friends are for. And that's why friendships should not exist between managers and their employees. Managers can't afford to put personal considerations above the jobs that they were hired to do and the results that they are expected to deliver.

Let's explore the case of James, a manager of a team consisting of ten men and women. His employees' jobs are varied, but, as in most offices, dependent on one another in a variety of ways. James is a very agreeable fellow and a devotee of coaching and mentoring and all of their myriad tools and techniques. James does much of what's asked of coaches. He tries to run his office in a manner that makes each employee feel part of a productive team. He has established open communication and has frequent one-on-one sessions with his people. So far, so good.

Over time, however, James developed a strong personal affinity for two particular employees of his named Tom and Sissy. He found that he enjoyed being with them, beyond talking about business matters. And this led to the threesome, or sometimes a duo, doing lunch, going out after a day's work for a few beers, seeing a movie together, and, of course, chatting up a storm.

The leading problem in this scenario was the portending public relations debacle. That is, the remaining eight employees in the office were well aware of this relationship. They felt excluded, and, naturally, reasoned that James preferred Tom and Sissy to the rest of them. They firmly believed that James could no longer be fair and impartial in managing the whole team.

One of the excluded employees, Bob, finally went to James and expressed his opinion that Tom and Sissy were being held to different standards from the remaining eight staff members. Somewhat startled by this perception of things, James said there was no special treatment being accorded either Tom or Sissy. But regardless of what James thought of his relationship with Tom and Sissy, it didn't matter nearly as much as what the rest of the crew thought.

What did he do? James reacted by abruptly cutting off his lunches and after-hours get-togethers with Tom and Sissy. They couldn't understand what the sudden change in their boss's behavior was all about, because they both considered James a friend. As human beings they were deeply hurt and felt that a trust had been violated—the trust of friendship. Predictably, these events made the work relationship between James and Tom, and James and Sissy, untenable.

## More Reasons to Keep It Strictly Professional

Do you still believe you can manage and be personal friends with some of your employees? Do you still believe you'll be able to make considered and fair business decisions without taking into account your friendships? Well, it's time to get real. What if a member of your staff, who is also a close personal friend, comes up for a promotion and is competing against another one of your employees, who is not a close friend? You don't believe the friendship factor will affect your decision in any way?

Scenario One: You select your friend based, of course, on the merits. You conclude he is the right man for the new job. Is the runner-up, not your friend, going to accept your decision at face value? Right or wrong, it's going to be perceived as favoritism.

Scenario Two: You tap your employee, not your friend, for the job. You base your decision again on strictly the merits. Your employee and friend is going to feel betrayed, even if he says he accepts your decision. How could a friend not "look out" for a friend and give him the upper hand? And then there's the possible perception that the promotion was given to the non-friend employee precisely to avoid the perception of favoritism to the friend employee. In other words, you are in a no-win situation.

Need more convincing? Let's venture into the ultimate and most difficult managerial decision, terminating an employee, and how that would prove very problematic for a coach and a friend. Think about this one.

Say you have an employee who's your personal friend, but who's not doing her job, what do you do? Keep her on board at the expense of performance, positive results, and a strong bottom line? How do you think the rest of your team will feel if they know a rotting piece of deadwood is languishing in their midst, simply because she's the boss's buddy? They'll be disgruntled. The aura of trust will be shot. The work atmosphere will turn sour. And you will never again be respected.

For argument's sake, let's say that you went ahead and did the right thing. You terminated this employee who wasn't doing her job, even though she was your friend. You made the right decision, but in the wrong circumstances. That is, you shouldn't be firing your friends, because you shouldn't be friends with your employees in the first place. Plus, you'll probably lose a friend. Friendship is bad for business—and very bad for friendship, too.

## The Sex Factor

There is no quicker way to destroy the coaching bond of trust than for a coach to be fooling around on the sly with an employee. It's commonly accepted wisdom that it's not good for employees to be dating one another, let alone a manager dating an underling. It brings an element into the workplace that is fraught with outside difficulties that are potentially explosive on the inside. No further explanation should be needed, but this most basic of business social edicts usually falls on deaf ears.

So, back to you and the mundane world of coaching. Consider this a public service announcement: It is crucial that you, in a position of authority, keep personal friendships and romantic relationships at arm's length and out of the managing equation. Managing is complicated enough even when conducted under the most optimum of circumstances. Anything that can be said for the problems associated with coach-employee friendships goes double for romantic liaisons.

Sure, keeping romance at bay might require self-control on your part. But self-control is part of virtue. Virtue in business is ostensibly what coaching and mentoring is supposed to bring into these ultra-competitive settings. If you don't exhibit professionalism in your every action, don't expect your employees to exhibit it in their attitudes and behaviors.

# Caring about Your Employees Without Crossing the Line

There are many considerate actions that you can take that are given the coaching and mentoring imprimatur. There are behaviors that show you care about your employees in both their personal and professional lives, while simultaneously maintaining that all-important personal detachment just discussed.

**QUESTION?**

**What is the "look out for them" principle in coaching and mentoring?**
It's a principle that implores coaches to look out for their employees and their careers by fashioning work environments of continuous learning and opportunity. It does not mean that coaches establish personal friendships with members of their staffs.

Personal detachment doesn't ask that you remain ignorant of your employees' personal lives or that you ignore events in their lives (like birthdays, deaths in the family, and so on). On the contrary, offering congratulations and condolences when appropriate is something you should feel free to do. Being detached doesn't mean you function in a different dimension and forget you're managing a close group of people who truly care for one another.

Here are some little things you can do for all of your employees that showcase your caring side as both a boss and concerned coach. If these things are meted out on a consistent and even basis, they won't get misconstrued as manifestations of personal friendship or signs of favoritism.

## Say Thanks

Say thank you for a job well done. On a regular basis, let your employees know that you appreciate what they're doing (and continue to provide them with positive feedback when warranted).

## Reward Progress

Reward progress—not just final results. Depending on what's at your disposal (spot bonus, gifts, recognition in the company newsletter, and so on), let your forward-moving employees know you see and appreciate their progress. This is a great self-motivating technique. There's nothing quite like giving deserving employees a day off, or half-day on Friday, as a reward for a job well done. A gift holiday, not taken out of their vacation time, generates good feeling.

In all your coaching efforts, you should reward progress and not only final results. Throughout employee performance plans and their various job tasks, pay special heed to employees making real progress in reaching their goals, and reward them with kind words, a bonus, or a gift of time off.

## Do Lunch

Take a deserving employee out to lunch. If you've established a criterion for such events, there's no reason for anybody on your staff to misjudge the lunches as acts of favoritism. However, make certain these lunch moments are special occasions with a purpose (reward for a solid performance, discussion of an important new job or promotion, and so on). Pal-to-pal lunches are frowned upon, as you know.

## Pass Along Compliments

Pass along any compliments about an employee that come your way. Whether they come from a person within your organization, or a pleased customer on the outside, don't let such positive expressions live and die with you. An employee who is complimented merits knowing about it. It's a two-bagger in one sense. Your employee gets complimented by a third party, and, at the same time, gets complimented by you, the big cheese.

## Keep a Permanent Record of Good Performance

Employees always welcome positive performance reviews. When your employees do their jobs, prepare performance reviews for them. Detailed performance reviews pointing out their solid efforts and achievements are confidence boosters. They tell your employees that you both notice and value their special efforts in overcoming obstacles, solving problems, and achieving their goals.

Writing a positive letter for an employee's personnel file is a well-earned reward for a deserving member of your staff. Such letters show your employees that you care for them in the here and now, but also that you are thinking about their futures as well.

Write a letter for an employee's personnel file detailing any exemplary achievements on the job. Give the employee a copy of the letter, and let him or her see what you've written. Words on paper are permanent records and more powerful than verbal feedback, or even a bonus or raise. Letters are living testaments that'll be forever part of an employee's record.

## Make Little Things Count

All of these seemingly little things really aren't little things at all. Little things mean a lot. Some managers rely on the showy Christmas party, or a Memorial Day gathering at a posh resort by the sea, as a substitute for all of these so-called little things. They believe these extravaganzas show they really care about their employees. And there's nothing wrong with pool parties and the like, but they shouldn't be substitutes for showing appreciation to individuals on a one-on-one and regular basis.

## Be Warm

Never underestimate the all-consuming power of kindness to make the workplace a better place. When employees are happy at their jobs, they are more productive and are more willing to reach for the stars, as it were. Simple gestures and a pleasant work aura can really make a positive difference in an employee's job performance and overall satisfaction with his or her job.

You can show your employees that you care for them and appreciate their work by doing a host of little things, including saying "thank you" along the way. This lets them know that you are aware of, and grateful for, their efforts.

The business world, in general, has got a reputation for being rather cold and sometimes even cutthroat. And it is a reputation that is well earned. Free-market capitalism, nevertheless, is still the only economic system ever devised that improves the lots of the greatest number of people. So, if a people-oriented management methodology like coaching and mentoring can ameliorate some of the harsher aspects of life in the corporate world and under the capitalistic thumb, it has to be welcomed with open arms. And this is in fact why it's becoming more widespread in management circles everywhere. Coaching and mentoring practices are civilizing influences when done right. They never disregard employees' personal lives or their feelings. This is progress.

Chapter 15

# Coachable Moments

The greatest challenge facing you as a coach on the rough and tumble of today's business frontier is lighting a fire under your employees to perform at consistently high levels day in and day out. This chapter explores the vital coachable moments that must never be overlooked or bypassed if you sincerely hope to sustain strong productivity and achieve long-term positive results.

## *Using Positive Reinforcement*

It's your job to set the right professional behaviors in motion from the start of your relationship with each and every one of your employees. This requires that you not only verbalize what is expected of each one of them in doing their jobs, but that you clearly identify the right behaviors in the practical reality of the fast-paced workplace. In other words, it's your job to instruct members of your staff on the rights and the wrongs of the operating workplace—on the spot and in living color.

Simultaneously, you need to reward your people with positive reinforcement as their job roles unfold and flourish over time. In doing so, you're teaching your employees to behave the "right way" as a rule, and eventually these good behaviors will become second nature to them. Your staff won't have to think twice about whether or not they're doing things right and behaving as business professionals. Aware and assertive coaching can make a huge difference here.

An important coaching technique is positive reinforcement. This entails first identifying the right behaviors in your employees and then rewarding them with positive feedback and other tasty carrots. Positive reinforcement of the right workplace behaviors encourages employees to exhibit these behaviors as a rule and not the exception. Optimally, this is what you want from your people.

We've discussed the many rewards that are used in the business world (bonuses, gifts, and so on), and you can parcel out variations of these to your deserving employees at any time you think it appropriate. However, it is most important that you recognize and note the good behaviors when you see them in action. Positive feedback, or words of thanks and encouragement, is the way to go here in making certain that the positive reinforcement hits its intended target—the particular employee who's performing in a manner that pleases you.

The flip side of the positive reinforcement coin is permitting bad behaviors to go unchallenged. By ignoring any kind of unprofessional behavior in the workplace, you are in essence encouraging it to continue. Maybe that's not your intention, but it's nonetheless the result. And to compound your managerial misery in this area, you are, in practice, rewarding the perpetuators of these bad behaviors. Yes, rewarding them! This is negative reinforcement, which will lead to more and more similar behaviors. Behaviors, by the way, that will guarantee that you won't maximize the performance of your team and achieve the best possible results from them.

Bad behaviors on the job should never be swept under the office rug. Some managers, who take the path of least resistance, reason that, "What's done is done and I can't do anything about it now." Is that so? When Lenny screws up and you don't say a word about it to him, what do you think is likely to happen next? Lenny's going to screw up again and again. When Sylvia misses her project target date, and you remain mute about it, what do you think is the inevitable consequence? Sylvia will miss her next deadline, and the one after that, and will probably fall way short of her performance targets and goals.

Positive reinforcement can't be overstated, because it's the ball that your employees will run with. True, it is up to your employees to motivate themselves to work hard and reach their full potential. But they've got to be shown the right and proper paths to forward movement, too. And this is where your coaching skills come into play. If you fail to show your employees the right paths to navigate (for growing job skills, job satisfaction, and career advancement), then you've been remiss in your role as coach and leader.

**ALERT!**

As a coach, you must be particularly attuned to the coachable moments that come your way. These are the times in your coaching when the circumstances are ripe for extracting valuable lessons to impart to your employees. Coachable moments are situational learning opportunities for coaches to pass on to staff members.

When men and women attend Alcoholics Anonymous (AA), they hear the recurring adage, "Only you can help you." They see it displayed on placards hanging on the walls of meeting rooms, too. But AA is about showing people the ways to quitting drinking, while freely and honestly talking about the right and wrong behaviors that define recovery. Ditto for the workplace and your role as a coach. You can never retreat from your job responsibilities by claiming that your employees have to help themselves and show initiative and a willingness to learn and grow. They do indeed have to do all those things. But you are empowered to help your employees help themselves. That's what you were hired to do. And that's why you're called a coach.

## When to Employ Coaching Techniques

Before the term "coaching" was ever applied to managers and consultants for hire in business circles, it was the province of men and women in sports. There were coaches in other fields, sure, but it was likely a professional sport, school team, or maybe a peewee league, that was being discussed when the word "coach" tumbled off your tongue. When the coach appellation took the business world by storm, it naturally brought with it a powerful connotation—a sports metaphor. That is, the word "coach" was loaded, courtesy of its long history on sports playing fields, and in a few other areas where teaching, organizing, and strategizing were par for the course. Do you recall the good old days when you played high school sports (or watched them from the bleachers)? Think about those coaches of yesteryear. What were their roles? What were they expected to accomplish? Did they impart useful lessons and encourage self-motivation to play hard and play smart?

**FACT**

The right behaviors of your employees refer to their professionalism and work ethic in the workplace. As a coach, you are responsible for managing your employees' behaviors and helping them achieve maximum performance results. You must always be on top of how each individual on your team is performing and how this impacts on the overall job results.

Fundamentally, your high school coaches looked for coachable moments in which to take charge and improve the performance of the entire team. By dealing with each individual's shortcomings and strengths, and then working on bringing everybody together in a concerted team effort, high school coaches valiantly labored to win games—for their own personal satisfaction, for you, and for the esteem of the school.

Coachable moments are what define the nature of coaching—either on the playing field or in the office. The moniker "coach" means something. We've made the case time and again throughout this book that the managers who call themselves "coaches" are operating in a decidedly different way than are more traditional managers. When you manage as a coach, you're not quite the football coach (no whistle, remember) or the Lamaze coach, but you're similar in one important respect—you understand how the game is played, you identify the coachable moments, and you're able to act upon them forthrightly and effectively.

## Timing Is Everything

The coachable moments that you should be particularly tuned in to run the gamut, and as you acquire more and more experience in your role as coach, you will seize upon these moments with great alacrity. This isn't some New Age concept. It's rudimentary human behavior—people learn more in circumstances germane to the lesson. That is, they learn more on the job than from theoretical lessons taught in a staid classroom. Your coaching is most effective when you're playing show and tell, as it were.

Coachable moments await you and will test your mettle time and again. It is during these times when you can upgrade your employees' skills—both hard and soft—and show your people what professionalism means in their daily efforts. But timing is everything, even in coaching. To put these coachable moments into a coherent context, here's a general overview of the kinds of actions or achievements your employees will demonstrate that will compel you to do some coaching:

- Positive performance results
- Job-task progression
- Innovative thinking

- Negative performance results
- Job-task retrogression
- Slip-ups

Ah, yes, the impromptu coachable moments. You never quite know when a golden opportunity will arise for you to really strut your coaching stuff. This isn't, of course, to suggest that coaching is something that you turn on when you wake up in the morning and turn off when you lay your head down at night. You are a coach some of the time in your personal life, but all the time in your work life. It's just that there are prime moments in managing when your coaching can make very demonstrable and positive differences. You've got to identify these moments, and then vigilantly extract the important lessons to be learned from them. Let's discuss each one individually and at some length.

## Positive Performance Results

When you spot positive performance, you've got to extract lessons from it. You can't just let out a whoop and a holler and move on. Your coachable moment here involves you meeting with your high-achieving employees and dissecting their successes. You know all about communicating along the way (via constructive feedback, and so on), but the importance of thorough wrap-ups needs to be underscored as well.

When employees' goals are reached or exceeded, you've got to reward them for their achievements. You can, for instance, write performance reviews detailing all the things that went right—A to Z. Allow your employees to glean positive lessons from their performances. Don't hold back even the most picayune details of what contributed to their strong performances. Indeed, break down their performances into the various ingredients that contributed to the stellar showings. Look at:

- **Preparation.** Just how did the employees' preparations for their jobs and specific tasks lead to their successful performances?
- **Skills.** Just what skills did they utilize in doing their jobs that made positive differences?

- **Attitude.** Just how did their overall approach to their jobs and work ethic contribute to the final results?

By breaking down the positive performance results into such categories, your employees can more fully comprehend their successes, and thus be more capable of moving to the next level, whether it's duplicating successes or perhaps improving on their already strong performances. Recognizing positive coachable moments is just as essential as dealing forthrightly with the myriad problems that come down the workplace pike—when those "negative" coachable moments rear their ugly heads.

**ALERT!**

Where there's positive reinforcement, there is also negative reinforcement. Be especially vigilant not to reward the negative behaviors of your employees by ignoring them and permitting them to slip through the workplace cracks. Even if it's not your intention, this is, in effect, negative reinforcement of such behaviors.

Another key area to explore in this summary of your employees' positive performances is outside influences. Did outside factors of some kind contribute to their performances that were not considered at the beginning of a performance plan or at the start of a particular project? Sometimes these weigh in on the positive side; other times on the negative side.

These outside conditions range from an economic upturn (or downturn), to a cultural fad, to breakthrough technology, to personnel changes in the company, to a wide assortment of other possibilities. So many things on the outside are, yes, outside both you and your employees' control; things that can seriously impact performances. And it's part of your job to identify them when they happen and find lessons to extract from the experiences.

For instance, an economic upswing and shift in consumer confidence can make a huge difference in performance results, depending on your department and the products or services that you offer. The lesson learned could be how to take advantage of these shifting economic winds by recognizing the shift early on and adjusting performance methods and approaches accordingly. Obviously, the same thinking would apply to an economic downswing. Your job is to always impart lasting lessons—where you can and when you can. One of the most important coaching lessons you can communicate is learning to adjust plans and approaches at a moment's notice. Resilience is so key in countless business as well as life situations.

## Job-Task Progression

On to another coachable moment. This one happens when you detect job-task progression in your employees. This is your chance to reward progress and not just results. But part of these reward efforts on your part should involve going beyond mere recognition of progress to the extracting of genuine and lasting lessons. Lessons, that is, steeped in the many factors behind the progress—behind the forward motion of your employees.

You follow the same course as you do with positive performance results, except that you don't wrap up this time. Instead, you dissect, examine, and convey lessons to your employees to keep them doing what works for them. At this time, you also make note of the behaviors and attitudes that could be improved upon to take the progress to an even higher level.

## Innovative Thinking

Innovative thinking on your employees' parts enables them to leap over hurdles by using their smarts and their skills, and by tapping into their special talents. Performance plans and various job projects follow timelines, and there are always crucial moments in them that will essentially make or break their success. As a coach, you've got to be keenly aware of these moments and reward your employees for their ingenuity, or poke and prod them to be more adaptable and clever at making things happen.

We've said it before that people's potential as work entities often remain dormant or not fully tapped. Coachable moments and bringing out lessons in these special situations are where good coaching really earns its kudos. Dinosaur managers are certainly not keeping their eyes peeled for these moments.

# The Flip Side of Coachable Moments

The flip side of positive coachable moments—positive performance results, job-task progression, and innovative thinking—are negative performance results, job-task retrogression, and slip-ups. As mentioned previously, these are also coachable moments. The same approaches are called for. You dissect the performance or the attitude, and identify lessons to be learned. The lessons, this time, are rooted in correcting wrongs and showing employees how to get on the right tracks.

Coaching for these negative moments can be summed up in a three-part process:

1. Review the moment.
2. Extract a lesson or lessons.
3. Apply the lesson or lessons to another set of circumstances—the next phase of the job, another job, or a career move.

In essence, you take negative circumstances and turn them into positives by applying your coaching skills to help your employees learn from their errors and improve their performance.

# Teaching Your Employees How to Learn

Teaching your employees how to learn may sound like instructing grade-school kids, but it's not. As you've just read, coachable moments call upon you time and again to pluck out important lessons from a wide range of work situations. When you correctly identify the consequential lessons to be learned, and scrutinize and discuss them with your employees, you're equipping them to learn on their own. That is, you're giving them the tools to recognize the genuine opportunities for learning in their own work experiences. You're showing them how to learn from these experiences and move forward.

Learning how to learn essentially means your employees respond to your coachable moments and absorb the lessons therein, and are better prepared to grow their skills, take on more responsibilities, and meet any future job challenges. They are more self-sufficient and more capable of seizing opportunities available to them. And employees who are more confident in their jobs and more accomplished at navigating around the many workplace hurdles are the prime candidates for advanced learning.

**FACT**

There is truth in the old adage that "Only you can help you." But don't expect your employees to help themselves without a little help from you. Your job as a coach entails showing your employees the paths to learning and career advancement. Walking the paths is up to them.

## Locating Opportunities for Learning

When your employees reach the advanced learning state, they are keenly aware of what's going on around them. They are mindful of their progression in their jobs and what it means for both their immediate and long-term futures. They are on red alert for opportunities to better themselves. Indeed, when your employees are in this heightened state of awareness in the workplace, they are open to any and all learning situations. They are not only delighted when learning opportunities come their way, but they make things happen by creating their own opportunities.

### Looking Outside the Work Environment

As a coach, encourage your staff to look outside the immediate work environs for materials to advance their skills and enhance their performances. Learning opportunities abound in so many places beyond you, your coaching efforts, and the immediate workplace. You should point your employees to good books and magazines on subjects pertinent to their jobs and special skills. Depending on what you and your team need and want, the reading materials could concentrate on subject matter ranging from highly technical skills to professional and leadership skills.

Colleges and universities offer relevant courses on technological advances, leadership tools and techniques, and just about everything else related to the workings of business. Keep your eyes open for these learning opportunities and match them up with your hungry employees in the advanced learning state. Also consider taking advantage of the many seminars and workshops available which offer a vast array of business-related subjects pertinent to managing and working in the corporate environment. Again, finding the right employee for the right learning moment is part of your job. And if this means sending an employee from the New York office to a seminar on cutting-edge computer skills in Los Angeles, you might consider committing to it. That is, if you truly believe that attending will make a positive difference for you and for your employee—one that justifies the expense and time away from the office and the job.

Remember show and tell in grammar school? Well, so much of coaching is a variation of show and tell. That is, you seize on any and all opportunities to impart business and life lessons, on the spot and in real time. These are the most powerful kinds of lessons.

## Looking Inside the Work Environment

There are learning moments less costly than expensive seminars and the like. It doesn't cost any company dollars for you to instruct your employees to talk to the people whom they encounter in their daily grind on and around the job. Tell them to listen to customers, to coworkers, and to peers in other departments of the company. Convince them of the benefits of hearing what others have to say on business matters ranging far and wide.

Many men and women are successful businesspersons because, they say, an important and influential person or persons gave them some advice or showed them some technique that was instrumental in advancing their careers. Of course, these influential persons are often mentors within the organization, or good coaches like you, but sometimes they're outsiders.

That is, they're persons who just happened by that made substantial and positive differences in their lives.

When you grow your employees' skills to the point where they are self-confident and accomplished at navigating around workplace hurdles, you've got candidates for advanced learning. Seek to broaden their learning opportunities with books, seminars, mentoring, and more.

There are many people out there with much to offer. But they're not going to come to you; you've got to go to them. They need to be drawn out. So, when you tell your employees not to be shy about asking questions of you (a basic tenet of a coach's communication), you should also extend this advice further. Tell your employees to network. Encourage them to talk to people within the organization and on the outside, too. Talk, question, understand, and learn.

## A Yogi Berra Lesson: Observe by Watching

The philosopher Yogi Berra once opined, "You can observe a lot by watching." And, as usual, Yogi was right. When you unleash your employees to travel to the ends of the earth—metaphorically speaking—to learn, grow their skills, take on new responsibilities, and welcome challenges with confidence, you've created not a pack of Frankenstein monsters, but human beings on the way to realizing their work potential. And doesn't it always come back to that? The purpose of the coaching and mentoring managerial methodology is to take people to their outer limits, not by threats of violence or loss of jobs, but by affording them the knowledge and the opportunities to get there. As a coach, you teach, teach, and teach, and then it's up to your employees to help themselves and achieve great things. You show the way and your employees determine whether or not to venture beyond their comfortable parameters. If you provide your people this kind of stimulating work environment, you've done your job and done it well. And, sure, not everybody in your employ will thrive under your tutelage, but most will, and some will do so at extraordinary levels.

Chapter 16

# Altering the Corporate Culture

When an organization adopts coaching and mentoring managerial strategies, it's getting something more than a finely honed roadmap to profit maximization. It's actually agreeing to full and absolute cultural upheaval, whether the company knows it or not. This chapter will take you through the ways and means of these extreme cultural makeovers.

# Understanding How Corporate Cultural Shifts Occur

Cultural shifts in business don't happen overnight. A revolutionary cultural change in a corporate setting isn't consummated with scattershot applications of coaching tools, techniques, and haphazard mentoring.

## How Coaching Overhauls the Culture

An absolute cultural makeover entails that companies fully embrace coaching in their management from the top to the bottom of their organizations. That is, companies must employ coaching and mentoring methodologies everywhere, and not in isolated spots and chosen moments. The companies that fully implement coaching as a managerial art are the ones that are radically altering their colors.

A cultural overhaul in operations means that the old way of doing things—planning, decision making, problem solving, rewards, promotions, and so on—is supplanted with a fresh new way of running the entire show. So, if you're managing as a coach in one department of the organization, a coach is running the office in another department. And coaches are likewise in place and managing on the next level in the company, too. One of the most conspicuous aspects that distinguishes traditional, directive-style management from coaching is that coached employees, unlike those in other organizations, are welcomed into the decision-making process, encouraged to be self-sufficient, and made to feel an integral part of the company.

**ALERT!**

When the entire corporate culture is rooted in the respect of individual employees, you know that coaching and mentoring practices are in place and getting results. Results, by the way, beyond mere bottom lines and big profits.

## Dysfunctional Cultures Can Be Tough to Change

Ideally, a corporate family, like any family, should respect all the members within it. Think of a dysfunctional family with parents who raise their children in a crude and contemptuous atmosphere. You know how it goes—the kids are always put down and are cruelly mocked. And it invariably starts at the top (just like in business). Mom badmouths Dad. Dad strikes back at Mom. Any of their kids' hopes and dreams are squashed and deemed unrealistic or foolish. Guess what? The kids will likely grow up and repeat this noxious process all over again with their own kids.

Corporate families that practice this same pestilent pattern of contempt never recognize the vast human potential of their employee pool. Instead, they hire people to work in specific jobs and do nothing to foster further learning and expansion of their knowledge and skills. Because there are no challenges and opportunities for advancement, these dissatisfied folks leave their jobs sooner rather than later, and the process is repeated over and over again.

Coaching is the best managerial method for making the workplace both a productive and a contented place. And the reason is that coaching and mentoring and their tools and techniques are designed to do just that. No other managerial methods marry productivity with satisfaction in such a conspicuously coherent way.

# Respecting and Encouraging Individual Initiative

Courtesy of its ironic origins and associations with discredited political ideologies and enemies of the free market and liberty, the expression "power to the people" has a somewhat notorious reputation.

Ah, but leave it to coaching and mentoring to clean up the slogan. This managerial art believes in ceding power to the people (employees) by highly respecting their individuality and celebrating their initiative. And that's the real thing—genuine power to the people. People are unique individuals with special talents who need to be set free both at home and at work.

When people look for jobs in the corporate world, they want to work in places that fulfill them. That is, they want to do important things and have some power over their destinies. People want to be in roles that unleash their full possibilities as worker commodities and, as seen in prior examples in this book, as more thoughtful and wise human beings, too.

An important personal attribute that coaches must always embrace is humility. As a coach, you should not view your position and role as the be-all and end-all. In order for coaching to connect with employees, the coach can never be perceived as being imperiously above the fray. Good coaches never patronize employees.

# Company Politics: The Last Campaign

Comprehensive coaching in an organization means that all its former company politics are put to bed. Employees can readily see and viscerally feel when politics dominate a company's decision-making process. Indeed, when politics rule in the office, people feel a sense of powerlessness in performing their jobs in the present, with a corresponding sense of hopelessness as far as their futures are concerned. They feel that no matter what they do on the job, company politics will eclipse even their best efforts.

So, yes, we've got another vital coaching job for you. And that's removing any overt politics from the office, which is your little part of the company—your domain and responsibility. When you work at eliminating this blight, you're handing more power over to your employees. You're raising their levels of satisfaction vis-à-vis their job roles and within the company at large, because the workplace is now unfettered with relationships and decision making clouded by company politics. Just what is meant by company politics? Here are some examples.

## The Blame Game

Deleterious company politics often spawn the blame game, in which the buck never seems to stop on any boss's desk and employees shoulder the lion's share of the blame for what goes wrong. As a coach, you must put an end to the blame game if it exists. Replace the blame with accountability and personal responsibility.

Never play the blame game in your office. Make responsibility and accountability the rule, for both you and your employees, and the blame game will become yesterday's news. Work with individual performance plans and goals, and hold each individual strictly answerable for his or her results on the job.

That is, put responsibility for doing a job in the forefront of any job assignment or project. Employees then know precisely what they are responsible for accomplishing. They have performance plans to guide them and have settled on goals to strive for. The blame game plays no part in a workplace where there is complete and defined accountability.

## The Distinctive Relationship

Another area of office politics revolves around what can be called the "distinctive relationship." Not only the obvious ones between managers and employees, but relationships between and among employees themselves that exclude others. And we're not talking about exclusion in a personal sense, but in a business sense, where employees do not sufficiently share information or work loads as a team (both of which are so essential these days in getting a job done right).

You've got to be eternally vigilant that these types of distinctive relationships don't take root and cause disharmony and disarray in your office environs. You must foster relationships that you know from experience promote team rapport and competent, concerted efforts. In your office, there should be no secrets.

## The Aura of Superiority

Company politics sometimes permit an aura of superiority to prevail in the office. An office caste system, if you will. Yes, you're going to have high-flying employees, the big achievers, whom you will rely on and groom for advancement. That's a highly desirable scenario. But you must be ever mindful not to tolerate your team splitting apart into factions based on skill levels or for any other reasons.

You're responsible for taking any aura of superiority and turning it on its head into an aura of generosity. Those in your employ with more advanced or sharper skills should be encouraged to impart their knowledge and skills to their coworkers (mini-mentoring)—without displaying an attitude of superiority or condescension. No employee appreciates feeling like a grade-schooler on the job, patronized and inferior. A team that produces results must share in so many critical ways, and every member of the team should be made to feel like an important part of the group effort.

**ALERT!**

Never allow an aura of superiority to hover over your office like a dark cloud about to rain down on it. Keep your team from splintering apart based on skill levels and other factors. Foster an aura of generosity instead, encouraging the sharing of knowledge and teaching of skills.

## Undue Delegation

When company politics reign supreme, even delegation of authority suffers, and sometimes gets twisted like a pretzel. Undue delegation, also called passing the buck, is in reality no delegation at all. It's an abrogation of somebody's responsibility.

**ESSENTIAL**

Coaches delegate, then delegate some more. It's all part of showing confidence in their employees and offering them added responsibilities and more challenges. But it's not delegation at all if it amounts to passing the buck. When you delegate, you delegate based on merit and ability to do the assigned work.

You know by now that coaches regularly delegate important assignments and jobs to their employees. As a coach, you are morally obliged to delegate, and as often as you possibly can, or you're not a coach. But you base your delegation of important job responsibilities on what you have to work with in talent and skills. Don't ever pass the buck and call it delegation. That is, don't get your employees to do your job for you in any way, shape, or form. And don't allow members of your staff to get their coworkers to do their jobs for them in any way, shape, or form, either.

## The Exclusive Clique

The last of the company politics issues we'll tackle is the notorious "exclusive clique," which is in some ways an extension of distinctive relationships in that it deals with interoffice alliances. The difference is, the exclusive clique sets the rules on how things get done—everything from soup to nuts. This is the way it's done, period, end of story! And nobody is going to come along and tell them otherwise.

In companies that don't practice coaching in management, it's not unusual for new managers, let alone employees on lower levels, to run head-first into exclusive cliques and be rejected as unworthy of admission. Managers with new ideas or methods are rebuffed; employees with any initiative are shunned. You get the picture. Your job as a coach is to implode any exclusive cliques if they are around, and replace them with teams of achievers. Also, you must be circumspect in not allowing any of these cliques to spring to life and grow on your watch.

Sometimes these cliques can sprout up without you ever realizing it. You're only human. When you're working with the same people day in and day out, a certain comfort develops that can lull you into an unsuspecting repose, and yes—a rigid way of doing things. You're in trouble when your way of doing things excludes others from contributing their ingenuity and talents. However, if your way of doing things is coaching in an enduring learning environment, you are, in effect, overseeing a team of self-starters, and that's what you want to be doing as a coach. If you want to get the best possible results in overall employee satisfaction and performance results, don't ever find yourself hunkered down with a cozy clique of favored employees.

## Hello Support, Goodbye Hierarchy

If you are indeed to work your magic as a coach and manager of people, you're going to have to supplant rigid hierarchy with support.

## Removing Barriers Between Managers and Employees

Traditional management methods regularly erect proverbial brick walls between managers and employees. If an organization sees fit to christen you a coach and grant you the leeway to apply the tools and techniques of coaching and mentoring, it is in effect saying to you, "Make things work." And, as a coach, you know what makes things work. You have to tear down any barriers and implement strong support systems. When you supersede strict hierarchy with support (and this covers everything that we've discussed relating to fashioning a healthy and productive work environment satisfying to your employees), you've taken a giant step in creating a corporate family in the office.

## Employing Coaching and Mentoring Across the Board

There are companies aplenty that don't endorse coaching and mentoring, but nevertheless have wise managers at the helm in various places in the organization applying very sound tools and techniques. In fact, it's a very commonplace scenario. But there are inevitable problems in the offing when everyone in the company does not practice coaching and mentoring.

**FACT**

Coaching and mentoring managerial practices attempt to displace the corporate hierarchy with a strong support system. They seek to make the customer the center of the office universe and not the manager, the coach. The coach is the leader, but the customer is the king.

For example, Eva works for Heaven on Earth, Inc., and is delighted with her job and thoroughly enjoys working for her manager, John. She is given increasing amounts of responsibilities and challenging job assignments, and her job has evolved nicely over time. Eventually, John recommends her for a new position in the company, a climb up the ladder. Eva is overjoyed at the chance for a promotion, and, of course, the nifty salary increase that goes with it. Her only regret is that she'll be leaving John and her coworkers, whom she thoroughly enjoys working with. But of course, she reasons, she will quickly acclimate to her new surroundings. "Don't look back," her boss John tells her. As a general rule, this is sound advice.

Well, unfortunately, Eva does look back, almost immediately as a matter of fact. Even though she has more prestige and more money in her new position, her superior is no John—not even close. Eva's new boss does not employ anything resembling coaching in his managerial conduct. But how could this happen, you ask? Very easily when the whole of the organization is not singing the same tune. When one manager is hitting the high notes like a veritable Pavarotti, and another manager is croaking along like Edith Bunker, you've got an organizational problem. Manager John shouldn't be standing alone in a corporate hierarchy, supporting his employees by lending them his expertise and understanding, only to promote them into a work environment that's the antithesis of the positive and healthy one he presides over. This runs counter to the totality of coaching and mentoring; coaches have to know beyond a shadow of a doubt that their employees have a place to go in the company—a place that will further their growth and not stunt it.

## Satisfying the Customer

We're all the customers of countless companies across a wide spectrum. The corporate world exists because of customers. Regardless of what the product or service is, performance results on the job invariably mean pleasing customers in one way or another. Even if the customers are somehow far removed from the workplace, this doesn't mean they're any less important. A powerful thread running through coaching and mentoring is that they seek to shift the emphasis from pleasing the boss to satisfying the customer.

### Leading and Setting the Tone

You are the leader and tone setter, of course. As such you must be humble enough to shift your employees' focus from you to your customers. That is, to the people you, as coach, and all of your employees are laboring in key ways to please. Yes, you do the hiring. You communicate. You teach. You work with your employees in devising their performance plans and setting their goals. But this is all about achieving the best possible results for the customers.

You want your employees to deliver results that are pleasing to them, of course, to you, naturally, and to the company, yes indeed. But most of all, you and your employees have to deliver results for the customers, because without customers, there would be no company, no coach, and no employees. If you've had the good fortune—or misfortune in some instances—of working in a retail or service business, then you know full well that dealing with the walk-in public is not always an easy task. Never mind the physical work required of you, which is often grueling enough. It's the mental drain that's debilitating sometimes, as various customers say and do things to test your patience and very often your sanity. Servicing customers isn't always pretty, but it's a necessity that's got to be done and done right, because satisfying them is what will in the final analysis determine whether a business lives or dies.

Role reversal is an important tool in the coaching and mentoring repertoire. Put it into practice when you want your employees to stand in the shoes of others (such as customers). By utilizing role reversal, you usher your employees into an all-important reality laboratory.

And this truism transcends working behind the counter in a drugstore, or as a waiter or waitress in a restaurant, where customer service is measurable at the point of service. So, while you may not work face-to-face with your company's customers, the company is still in the business of giving its customers what they want and when they want it. And if your company doesn't do these two things, somebody else probably will. For that reason, if you can take the spotlight off yourself and put it where it rightly belongs—on the customers—you'll be making the familial atmosphere of the workplace more cohesive, with everybody working together with the same objective in mind.

## *Reversing Roles*

When you frame a job in the simple terms of pleasing customers, it is an invaluable technique to ask your employees to engage in a little role reversal by putting themselves in the customers' shoes. We're all customers. We patronize countless businesses, utilize so many services, and experience widely varying results in the process. Results that make us want to use, or not use, a particular product or service again.

When your employees see things from a customer's vantage point, they put themselves in the place of the very people they're trying to please. They see things from an unmistakably different perspective. That is, you want each employee working for you to consider:

- How do I like to be treated as a customer?
- What can my company do that would please me as a customer?
- What can my company do to prove that we truly believe that the customer is king?

When you go a step further and ask that your employees answer their own thoughtful, open-ended questions, you're in effect asking them to think as entrepreneurs. And, as far as you're concerned, the pièce de résistance is putting these answers into action. By fully utilizing this role-reversal technique, you permit your staff to:

- Think in entrepreneurial ways
- Fashion flexibility
- Empathize with customers
- Sharpen self-awareness

In this role reversal, you are not only asking your employees to think like entrepreneurs, but also to fashion flexibility by seeing themselves as customers of what the company, yours and theirs, is offering as a product or a service, and how they are offering it. By doing this, you are effecting positive change and implementing new ways of thinking based on your employees' experiences in this reality laboratory. Yet another benefit of role reversal is that it enables employees to empathize with customers.

**FACT**

Empathy is defined as understanding what somebody else is feeling, or appreciating the circumstances that another individual is in. You can't empathize with another person unless you've shared his or her experiences in a comparable way. Thus, by asking that your employees see things from their customers' perspectives, you are asking that they empathize with them.

You are asking, in effect, that they translate this empathy and new understanding into a better product or service via better performances on their parts. And lastly, any kind of role reversal sharpens self-awareness. When you place your employees in their customers' worlds, you're asking them to look into their own lives and explore how they behave as customers—what does and does not satisfy them, and why.

# Chapter 17

# Enhancing Profitability

Coaching and mentoring in corporate management would be an unwelcome intruder if it did not produce quantifiably positive results. That is, if it did not sweeten bottom lines. This chapter details how coaching and mentoring managerial methods make companies—even large corporations—more profitable and, in the process, enhance their reputations, which are often seen as cold and bloodless.

## The Coaching and Mentoring Shock Absorber

We've got the global economy, the Internet, and downsizing and restructuring all coming together in a furious blend. It's a hard fact of business life we'd all better get used to because it's here to stay. In this decidedly turbulent atmosphere, unsuspecting managers and anxious employees alike are fearful about what the future holds. The future, however, is daunting only for those who don't fully appreciate that these tumultuous twenty-first-century business realities can in fact be harnessed. Tamed, that is, by a fresh way of thinking and managing people called coaching and mentoring. Coaching and mentoring are the modern workplace's shock absorbers.

Coaching and mentoring's tools and techniques aim to tame the often-harsh realities of conducting business in the new millennium. By making employees more resilient, self-confident, and better prepared to handle the stress and challenges of today's dog-eat-dog work world, a good coach can banish all fears of the unknown tomorrow.

As a coach and mentor, you're responsible for placing these shock absorbers in the engine of the workplace. Indeed, if you've got coaching and mentoring tools and techniques at your disposal, the inescapable shocks—problems and obstacles—that will come your way can be both competently and calmly managed without going into the crisis mode or sounding a red alert.

Big-shot companies are often out in front of so many important business trends. Hence, they understand that by instilling coaching and mentoring from top to bottom in their organizations, they're preparing themselves for the inevitable breakneck changes that come with the territory of conducting modern-day business. They also know full well that their competitors, who view on-the-job learning as finite experiences, will in short order be swept away by the winds of change.

## Flexibility Is Key

You're expected to be very flexible in your daily managing efforts—flexible in dealing with your diverse employees and flexible in your planning, based on the multiple factors associated with the faster-than-fast business realities of the present that we've just discussed. Flexible in dealing with people? You'd better believe it. We've confirmed time and again on these pages that employees laboring in today's corporate environs vote with their feet when their work wants and needs aren't addressed. That is, they leave their jobs for greener pastures and more fulfilling places to draw paychecks. And courtesy of this swishing and swirling labor pool, the companies that offer the most stimulating work environments—with the greatest opportunities for career advancement and other appetizing carrots—will come out on top. The companies with coaches at the helm are best poised to survive and thrive by attracting the best and the brightest.

## Coaching and Mentoring Is a Sound Investment

Because companies' initial training and orientation costs are more substantial than ever before, it's in their interests to get a premium return on their investments. Translation: They must invest their time and money in employees who will do a good job for them and not their competitors. The bloodthirsty corporate world of today is a free-for-all competition for cream-of-the-crop employees. And in turn, authoritarianism in the managerial hierarchy is breaking apart like a powdered donut dunked in a cup of coffee. Who wants to work for an unimaginative ogre these days when there are so many more pleasing alternatives?

And, on the other end of this sour spectrum, managers who rely on managing via e-mail are not about to inspire commitment from their staffs. Neither authoritarian nor indifferent bosses are going to keep the greatest achievers with the greatest potential in their folds. They're not going to extract the maximum human potential from their people because they're not both asking and allowing their employees to boldly go forward. Or, in the case of the mad e-mailer managers, they're not there in the flesh and blood to poke and prod them to perform. Enlightened companies know the score and are consciously training, and in some cases retraining, their managers to be teachers and counselors—coaches.

**FACT**

Many large corporations have justifiably sullied reputations in the area of caring for their employees' on-the-job well-being. Coaching and mentoring in management are striving to light a fire under these frosty reputations by transforming remote corporate countenances into something that more closely resembles a human face.

Human potential is more or less boundless. But it needs to be tapped like a keg of frothy beer to get its full kick. Companies with adroit management in place actively mine this vast human potential. But they always need stables of schooled coaches and wise mentors to get the job done. Otherwise all that latent talent and great possibility remains dormant and unrealized like some kind of buried treasure. People are brimming with ideas, including ideas on how better to do their jobs and perform at higher levels. They're chock full of skills and know-how that can easily go undetected and unused if there's no coach to find it and unleash it.

## The Coach as Detective

Leave it to corporate bigwigs to view their managers as detectives on a diligent search for getting the best possible results. After all, it's common sense. Successful businesses don't run on autopilot, because their employees don't run on autopilot. Employees need to be turned on. This subject matter was touched upon in Chapter 15 in a discussion of the utilization of "coachable moments" to spur on self-motivation. Yes, it's up to employees to ultimately do their work, but coaches have to click them on sometimes and adjust the controls. Time and again on these pages, you've seen that coaches wear many hats in their many roles. And one of them is a detective's fedora. So put it on and get ready for some intriguing detective work in the office.

For argument's sake, let's say that you're a fusion of detectives Jim Rockford and Lt. Theo Kojak. Rockford is a private investigator on the West Coast, known for his unorthodox approaches in doing his job. Kojak, on the East Coast, works within the confines of the New York City Police Department regulations, but falls back on his experiences from his regular detective work.

Coaching by its very nature is unorthodox as it tries new ways of doing things all the time. Decisions are often based on an individual employee's personality and skill level. This sharp and constant focus on individual potential falls well outside of traditional management parameters. By the same token, as a coach never lose sight of the fact that you work for a particular company with a particular vision. The Fortune 500 companies, for instance, are vigilant in guarding their reputations. Thus, you are afforded a lot of unorthodox rope to work with, but be careful not to hang yourself with it.

You ascertain what you've got to work with—that is, the people, their knowledge base, and their overall skills. You detect in them what they can do and, essentially, set them to doing it. It's absolutely vital to project a can-do spirit; however, this assertive posture maximizes performance results only when it's paired with can-do employees. Otherwise, it's more hot-air than can-do, which doesn't accomplish much in business or in life in general.

## Brainstorming Gets Results

From employees' perspectives, coaching means—among so many positive things—that their managers will listen to them and allow them ample say in both defining and navigating their jobs. In your magnanimous and wise presence, brainstorming permits your employees to sound off in freewheeling, candid settings. That is, your employees can express themselves without fear of the office thought-police coming down on them.

As a coach, you are expected to promote a can-do spirit in the office. You do this by exhibiting enthusiasm and setting bold but attainable goals for your team. You must, however, make certain at all times that you match your can-do spirit with can-do employees.

Your coaching methods and the overall office ambience shouldn't be patterned after a totalitarian state with you as the benevolent dictator. It shouldn't be a place where "oppositionists" are thrown into the office equivalents of prisons or gulags. Admittedly, you don't want oppositionists working for you who rail against your coaching program and all that you're trying to accomplish. But you don't want yes-men and yes-women on your staff, either. You want your people to freely speak their minds and go against the grain now and then.

**ALERT!**

Brainstorming sessions are, in many ways, microcosms of the relationships between coaches and their employees, because they represent communication without boundaries. And creative people relish this rhetorical freedom. They enjoy contributing their ideas and suggestions without fear of being ridiculed if their verbal offerings don't pass intellectual muster.

When word gets out that you lend an ear to your employees' ideas, people of talent and ambition will be viscerally attracted to your work environs, and employees will want to remain in such a warm and nurturing business environment. This is still another reason why big and small businesses alike are welcoming coaching and mentoring—and their bold approaches in letting employees have their say—into their organizational structures. Smart companies appreciate that letting employees have their say often means that they are more likely to want to stay.

## *Guidance Counselors: Coaches Supplying Answers*

Because the biggest companies are big—really big—it is not surprising that an employee gripe is that advice and real direction from management is hard to come by. And this is a big—really big—reason why coaching is being ushered into the corridors of many of these sprawling companies.

In all levels of education, there are guidance counselors. In grade school, high school, and college, they are in place and ready, willing, and able to help out. Exactly what are they ready, willing, and able to do? Ideally, guidance counselors are in place to answer students' questions and lend them support when and where needed. Grade school counselors' advice, however, is somewhat different from that of their high school counterparts. And college counselors, of course, dispense a different brand of advice altogether.

**FACT**

A coach's workplace is not patterned after the world's totalitarian states. In fact, just the opposite is the case. Coaches recognize that freedom of expression is a specially guarded right that they will defend to their deaths—as coaches, of course.

Above all else, this chapter illustrates the importance of replacing an unbending managerial hierarchy with a pliable support system. And this means placing the equivalent of guidance counselors—coaches and mentors—at all levels of the company.

Employees up and down the corporate ladder have never-ending streams of questions and concerns. They want and deserve to know so many things, from what is expected of them, first and foremost, in their jobs, to what possibilities await them in their futures. It's completely disheartening for employees in an organization to have a plethora of questions on their minds, but nary a soul to ask. So, yes, you're an answer man or answer woman as a coach. The company paying your salary is relying on you to thoroughly answer your people's job-specific questions and assuage any of their career concerns.

**ESSENTIAL**

Among the hats that you wear as a coach is that of guidance counselor. You must have lots of answers at your disposal to the many questions and concerns of your employees. There is nothing more deflating for people on the job than having questions and nobody to pose them to.

Putting this aspect of coaching in the forefront of the support system is rudimentary if once-faceless companies desire a more human face. For it is only this human face that will resurrect reputations. It is this human face that'll also maximize employee performance results—and, yes, profits—in today's business climate.

# Putting a Human Face on Corporations

While on the subject of putting a more human face on big companies, let's own up to the fact that many people are skeptical that it is even possible. For the many doubting Thomases out there, let's look at it this way. How many of today's medical students are choosing to specialize in the fields of cosmetic doctoring? Many more than in years past, that's for sure. Putting a human face on a business entity is a lot easier than performing plastic surgery on flesh and blood!

## Changing the Corporate Face

Advancing technology in plastic surgery techniques, coupled with runaway vanity, has made human face makeovers the "in" thing. From the hair atop the head to the point on the chin, people are opting to change their looks by rearranging their biological visages. In a similar vein, many businesses, courtesy of today's rapid technological growth, are changing their faces—their reputations—too, by rearranging the ways they manage their people.

## Almost Anything Is Possible

True, the technological advances in business are somewhat different in nature from those in medical science, but what they have in common is that they make what was impossible yesterday very possible today. Many businesses, big and small alike, are afforded very little wiggle room in the survival game. And depending on their product or service, and the stiffness of the competition, a face-lift is more often a necessity than a luxury.

Despite the stretching of this analogy, coaching and mentoring can never be perceived as mere cosmetic changes if they are to work effectively. In businesses where coaching and mentoring are seen as more cosmetic than real, they don't produce the results they should and could. Some outfits take bits and pieces of what they believe are coaching and mentoring, but don't lay the proper foundation of good management with integrity, which earns the respect and trust of their employees.

Some companies spout slogans such as: "Coaching begins with an attitude of helpfulness"; "Coaching is asking the right questions, not supplying the answers"; "Coaching requires commitment." And that's all well and nice. But if these enterprises don't back up the words with credible actions, their attempts at inspiring employees to commitment are seen as ludicrous.

## *Making the Face-Lift Permanent*

So, we can all agree: The coaching and mentoring methodology is anything but cosmetic. It is flexible and varied—always a work in progress—but it represents a permanent managerial face-lift. It's a face-lift that takes tired and worn-out traditional management approaches and turns them into young and sexy management styles befitting the new century and new millennium. For coaching and mentoring to deliver results, they've got to be both permanent and thoroughly applied throughout an organization.

As a coach, you want to appear "young" and "sexy" in managing your team. (Of course this is a metaphor, because coaching and mentoring never discriminate in their embrace of people of all ages and physical attractiveness.) It's about being vigorous and attractive in your managerial practices and outlook. It's about challenging your employees without appearing overbearing and expecting the impossible. It's worth repeating that both you, as a coach or mentor, and your employees or mentees can substantially benefit from a company's new face in so many positive ways.

# Chapter 18

# Managing Diversity

Coaching and mentoring's tools and techniques are tailored to address the increasingly important diversity issues in the workplace. This chapter reveals how this enlightened managerial approach handles the unique concerns of women, minorities, and other special groups on the job frontier. By carefully avoiding a one-size-fits-all style of managing, coaching and mentoring methods—and the people who implement them—are at the ready to meet any and all diversity challenges that come their way.

## *Breaking Through the Glass Ceiling*

A review of corporate middle management reveals that the numbers of women and minorities in managerial positions are at an all-time high. This is a breakthrough worthy of celebrating! However, above middle management, the numbers of women and minorities are not especially impressive, considering their overall percentages in the workplace. This conspicuous disconnect is sometimes referred to as "hitting the glass ceiling." The glass ceiling is not some media-manufactured illusion but an ingrained reality, even in the twenty-first century.

**QUESTION?**

**What is the glass ceiling?**
The glass ceiling is the term applied to the obstacles that women and minorities face in breaking into the senior management of corporations. In recent years, historic gains have been realized in middle management, but nothing quite as impressive above this level.

The logical question to contemplate now is "Why?" Why aren't women and minorities making the same sizeable strides into senior management as they are in middle management? It's the answer to this profound query that will help explain coaching and mentoring's short- and long-term role in breaking apart the glass ceiling shard by shard.

Is blatant sexism and racism the reason for the glass ceiling's persistence? Maybe thirty, forty, or fifty years ago, the answer would have been a resounding "yes!" But it's a vastly different time. There are strict labor laws in place now that prohibit discrimination based on gender, race, and any number of things. This isn't to suggest that there aren't some very biased souls running around in important positions in the corporate sphere. There sure are. But it's not these less than enlightened folks who are the chief custodians of today's glass ceiling.

Instead, we need to look at the invisible hand that's literally holding back countless women and minorities from moving on up the corporate ladder. For instance, many mentoring and mini-mentoring relationships are in the invisible hand's tight grasp. That is, senior managers, by and large, groom people to work alongside them or to succeed them, and they choose people they feel most comfortable with and trust. And who do you feel most comfortable with and trust? People who share your background, interests, life reference points, and such. To put it bluntly, people who are most like you. This cultural connection cannot be minimized in understanding why white males tap mostly white males to be their on-the-job peers and heirs to the thrones, as it were. This isn't necessarily sexism, racism, or xenophobia. In fact, it has more to do with sociology. Generally speaking, people tend to socialize with others who are most like them. It's just the way it is.

This is a roundabout way of saying that the old boy network exists because old boys prefer to play with other old boys. Today's focus on political correctness may in some instances lead people to jump to conclusions and to frame situations in terms of barefaced discrimination and other nefarious motives. This posture champions more government intervention in hiring laws, and so on, compelling corporations to get with the program— programs that give people a leg up based on gender or race, and not, foremost, on knowledge and skills.

**FACT**

The invisible hand in many mentoring and mini-mentoring relationships is a big reason why the glass ceiling still exists in the workplace. That is, white males in senior management tap other white males to work alongside them and succeed them. They do this based on familiarity—common backgrounds, interests, and reference points—more often than prejudice.

No matter what benign labels politicians and the media minions apply to these policies, they are nevertheless unfair and counterproductive. Selecting employees based solely on gender or race was wrong fifty years ago, and it's equally wrong today. Opinion polls reveal that large majorities—regardless of race, gender, or ethnicity—agree that these kinds of preference policies are way off beam. All people want to be judged on the merits of what they can do as individuals. Fortunately the coaching and mentoring managerial approach is geared to forthrightly deal with genuine gender, race, ethnic, and cultural concerns, while not sacrificing the all-important meritocracy that is the bedrock of a fair, contented, and productive work environment.

## Making Equal Opportunity Mean Just That

Remember that "opportunity" is always your coaching trump card. That's what you offer your employees from day one on the job; that's how you attract new talent to come work for you. The word "opportunity," as a matter of fact, is sprinkled all over the pages of this book because opportunity is such a valued principle in the coaching and mentoring philosophy. In this people-intensive approach to managing, opportunities for learning, new challenges, and, of course, advancement in the company have to always be available to your employees. But the opportunity bell rings rather hollow if it doesn't mean genuine opportunity for all, regardless of gender, race, or ethnicity.

You can talk the opportunity talk all you want, but if Beth sees Sean, Will, and Christopher advancing at a faster clip than she is, even though she's equally or more qualified than all of them, then you've got a lot of explaining to do. Likewise, if Fred, Eugene, and Donald find themselves passed over for a promotion in favor of Ellen, who hasn't earned her on-the-job performance stripes, you've simultaneously got a credibility problem and a morale problem on your hands.

So, what exactly do you do to ensure that your talk of equal opportunity means just that? How do you factor in the sober reality of the glass ceiling? How do you ensure that women and minorities aren't excluded from those special relationships (mentoring and mini-mentoring) that play a considerable part in the opportunity equation?

### Understanding the Role of Affirmative Action

Affirmative action is a much debated and contentious public policy issue. So, we'll leave the issue debate to a book on politics and public referendums. The history of affirmative action nevertheless reveals that it was originally crafted as a government access program, not any kind of set-asides or preferences for one group over another. Your job as a coach is to practice affirmative action in the workplace as it was originally and very nobly conceived. That is, you've got to make certain that women and minorities are apprised of all the advancement opportunities in the workplace and are afforded genuine shots at competing for them.

In the office environs—and it doesn't matter if you're a man or a woman—your role as a coach is to level the playing field, not the results. A level playing field doesn't mean establishing different standards for people based on gender, race, or ethnicity. Instead, it means that you're fully aware of and understand the roles that invisible hands play in the workplace, and you make compensatory allowances and adjustments for them.

When mentors are assigned to employees, for instance, it is often the case that women and minorities bear the brunt here based on an entrenched and long-standing pecking order. Mentoring (see Chapter 4 for a comprehensive overview on the subject) often entails higher-ups in an organization advising and providing career counseling to employees on lower rungs of the corporate ladder. And, as previously noted, there is a propensity for male bonding in these relationships that perpetuates the dearth of diversity in high places. There is this prevailing mentality: "These are the kinds of guys I hang around with, live next door to, and talk to about all things. So, naturally, these are the kinds of guys I want to work with, place my trust in, and groom for bigger and better things."

In order for you to promote diversity without controversial preferences, you've got to both understand and value the difference between *equality* and *equivalence*. Equality of office standards and performance expectations that everybody must abide by and meet are a must. Equivalence in individual employee treatment, however, is not part of the coaching and mentoring playbook.

Okay, let's get a little more specific in how you can level the playing field without losing your credibility and authority as a coach and manager. Foremost, you need to clearly distinguish between equality and equivalence in the workplace. The words are not one and the same when it comes to managing people. This shouldn't be too difficult for you to fathom, because your coach's toolbox is crammed with tools and techniques designed for making such critical distinctions.

## Upholding Equality

Equality is a principle that everybody who works for you is expected to uphold by abiding by certain rules of conduct, ethical boundaries, and, of course, meeting performance expectations. Equivalence, on the other hand, is not part and parcel of coaching. In fact, it runs completely counter to it. Every employee in your charge is a unique individual. Therefore, equivalence in treatment doesn't ever wash with wise coaches.

**FACT**

Performance standards don't ever need to be lowered to accommodate diversity. You need only afford genuine opportunities to those who fall under the diversity umbrella and allow them to meet those standards and advance based on merit and merit alone.

Now comes the hard part. Sure, you fully accept your responsibilities in handling all the behavioral challenges and skill deficiencies in your employees that come down the pike. After all, you're a coach, and that's what coaches do. But now you're being asked to manage differences that are very apparent (gender, race, and ethnicity), but also very complex.

## Keeping Firm Standards

No need to panic. Managing diversity is the kind of challenge you address with the firm standards you already have in place—standards that all of your employees are measured against. You deal with your employees on an individual basis, yes, but you never alter your bedrock principles or lower your performance expectations—for anybody or for any reason. Sure, diversity issues are the most ambiguous of all. You've got to look at gender, race, ethnicity, and other cultural differences in a manner quite unlike the way you would address poor attitudes or skill deficiencies.

The obvious question that springs to mind right now is "Isn't this discussion leading to a call for lower or different standards in accommodating diversity?" The answer is a resounding "No!" If you reinforce both the company's expectations and your own expectations, you will always remain on solid ground. The problem of a lack of diversity atop corporate managerial hierarchies does not require anybody to lower standards to ensure more of it. Rather, the solution asks us only to furnish more opportunities to the diverse among us to meet universally high standards and to move onward and upward.

## Putting a Premium on Skills

In your day-to-day coaching, you make opportunity a reality for everyone because you conduct business in a vibrant and unrestrictive learning environment, which puts a premium on growing employees' skills. And, automatically, this means that you're encouraging diversity because your staff of employees is in all likelihood a very diverse brood. If you assiduously navigate the coaching course as described, you most certainly will be grooming star pupils from all walks of life.

Hence, your employee pool of bright stars will be diverse, and not because of a quota system, but because you devote your regular, everyday coaching activities to building up people—all people, regardless of gender, race, or ethnicity. You can uplift people by taking into account all aspects of their personality makeup, including diversity, and not ever run counter to your doctrine of equality. This is the course you should always travel.

## Why Gender and Ethnicity Issues Matter More Than Ever

Managing as a wise coach (and that's what this book is all about) consequentially guarantees more women and minorities getting mentors and taking full advantage of other career-boosting opportunities. When you're managing as a confident coach, you don't hesitate in assigning mentors to any and all of your performing employees regardless of their race, gender, or ethnicity. You don't hesitate to groom them for promotions and furnish them greater and greater challenges. You don't refrain from promoting employees of all stripes because you are absolutely sure that your coaching methods are the right ones in developing highly competent, temperamentally suited, and peak-performing employees.

**FACT**

A coach need not be color-blind or gender-blind. On the contrary, a coach sees everything, evaluates everything, and considers nothing inconsequential with regard to decision making, finding solutions, and seeking positive outcomes to any and all situations in the workplace.

## Nothing Is Inconsequential

While gender, race, or ethnicity shouldn't be factors in hiring or promoting people, don't believe these factors no longer matter in the workplace. When you sit down with a highly sensitive employee for one of your many coaching conferences, be it a get-to-know-you-better meeting, a performance planning session, a performance review, or a problem-specific chit-chat, you treat your sensitive employee differently from the way you interact with the more thick-skinned employees in your ranks. And the same logical reasoning applies to matters of diversity.

Coaches, for example, have to acknowledge that foreign-born employees who work for them have distinct customs and perhaps see the world from perspectives a little different from the native-born. So, when you coach employees from alien backgrounds, you can't disregard these cultural realities. This doesn't mean you bend your workplace standards to accommodate foreign workers in any way. It merely means that you consider *everything* in the makeup of the unique individuals on your team.

## Avoid Extremes

Managing diversity is often a very challenging affair for some coaches. But it's not something that should ever intimidate you. It is, in fact, the managers who are intimidated in this area who tend to create more problems for themselves than need be. They either err on the side of condescending to diversity, for fear of getting branded a sexist or racist, or they preclude diversity because they don't know how to deal with it, and think that it's more trouble than it's worth. Both of these unseemly postures invariably explode in their practitioners' faces. If you don't manage diversity as you manage everything else, with calm and consistent assuredness, you will eventually have a mutiny on your hands.

If you seem to be twisting your standards and moving away from the all-important workplace meritocracy, you will lose your credibility in a heartbeat. If you show blatant favoritism on the other end of the spectrum, you will similarly be viewed as not living up to your own words and principles. The bottom line is, you must allow everybody to get in the game on your coaching field. That is, you must permit every employee to progress based on his or her merits. You must never construct any roadblocks based on gender, race, or ethnicity.

**ALERT!**

In all your coaching endeavors, it is imperative that you avoid the polar extremes of managing diversity issues. That is, don't condescend to diversity by granting special privileges based on gender, race, or ethnicity. Conversely, don't ever impede diverse members of your staff based on unfounded fears or prejudices.

If you always coach with a wise and understanding hand, you will come to realize that it is an even hand. Diversity will naturally occur in such a properly run workplace. And there will be no dark cloud hanging over your coaching efforts and raining down on all that you've accomplished in productivity. There will also be no stigmas attached to those who are conferred more challenging job responsibilities, and those who get promoted and move on up in their careers. Everything that transpires will be based on merit.

## Avoiding the Assumption Function

To keep you on the straight and narrow, there are a few things you must absolutely avoid practicing in your coaching duties. Stereotyping your employees based on gender, race, or ethnicity, for one, is a big no-no.

Remove stereotyping from your thought process if you want to see diversity come to pass. In fact, coaches never work with the *assumption function* that everybody from a particular group does things in a particular way.

Take George, a department manager, who assumed a lot of things that just weren't so. He managed quite a diverse group. But he tended to parcel the greatest responsibilities and biggest challenges in job roles to the male members of his team. And when a highly able female in his employ, Laurie, questioned him on her perceptions that something was rotten in Denmark, George informed her that he couldn't afford any interruptions in the important job projects for which he was responsible.

Laurie couldn't quite figure out where George was coming from with such an explanation. What did "interruptions" in job projects over a period of time have to do with gender? Upon further pressing of her concern, George admitted that in his last job, he managed a team with an employee who left on maternity leave in the middle of an important project that was very dependent on her knowledge and skills. From that moment on, stereotyping consumed George's thinking and he assumed that every woman in his path was poised to begin or enlarge a family, cutting him adrift and causing overall performance to suffer. Laurie apprised him in no uncertain terms that he was managing with a sexist stereotype and discriminating in the process. She made it clear that his stereotyping was not only far off base but against the law as well. Laurie told him to clear his head and alter his way of doing things and she would avoid lodging a formal complaint. Suffice it to say, George heaved a sigh of relief at her magnanimous offer.

Coaches don't work with the assumption function. That is, they don't assume that every member of a particular gender, race, or ethnicity does things in the same way. Similarly, they do not assume that a group doesn't possess particular skills or can't do certain jobs. Assuming such things are bad enough, practicing them is against the law.

If you assume that employees cannot do certain jobs or learn particular skills based on gender, race, or ethnicity, you're very silly and not coaching timber. You're also asking for a mess of trouble. Discrimination lawsuits in the workplace are routine these days and nothing to sniff at. This is something you've always got to be cognizant of while managing in the twenty-first century. Even if you view certain lawsuits as frivolous and without merit—and many of them are—it doesn't mean that they're not going to cause you and the company you work for a lot of heartache—and, perhaps, cost a lot of money, too.

**ALERT!**

In your work domain, it behooves you to adopt a zero-tolerance policy toward off-color humor, abusive language, and exclusionary practices of any of your employees based on gender, race, or ethnicity. Such a strict policy in place—and enforced—will make the office environs both a more productive and more serene place in which to work.

Communicating with and getting to know your employees are the building blocks that make coaching, the managerial art, rise like a colossus. If you permit groundless assumptions to preclude you from digging deeper and unearthing what your employees can do, you're being very shortsighted and foolish. And foolish folks with blinders on and silly prejudices don't make the coaching grade.

The glass ceiling is not a figment of people's imaginations. It hovers up above and does so because of exclusionary practices—conscious or unconscious—but exclusionary nonetheless. No employees, for any reason, should ever be excluded from opportunities to do their jobs and do them well.

## Eradicating Unhealthy Behaviors

There is a whole roster of behaviors that you'd be wise to eradicate from the office environs sooner rather than later. In order to preside over a healthy and productive work atmosphere, you've got to make it a civil one, and that means that you must enforce zero tolerance on the following common practices.

## A Joke Too Far

This covers a lot of ground. Insult comedians often make for entertaining performers. However, a clone of Don Rickles as an employee is altogether something else, and not a personality you could tolerate in the office. Even if an employee is "only joking," those on the receiving end of the "joke," or within earshot of it, are the ones who make that determination. There are plenty of comedy clubs to go to and comedy channels to watch, and that's where put-down, sardonic, and off-color humor can flourish. The corridors and cubicles of the office aren't the places for edgy comedy.

## Abusive Language

You also should be eternally vigilant in stamping out foul and abusive language of any kind. Remember that the workplace isn't an extension of the *Howard Stern Show*. And some people find working in a *bleeping* environment to be *bleeping* unpleasant and bad for *bleeping* productivity.

# Coaches as Risk Takers

Okay, you've opened up all the opportunity doors and everybody is welcome to enter. You've done your job well. But it's ultimately up to the individuals themselves to walk through these open doors, and sometimes this involves taking risks. There are various lessons that you can impart to those diverse members of your staff who might otherwise feel intimidated in moving into uncharted territories. Many people in the workplace are averse to taking genuine risks, particularly women and minorities who have been shut out from reaching certain levels. Indeed, it's human nature to allow cautiousness to take over when boldness is called for. The fear of striking out, which cuts a wide swath in the workplace—men, women, all races, all nationalities—often precludes many home runs from being hit.

Speaking of home runs, in baseball, to avoid striking out, a batter will sometimes choke up on the bat. This gives him more bat control and a quicker response time to swing at the ball. But it also cuts down on his power, because the shorter swing is calculated to hit the pitch and make contact. A bigger swing, on the other hand, is more likely to miss a pitch, but is also more likely, when contact is made, to send the baseball flying greater distances. The baseball player's choice is to play it safe or to go for it.

The same choices apply to moving up in the business world. Choking up on the job amounts to being cautious, which, in some circumstances, is a wise posture to take. Caution embraces thoughtful and deliberate thinking and a strong attention to detail. These are admirable traits and work effectively in certain jobs—but caution can also hold people back. Sometimes boldness, or risk taking, is required to reach the highest levels of management in an organization. Risk taking is something you as a coach should always welcome, and you need to pass this principle on to your employees, particularly those who will be charting areas where their gender, race, or ethnicity is underrepresented. Trailblazing in any area involves throwing caution to the wind in many situations and moments.

## *Thinking Long Term*

Another important lesson that you should convey to all of your employees—but again, especially those under the glass ceiling—is to look at job- and career-related matters in the long term as well as in the short term. As we've seen time and again, coaching and mentoring attempt to bridge the short- and long-term goals of the workplace. Coaching pays very close attention to the job at hand but links the lessons learned to employees' long-term goals.

**FACT**

Coaching is uniquely qualified to deal with diversity issues because it is the mosaic of managing. That is, it is a work in progress that celebrates individuality. Coaching and mentoring places minimal restrictions on its coaches and mentors. It is, above all else, an open and malleable managerial methodology.

Women and minorities who feel they must work harder to climb up the career ladder sometimes devote all their time and energy to succeeding beyond their wildest imaginations in the present, and give short shrift to planning in the longer term. This is understandable behavior that your coaching can more properly align, leading, of course, to more opportunities for advancement.

You should drum into your employees on the diversity frontier that they should indeed keep focused on improving themselves in the here and now. But that they should also be thinking about where they want to be in one year, five years, and ten years. The bottom line is that if you insist on your people perpetually learning and growing their skills, their futures will shine bright—guaranteed.

Chapter 19

# The Next Frontier: Retail and Service Industries

This chapter takes coaching and mentoring and their methodologies into the retail and service industries, charting a bold and new frontier in the process. Here you'll discover that most of your coaching and mentoring tools and techniques can be readily applied to managing walk-in retail or service-oriented businesses.

## Meeting the Public Face to Face

Really, there are few places on the business landscape that clamor more for a people-oriented approach to managing than the customer-intensive retail and service sectors of the economy. Why? Because, first of all, increasing numbers of people are finding themselves in jobs where they must deal face-to-face with living and breathing customers—and this kind of interactive work is fraught with unpredictability and stress. For a variety of reasons, the atmospheres in many of these work environments are unhappy and unhealthy for both employees and the customers they serve. These particular slices of the retail and service industries are crying out for a fresh kind of leadership—one that appreciates employees' unique needs and wants in these demanding job roles, but that also holds them to high standards of professionalism.

Because you interact with the public in retail and service businesses, you've got to make clear—even more so than in office jobs—the importance of learning, building skills, and gaining experience. You've got to extract lessons from every job and every situation and point them out to your employees.

## It's Easy to Forget That the Customer Is King

Long before the terms "coaching" and "mentoring" wound their way into business circles, you, as a customer yourself, experienced various treatments in retail and service settings. Sometimes the red carpet was rolled out for you; other times you were treated with a detached indifference or worse, made to feel unwelcome, as if you were an intruder. The businesses that rolled out the proverbial red carpet for you were the ones that put their principles in action—principles that they instilled in their employees. They accentuated and practiced good customer service. And considering that businesses live and die based on satisfying their customers, this "customer is king" mantra isn't a bad idea, nor is it revolutionary thinking.

You'd think sometimes today that granting the customer a modicum of respect is in fact revolutionary, because such respect seems to be getting scarcer with each passing day. Is there any hope of reversing this unfortunate trend? Can coaching and mentoring's latticework wend its way down into these retail and service businesses that so often get overlooked as being too dirty for so contemplative a managerial approach? Ironically, it's in these very retail and service businesses where the greatest numbers of people can reap the benefits of coaching and mentoring.

**ALERT!**

Some coaches prefer to work with the slogan "the customer is always right even when he isn't." This catch phrase exemplifies the great latitude that must be given to the very customers who make or break businesses every day. In business, you just can't live without them!

## Motivating Service and Retail Employees

We've all patronized places of business where a clerk or cashier delivers a memorized spiel: "Hello and welcome to Happy Burger. If you have any questions regarding our vast and varied menu, please do not hesitate to ask. Today's special is the double Swiss-cheese burger with our own special barbecue sauce. How may I assist you today?" Now, consider your reaction to these rather robotic renditions of common courtesy? Some customers understandably deem this kind of thing very annoying, and liken the experience to being serviced by an army of androids. For others, however, this robotic brand of courtesy is better than the alternative—no courtesy at all.

The reality is that this indoctrination of a short "welcoming the customer" speech is at least a start. It's what managers attempt to do first and foremost with a workforce of men and women who need a mother lode of training, particularly in the soft skills of interpersonal communication. Indeed, when you're confronted with employees who lack even the most rudimentary social and professional skills, it's generally prudent to ask them to commit to memory a few sentences of civility and regurgitate them on cue. And then you can take it from there.

## Motivate with Few Motivators

In addition to the lack of social skills, perhaps the most difficult hurdles that managers must leap over in retail and service businesses are associated with employee commitment and self-motivation. If you're managing in a busy restaurant or big chain store, for instance, you're more than likely expected to work many long and hard hours. You're asked to motivate yourself in doing a tough job without the most obvious of rewards, and to instill that same push and determination in your employees. This isn't an easy task in the office place, and it's a more difficult one, as you might imagine, in a retail or service business environment.

Respect up and down the workplace is critical to achieving positive results. This means you must be respected and respect others. It is particularly important in retail and service businesses to elevate respect to its highest level, as many employees don't respect their jobs or feel respected in doing them.

For starters, the paycheck and benefits in most of these jobs are not as fleshy as in corporate office jobs. And when the pay is on the lower end of the scale, it's very hard to sermonize on the many benefits of going all out in the job. Another problem is that the range of opportunities for advancement in these businesses is ordinarily very limited. In other words, it's tough for you to convince people that the sky's the limit while working in a coffee shop or a sneaker store.

## Honesty Is the Best Policy

So, what you must do first in any kind of retail or service management position is tell the whole truth, as you would anywhere else. That is, don't make promises that you can't keep—or that nobody believes—and don't manufacture promotion opportunities that exist only in people's imaginations: "If you work your buns off here, you've got a chance to be the next Ronald McDonald and make personal appearances all across the country.

You could be earning a six-figure income in no time flat." People are a gullible lot, but not that gullible.

Since you can't always offer better job opportunities, your coaching stance must place the emphasis on where it properly belongs—on continuous learning on the job, and the growing of skills wherever and whenever possible. At first glance you might think that the notion of a continuous learning environment thriving in a fast-paced retail or service setting is ludicrous. You might also determine that you be perceived as the court jester if you opined on growing skills and career advancement to a gaggle of underpaid and overworked employees.

Well, you'd be greatly mistaken if you accepted this negative scenario as inevitable. Let's say, for example, that you're managing in a hustling and bustling eatery. You could assume that your staff—waiters, waitresses, and so on—would turn a deaf ear to your preaching about acquiring knowledge and building skills on the job. But why assume this? Really, your success here boils down to your communication abilities and the bond of trust that you establish between yourself and your people.

Many managers in high turnover retail and service businesses opt to sugarcoat reality. They paint rosy pictures at odds with reality and promise things that will never see the light of day. They go this route because they believe it's the only way to raise the performance level of their employees. It's an approach that usually gets them nowhere fast. If, on the other hand, you make the case that learning on the job—any job—transcends the job role itself; if you make the case that growing skills—any skills—encompasses more than meets the eye, you will witness performance progress.

Let's return to your job in the restaurant. You're a coach rather than a traditional manager. In this setting, you'd be charged with making the case that beyond waiting tables—a skill in itself—is a steep learning curve with copious learning opportunities. Further, your responsibility as a coach would be to illustrate the many lessons learned in waiting tables. For instance, dedicated waiters and waitresses acquire invaluable people skills while ministering to hungry customers. In the fast-paced environment of a restaurant they also learn conflict resolution, which is another indispensable and highly coveted skill in any job.

And since many people—including some college graduates—find themselves working in fast-food joints these days, let's patronize one to illustrate another point. Deep-frying chicken fingers may seem like a dead-end job—and, admittedly, it is to some people—but believe it or not, there's a lot of learning and growth potential downdraft of that hot oil (with no trans fats, of course). Coaching in this particular situation would ask that you turn the chicken fingers into chicken cordon bleu. That is, if you see learning opportunities as more than just completing tasks competently (frying chicken fingers to perfection, etc.), you venture beyond the narrow parameters of the job itself and take in such important job skills as responsibility, ability to follow directions, customer service etiquette, and the overall work ethic. You thus make every task that you assign your staff a multilayered affair with important lessons therein.

Experience is priceless. Coaches in retail and service management positions need to emphasize this time and again. They need to show how gaining knowledge and growing important skills, such as responsibility, customer relations, and overall work ethic, are invaluable and can lead to bigger and better things.

If, in such coaching exertions, you convince your employees that what they do today truly matters—no matter what their job roles—you'll have successfully upgraded a work environment that sorely needed upgrading. You'll have upgraded, too, a group of people who sorely needed a boost. You'll have altered a job culture for the better.

## Starting Coaching and Mentoring in New Places

To further expand on the most conspicuous problem in many retail and service businesses—that by and large the labor pool doesn't know how to properly service customers—both managers and employees alike need evaluation. As the old adage goes, "The fish rots from the head down." Everyone knows there is a genuine and growing customer service problem, because we've all personally been on the receiving ends of poor treatment from both managers and employees at some point while shopping, dining out, hiring contractors, etc. We've all seen managers looking on in stony silence while their employees run amok. Worse yet, sometimes we've received lousy treatment from the men and women who called themselves managers—at least that's what their name badges said. They weren't coaches—that much is obvious.

If commonplace circumstances like these don't cry out for coaching and mentoring—a finely tuned retail and service business version of it—then nothing does. When these types of businesses care enough to commit themselves to bettering both their employees' job satisfaction and customer service at the same time, a coaching approach will be welcomed with open arms into management. And soon thereafter, just as in the corporate office, the retail and service businesses that go down this managerial pike will get noticed for offering not only a better product or service, but top-notch customer relations as well. But, as noted time and again on these pages, businesses have to commit themselves from top to bottom to coaching and mentoring approaches, or they are not going to happen.

The Best-Foot-Forward Doctrine is something all coaches should bear in mind. It says that employees attempt to make the best first impressions possible by giving their all in interviews and during their first days and weeks on the job. If they unfailingly violate this doctrine, you don't want them around for the days, weeks, and months to come.

In franchise operations or department store chains, for example, coaching and mentoring need to be welcomed aboard, yes, but also systematically placed into management at all levels. Senior management in these businesses has got to take the lead and insist upon instituting this new managerial methodology, funneling it all the way down to in-store managers. They've then got to diligently search for the right people to place in these managerial slots—men and women who could assimilate the tenets of coaching—and give them the absolute authority to manage as coaches.

Coaching in the retail and service sector is poised to make the many jobs available there more appealing to employees and would-be employees alike. And better customer service will be the natural by-product of overall job satisfaction and a more healthy work environment. It's a win-win proposition.

## The Way We Were

If you're old enough to remember the good old days, you recall when you walked into a store—from the small mom-and-pop sort to the huge department store—and the help was actually helpful. Not too long ago, it was the rule rather than the exception that employees were to behave in a particular way and do certain things in assisting customers. And if they didn't cut the mustard, they were shown the door. And, all the while, managers meticulously enforced comprehensive and unbending customer service policies. So wait a minute! What happened? Did a coaching-style management exist in the past and somehow vanish into the ether? No, not quite.

The Texaco guys, who would emerge from the interior of the gas station the moment customers pulled up to the pump to check their oil, tire pressure, clean their windshields, and service them with a smile, were not being managed by a 1950s version of a coach. Yes, their actions mirrored the high expectations that Texaco had for all of its service station owners and employees. But the real reason the Texaco guys served customers so well was because the cultural mores of yesteryear were at odds with today's. Simply put, people in those days of yore treated each other better in the public square and had more respect for the work they did and jobs that they held.

This isn't to suggest that all was hunky-dory for the Texaco guys and for employees at five-and-dime stores, malt shops, and the like. It surely wasn't. But if you talk with men and women who worked their first jobs in the 1950s, 1960s, and 1970s, they more often than not express a certain nostalgia about them. They admit to having learned a lot while laboring behind the counter of a drugstore or clerking in the stereo section of a local department store.

## The Retail Coaching Moment

Years ago in retail and service jobs, employees learned and valued the importance of responsibility—showing up for work on time, practicing good oral hygiene, wearing clean clothes, and functioning in a role with the best possible attitude. Today, these simple rules of conduct are often missing in action. For many of today's entrepreneurs, their most difficult and depressing duties involve staffing their businesses. They find it near impossible sometimes to find competent and reliable employees to work for them. The pickings are usually very slim, and the prospective employees' attitudes are more likely negative than positive.

**FACT**

There are few coaching and mentoring tools and techniques that can't be applied to retail and service operations. So, whether you manage a restaurant, department store, fast-food chain, or meat market, the fundamental managerial principles of coaching and mentoring remain the same and produce the same results.

It is a long-held and generally accepted view that people desire putting their best feet forward in their job interviews. This makes perfect sense. Likewise, upon getting hired, they want to be on their best behaviors and make the best possible impressions during the first few days and weeks on the job. This again makes perfect sense. As a coach, you're conscious of this in interviews (see Chapter 12 for the full lowdown on interviewing prospective employees) and in the infancy of any new work relationships. But ask around and you'll hear—if you haven't seen it up close and personal yourself—that many managers are witnessing new employees making very bad impressions immediately. They're making bad first impressions, not because they're trying too hard and are hopelessly inept, but because they aren't even making a good-faith effort to look good.

Strange as this may sound, it's not even on many employees' things-to-do list. These employees do not even entertain the thought that it's important to make good impressions at work, particularly when beginning a new job. Bad first impressions reveal themselves in the offices of corporate America, but they're epidemic in retail and service jobs.

For the small businessperson or manager on the retail and service frontlines, the Best-Foot-Forward Doctrine, once inviolable, is regularly breached by today's employees. New employees arrive late on their first day of work. New employees call in sick a couple of days during their first week on the job. New employees complain about their jobs from the get-go.

## Managing on Two Levels

Actually, you coach retail and service employees on two levels. You manage people on the conventional level of assigned jobs, performance expectations, and the like, but you also manage them on another important level, too—customer relations. You see it happening in some of these businesses already—and they stand out from the pack because they are a distinct minority at the moment. Nevertheless, virtually every coaching and mentoring tool and technique can be transferred out of the office and applied to the retail and service frontlines—with some modifications, of course, but with the core principles intact.

Even though you might not be able to plan too far in advance because of the high turnover in the retail and service industries, you still must draw up performance plans, even if only for the short term. You can set goals with your employees and utilize action plans. And you can measure your employees' progress on a recurring basis. You've got to get good performances out of your people no matter who's paying your salary—IBM or Tony's Pizzeria, it makes no difference.

**ALERT!**

Coaching and mentoring in managerial positions are desperately needed in retail and service settings, where poor employee morale is the rule and lousy customer service commonplace. Coaching instituted in retail and service environments could touch countless people—from employees to customers—in very positive and visible ways.

The trust you develop with your employees, and the integrity that you personify, loom larger than ever in the retail and service world, because the leeway your employees will afford you is decidedly less than in the confines of the office. Why? Because most of these employees know they can walk down the street and get another job in the same sector tomorrow. So, what you've got to do is underscore trust and expand the field of learning. Talk often about the value of gathering experiences and pride in successfully working at jobs—any jobs—and mean it. Make your instruction plausible and cite examples from your own job experiences and the incalculable lessons that you have learned along the way.

## Curbing Bad Attitudes Where They Are Rampant

Bad attitude in retail and service jobs is the "in thing" these days among employees. It's hip to be negative. Indeed, this is the roughest road managers in these kinds of businesses must traverse. Unhappily, for many bosses of these disgruntled minions, the result of their efforts is unmitigated failure. We've mentioned the myriad reasons for the poor attitudes in retail and service jobs—low pay, restricted job roles, general resentment, and, yes, dealing with Mr. and Mrs. John Q. Public.

### Working with Customers in the Flesh Isn't Easy

Mr. and Mrs. John Q. Public can be tough cookies to please. In fact, it's in the area of customer relations where you, the coach, must work diligently to convert employees' bad attitudes into good ones. The learning environment that we've talked at length about in this chapter is very often grounded in relating to customers and satisfying their needs. For those of you who have never worked with the general public, you've missed out on the learning experience of a lifetime. Catering to walk-in customers is a neverending challenge because you never know what's going to happen to next. A smooth work road invariably hits a bump, and sometimes even a crater, without any warning at all. However, if you instruct your employees on how to properly service the public, you'll see a more resilient group of people developing before your eyes, and an increasingly more relaxed bunch over time. And, yes, this will redound to better customer service. You don't necessarily have to roll out a red carpet for customers, but you've got to remove the hot coals from the paths that so often greet them in businesses today.

## Customers Aren't the Plague—They're the Paycheck!

You must disabuse your employees of the notion that customers are a plague of locusts that descend upon them. There are people whose jobs require them to stock shelves and they go at it with an artist's aplomb. The problem is that some of these same folks testily bristle when customers come along and purchase things off the shelves, thus messing up their works of art. In this example, you've got to get the point across that the reason for packing shelves up to the hilt is so the buying public will buy the very things packed on them. And, further, that if the awe-inspiring packed shelves remained so, you and your employees both would be out of jobs.

Who isn't familiar with the business maxim "the customer is always right"? This sentiment is far-reaching, longstanding, and loaded with meaning. While it boldly declares that customers are always right, it's not meant to be taken completely literally. Those who toil in retail jobs would be glad to hear that.

What "the customer is always right" motto asks of managers and employees alike is that they accord their customers a tremendous amount of leeway. Pleasing customers has to be at the top of the agenda of any business and not just a mere afterthought. One of the most dogged problems in customer relations today is that employees are not taught to understand, let alone respect, the true meaning of "the customer is always right" maxim. In fact, many retail and service business managers set the inappropriate and counterproductive tone of criticizing or mocking customers behind the scenes, and sometimes even engaging them in antagonistic skirmishes for all to see. This negative tone setting creates the unfortunate ripple effect of marring the customer relations landscape. Predictably, employees then get in on the act with the imprimatur of their bosses.

ALERT!

The popular adage, "the customer is always right," should be ingrained in your employees' thinking. Not to be taken literally, its meaning must nevertheless be well understood. That is, customers must be afforded ample leeway because they're why businesses and, yes, jobs exist in the first place.

Your coaching, on the other hand, should set a decidedly different tone—a positive one—where you instill in your employees the mantra that the "customer is indeed always right, until proven otherwise—and even then sometimes." As a coach you must make certain that the inescapable bad apples in the customer barrel aren't permitted to spoil the whole bunch. The daily grind of working with a constant flow of customers often causes employees to lose sight of an important fact: The vast majority of customers who shop, eat out, and the like are decent people. Indeed, most consumers don't initiate any grief at all; most folks just want to buy their pound of seedless grapes, order their breakfast omelets, get their bags of chunky dog food, pay their tabs, and go on their merry ways.

## Dealing with Problem Customers

Unfortunately, it's the silent majority of good customers who bear the brunt of the distinct minority of problem makers. It's the handful of griping customers who cause managers and employees to view, and hence treat, all customers as the enemy. As a wise coach, you've got to act as an aggressive iconoclast and destroy any false and destructive impressions, because the customer mischief-makers are—really and truly—the exceptions and not the rule.

If you highlight repeatedly the positive transactions between your employees and customers, you will be accenting the true reality—that dealing with the public is predominantly a positive experience, and shouldn't be viewed as a negative one. When the problem customer does come along, you can position the interaction as a learning opportunity in a reality laboratory. Emphasize that these bad experiences with customers are quite rare. If you can make the retail or service setting a positive place, you will see that your employees respond favorably and handle confrontational moments more professionally.

## Respect Is Key

Retail and service businesses are joined at the hip with the aforementioned confrontational moments. You can't have one without the other: confrontations not only between employees, but managers versus employees, and—yes—employees versus customers. This unpredictable multidimension is what makes managing in these types of businesses such a formidable undertaking. Respect is often in short supply. Employees often feel diminished on so many fronts.

Many people look down upon retail and service workers, and treat them as the help, as it were. Some smug sorts couldn't conceive of coaching and mentoring's tools and techniques applied in such rough-and-tumble business environments. But, as we've carefully laid out in this chapter, coaching and mentoring not only belong in retail and service businesses, but could supply a necessary uplift for countless disheartened employees and many battle-weary customers, too.

# Chapter 20

# Coaching and Mentoring: A Legacy

On the business frontier, coaching and mentoring is not merely an alternative management philosophy to implement in the here and now. This chapter explores the role of coaching and mentoring as a vital lifeline for the continued performance and growth of organizations in a variety of fields in both the private and public sectors. Among its countless benefits, coaching and mentoring molds the critical talent of tomorrow. Wherever they are applied, coaching and mentoring methodologies are intended to leave in their wake positive and lasting legacies.

# Demographic Challenges: Baby Boomer Retirements

The specter of millions of retiring baby boomers looms like a colossus over the nation's social and economic fabric. The potential calamity of the so-called "boomers" and their imminent departure from the workforce is a genuine concern for both business organizations and government institutions alike. Courtesy of their considerable numbers, the actions of baby boomers have indisputable consequences on matters far and wide. No, this section isn't going to ring another Social Security warning bell. It's not going to discourse on the budding crisis that swirls around the recompensing of this sprawling generation in its golden years. Nevertheless, what is addressed here is a matter of equal import.

**FACT**

The baby boomer generation is widely considered to consist of the men and women born between the years 1946 and 1964. Some demographers end the baby boom in 1962. Approximately 78 million boomers were born in the United States between the years 1946 and 1964. Boomers International estimates that there are roughly 450 million baby boomers worldwide.

## Different Organizational Faces

The wholesale exiting of baby boomers from the workforce over the coming decade will leave many organizations with huge holes to fill in the talent and skills department. Businesses' abilities to fill essential job roles will be severely tested in the coming years. This employment reality is a gathering storm. In fact, it's already a budding problem for numerous organizations in both the private and public sectors.

In the imminent future, many enterprises will encounter *critical talent vacuums* unlike anything they've experienced before. Finding individuals with the requisite educational backgrounds, temperaments, and abilities to assume indispensable jobs and occupations is guaranteed to be a huge challenge. This widening skills chasm on the employment frontlines is why coaching and mentoring methodologies are more important than ever before. Unlike traditional management approaches, coaching and mentoring methods instill in employees knowledge and skills that not only perform admirably in the present, but neatly bridge to the future as well. Ideally, coaches and mentors educate individuals under their patient and far-sighted tutelage to be the movers and shakers of tomorrow.

**ALERT!**

The Bureau of Labor is warning of shortages of qualified personnel in occupations running a wide gamut from social workers to police to photographers to teachers. And, needless to say, it is increasingly difficult to fill those many corporate office chairs with competent fannies. The talent and skills shortage in the labor market is not a mirage.

## What's So Special about the Baby Boomer?

The ubiquitous baby boomer is not blessed with a higher IQ than previous and subsequent generations. As a group, baby boomers have no extraordinary qualities that make them any better than the preponderance of humankind. Boomers have, on occasion, been branded an uncomplimentary thing or two.

The baby boom generation succeeded what newsman Tom Brokaw labeled the "Greatest Generation" in his best-selling book of the same name. *The Greatest Generation* chronicled the lives and times of men and women who lived through a Great Depression, fought a victorious war over a most depraved tyranny, and then raised large families—*of baby boomers*—in not always the most idyllic circumstances. Some thought that Brokaw's book reflected poorly on boomers, even if it wasn't the author's intention. (After all, Tom Brokaw is a baby boomer himself.)

So, this discussion is not a debate between the merits of baby boomers versus the Greatest Generation or Generation X or Y. It is a dialogue revolving around baby boomers and their work-specific skills—i.e., what they bring to the table vis-à-vis job attributes that are not being replenished in sufficient quantities upon their retirements. To be more exact, these are the skills urgently needed to both start successful companies and build on existing ones. They are the skills that ensure the efficient and effective running of all kinds of organizations. They are leadership skills. They are, alas, skills that are in shorter and shorter supply with each and every tick of the clock.

## The Educational System

Just why is it that when you need customer support concerning a computer glitch, you are invariably hooked up with a person on the telephone or in front of a terminal across a vast ocean? In many instances, it's simply a matter of education. Simply put, it's where the competent software engineers are. It's where the most adept troubleshooters call home. In other words, it's where the people with answers to your questions are. Sure, the wages paid are often much lower in those faraway parts of the world than they are here, but that's a completely different kettle of fish—one of corporate conscience.

The unpleasant reality is that the American educational system, as well as many others in the western world, is coming up a yard or two short. Today's primary, secondary, and even higher education leaves a lot to be desired. Schools from the basement to the penthouse are not cutting the mustard in turning out the necessary brainpower to keep pace with technological gains and all that these gains dictate. Schools are not arming students with even the most elementary communication and analytical skills.

### Why Less Isn't Better

One sometimes wonders how school kids of the past did it. They not only learned reading, writing, and arithmetic, but also came away from grade school with an ear for Latin and the ability to locate Sri Lanka on a classroom globe. For sure, the ways and means of education have been gradually changing over the decades, and most members of the baby boom generation were not compelled to learn all of the things that previous generations of school kids were taught—you know, in those one-room schoolhouses without electricity. But, by and large, baby boom children were an educated bunch and held to higher standards than succeeding generations.

The educational divide is most conspicuous in the aforementioned areas of communication and analytical skills. Indeed, once the baby boom slowed to a trickle, a gradual dumbing down of educational standards took root. Ironically, many within the fraternity of baby boomers are the architects of this "less is better" approach to learning that exists in all too many educational settings today. These instructive shortcomings are most evident in the increasingly shallow talent and skills pool on the labor market.

### Is It Really That Bad?

There are many talented and highly educated people of all ages in all kinds of jobs—just not enough of a supply to meet the demand. The point here is not to paint with a broad brush, or to tar any particular generation or generations, but to tread in reality. There is a genuine demographic predicament gathering over today's job market like a dark cloud about to rain down on it. Indeed, one generation's retirement portends fundamental problems for the future of business organizations as well as government bureaucracies. This truth cannot be glossed over in the hopes that it will evaporate into the ether.

In many business fields and assorted occupations, critical skills shortages are already a fait accompli. So, the big question is what can coaching and mentoring as a managerial art do to make these shortages shorter, as it were? What can coaching and mentoring do to fill existing skills gaps with the requisite know-how?

Coaching and mentoring can nobly perform a service by teaching tomorrow's leaders the skills to carry on with what works and what grows companies. Coaching and mentoring can light the way to organizational progress by handing off the baton of wisdom. In theory—and hopefully in practice, too—coaching and mentoring endeavor to maintain and build upon essential business lessons learned, rather than allowing it all to retire to Florida and the shuffleboard courts.

## Critical Talent: Missing in Action

The chief impetus behind the increasing relevance of coaching and mentoring in the workplace revolves around the subject of critical talent like the earth revolves around the sun. Coaching and mentoring in management seeks to broaden the pool of men and women with the skills to steer organizations' growth to new levels, as well as to inaugurate new companies. Everything that's been discussed in this chapter thus far can be reduced to the critical talent equation. What will it take to make certain that this critical talent is around tomorrow and the tomorrow after that?

Coaches are hired to get results without delay and to meet all kinds of deadlines—one month, six months, one year, etc., etc. But, just as importantly, they are in place to ensure that the vital critical talent to sustain and bolster companies' business performances is around for many years to come. In other words, coaches are unleashed so that critical talent is present long after they (the individual coaches) have moved on to greener pastures or into well-earned retirements.

**QUESTION?**

**What is "critical talent" in the workplace?**
The men and women who are the lifeblood of an organization's core success are known as critical talent. They are the individuals most responsible for taking companies—and other institutions—to the next level, as it were. They are the key personnel behind both businesses' basic functioning as well as their stellar performances.

## The Managerial Wave of the Future

Critical talent in the business sphere greatly varies from organization to organization. It is not always what you might think. Critical talent doesn't mean senior executives or even management, per se. For instance, truck drivers are critical talent in enterprises that heavily rely on knowledgeable and dependable truck drivers. Critical talent could also embody qualified sales help in fields where such selling is fundamental to a company's day-to-day operation and ultimate success.

Throughout this book, we've talked about coaching and mentoring finding its way into every conceivable business and non-profit organization, including government agencies. And one of the chief reasons why coaching and mentoring is the managerial wave of the future is that this method, by its very nature, confronts the burning issue of critical talent shortages. Coaching and mentoring cultivates talent from within organizations.

The hunt for critical talent is fierce right now and is expected to become even more bloodthirsty in the coming years. And just where do most businesses look for their critical talent? Most often, they cast their lustful eyes on their competitors. In the end, businesses poach from one another. It's a longstanding tradition.

Companies have customarily searched for critical talent at the doorsteps of their competition. Coaching and mentoring managerial practices aim to place more of an emphasis on development of talent from within rather than acquiring it from the outside. An important part of a coach's job responsibility is nurturing employees' skills and knowledge of how the company functions.

## *Development*

All too many companies are deeply rooted in a culture of acquisition. That is, of bringing employees in from other places to fill key job roles. While acquisition of critical talent and employees with desired skills is an absolute necessity at times for growing companies, it needn't be the be-all and end-all. With competent coaches in place, the focus shifts to development of talent and the retention of said talent over extended periods of time.

**FACT**

Developing critical talent from within organizations is unquestionably the wave of the future. It has to be. With the increasing scarceness of indispensable skills in the job market, companies are compelled by absolute necessity to teach these skills to their employees. When they cannot find the right help on the outside, they have to create it on the inside.

The current labor market is a very fluid one. In particular, the corporate workforce is in a perpetual state of flux. People just don't stay put anymore. They move on and then move on again, often in very short intervals. They laterally climb career ladders in multiple companies—and sometimes in totally unrelated fields. The phenomenon of working for one company for a job lifetime is quite rare these days.

Nevertheless, there are still organizations that retain their employees better than others. These are the businesses that promote cultures of development, development, and development of talent. They heavily invest in internal training and offer their people legitimate opportunities to advance within the organization. Paradoxically, many companies spend significantly more capital to recruit talent than they do in training their own personnel. This popular approach to conducting business is hardly far-sighted. And nowadays, bypassing in-depth training by relying on the locating of already skilled persons is becoming less and less practical with the dearth of existing critical talent.

## Passing on Knowledge to Future Generations

By its very nature, coaching and mentoring is a *knowledge transfer facilitator*. Sounds like something from a James Bond movie, but it's nothing so dramatic. It's merely a coach's tool—but, perhaps, his most important one.

With fewer and fewer alternatives at their disposal, business entities in a variety of fields will be compelled to pass down knowledge from on high. They are going to have to stop relying on lifesavers riding in on their white horses from the outside. Companies are going to have to shift their priorities and alter their battle plans—with less reliance on recruitment wars and more commitment to basic training on the inside.

In fact, business talent management approaches are in need of a comprehensive overhaul. Coaching and mentoring principles can facilitate this overhaul. Exactly how can this seismic change occur? If managers are also coaches on every level of an organization, they are, in essence, transferring vital knowledge to employees. They are advancing the skill levels of those who work for them. In other words, they are acting as facilitators of the company's ways and means and grooming their successors. Coaches enlarge skills pools on their watches and endeavor to keep as many talented employees both on the job and happy to be there. In the bigger picture, coaches are charged with ensuring bright futures for the companies who pay their salaries (even though there are no such things as ironclad assurances).

## Different Strokes for Different Folks

You can easily spot the differences between and among organizations as to how they perceive their human resources. Companies with unceasingly high turnover have this happening for very good reasons. Maybe the employee pay and benefit packages aren't too hot. Perhaps the job responsibilities are too much—or too little. Could be that the opportunities for advancement are nil or next to nil.

There are businesses that recruit and recruit, but do next to nothing when it comes to training the fruits of their recruitment. For instance, some companies recruit like mad on college campuses. That is, they hire recently graduated students—straight from the classrooms, as it were—without any hands-on experience in the thunder and lightning of the business sphere. Not a bad way to go if the organizations simultaneously train and grow the skills of these new kids on the block. But what you get all too many times out of this kind of arrangement is college grads who are more than happy to take first jobs that they know are merely stepping-stones to better jobs elsewhere. And what so many of these companies desire are not long-term employees rising up their ladders, but—to put it bluntly—cheap labor instead. Hey, it's not only wine makers who are on the hunt for cheap labor to pick grapes in their vineyards. Many white-collar outfits function with the same exploitative principles. Pay out as little as possible to new hirers, let them move on to greener pastures, and then repeat the process all over again.

## What Do Employees Really Want?

Aside from a competitive salary and all that obvious monetary stuff, what do employees really want from their employers? They want to be fully developed as talents. They want to do important things with the understanding that they can go places where they can do even more important things.

All too many companies miss the boat when it comes to acquiring and maintaining the best talent. They concentrate so much on finding qualified personnel on the outside, but then give short shrift to developing them to their fullest potential when on the inside. Above all else, these development possibilities on the job are what employees want.

Consider the things that you look for when seeking a job. It's probably not all about money and the things that money can buy. Very likely, you want to work for a company that cares enough to put its money where its mouth is. That is, when you go to the office, you want to go to the office. You want to work in a place that both values and expands your existing skills.

There are many individuals who happily assume entry-level positions in companies because they know they will be afforded opportunities to move up the corporate ladder within them. Indeed, businesses that root themselves in cultures of opportunity and advancement are the ones that are poised to thrive in this new reality of scarcer and scarcer skills in the labor market. Companies that ignore this reality do so at their own peril.

Qualified coaches in managerial positions are, in effect, talent detectors. By unearthing the myriad talents of the men and women on their staffs, they save companies oodles of dollars that would otherwise be spent on costly recruitment efforts. Good coaches develop, and develop some more, the talent on their watches. This is their supreme legacy.

Organizations that allow talent—often undiscovered—to languish in lowly positions are not going to survive in the competitive labor climate that permeates the twenty-first century. When companies neglect developing talent from within, they regularly bypass talent at their disposal—*because they don't even know that it's there.* Often they are recruiting talent—at a huge expense to them, by the way—that is already on their payrolls.

# Tapping Into Senior Executives Before It's Too Late

There is an old saying that goes, "It's never too late." Unfortunately, as many businesspersons and others have discovered: Sometimes it is too late. There's another more apropos old saying, "Nothing lasts forever." By merging these two oft-repeated bromides, there sounds a clarion call to senior executives everywhere. It's time for you folks—as well as others in high positions—to begin in earnest passing on your accumulated know-how to those beneath you on the totem pole. The reason is that nothing lasts forever, including many successful and thriving business organizations. Before it's too late, it is time to start building a legacy.

## Mentor, Mentor, Mentor

It's a fact: There are some senior executives in very high places who are utterly removed from the employees toiling beneath them. There is a disconnect between these men and women up above and the so-called little people. They don't have much respect for those in the trenches who make the wheels turn on a daily basis.

Human nature can be quite twisted at times. Many people forget where they came from. Senior executives are quite often worlds apart from the underlings in their companies. And because of this vast gulf, they consider it beneath them to mentor others. They testily bristle at the prospects of passing on their "secrets" to just anybody. In fact, they come to believe that nobody else can do what they do, and that nobody else is remotely capable of filling their shoes.

When senior executives view themselves as indispensable, what do they envision for the futures of the companies they work for? Do they think that they are going to live and work forever? If they do—how smart can they really be? Coaching and mentoring is a comfortable vehicle for executives and managers to pass on their acquired knowledge.

## *Playing Taps*

It always cuts both ways. Sometimes there are senior executives and persons in authoritative roles who are ripe for the picking. That is, they are perfectly willing to mentor and instruct others on the many things they've learned along the way. But, it seems, nobody ever approaches them and asks them to do it. It's imperative that companies have mechanisms in place to transfer knowledge—i.e., to tap into senior executives and so many others before it's too late.

Whatever your station is in a business environment, always endeavor to tap into the wisdom of people who have walked the walk. And this doesn't mean that you barge into private meetings of high-powered individuals; it merely asks that you pick the brains of persons who can help you grow your skills and augment your knowledge of the way things work. Don't miss opportunities to better yourself and enhance your value as both a human being and a human resource.

Turn on other people's taps when you have the chance. Don't let opportunities pass you by. Set up mentoring relationships wherever and whenever possible, even informal ones. Learn from others and pass on what you've learned. Companies with work atmospheres that encourage this kind of sharing are better equipped to succeed in the twenty-first century.

When coaching and mentoring is in place from top to bottom in organizations, they are armed with the equipment to effectively transition to the future. Since it is generally accepted that the coming years threaten a critical talent crisis, businesses and other enterprises that utilize what they have in human capital to the fullest will more than likely weather the impending storm. And, yes, this means tapping into senior executives and their know-how, but also instituting a framework of learning and skills enhancement all across the board.

## *Educating the Leaders of Tomorrow*

Tomorrow is taking shape and coaching and mentoring is going to play a significant role in what it looks like. From cover to cover in this book, coaches are rightfully placed atop a pedestal. Ideally, what they do on the business frontier transcends mere managing of individuals to get them to do this and to do that. When they do what they are supposed to do, coaches and mentors enrich and enlighten people. More to the point, they are the leaders of today who are simultaneously the educators of the leaders of tomorrow. And this education is more important than ever before because of the cross-pollinating realities of baby boomer retirements and a vastly underskilled labor pool available to replace them.

### *Tomorrow: It's Sooner Than You Think*

Many organizations are clinging to members of the baby boom generation in their employ. And not because they prefer gray hairs or are champions of senior power. They want to hold on to the particular individuals who have the skills that they need to run and build their businesses. Essentially, they want to hold on to their leaders.

**FACT**

Many companies are trying to retain key employees—who are also members of the baby boom generation—for extended periods of time past their anticipated retirement dates. They are offering them enticing carrots such as bonuses, telecommuting opportunities, better pension formulae, flexible schedules, part-time work, and, yes, mentoring roles.

Despite the critical talent dilemma facing both businesses and non-profit outfits alike, there is still a wealth of diamonds in the rough out there. There are leaders of tomorrow who are at the ready. In many instances, it's just a matter of them being identified and nurtured.

## Remedial Work

Where there are shortages of critical talent, there is always going to be a need for remedial education in the workplace. It's happening on the college level with students compelled to take remedial courses in such fundamental subjects as basic reading and writing. And, of course, this begs the question: What kinds of standards did these students' high schools hold them to? But, again, it's the reality that we live in. And it's certainly not going to change in one fell swoop. Wherever it is practiced—on the job or elsewhere—coaching and mentoring can adapt to the circumstances.

So, the current times demand remedial education. If businesses are going to overcome the critical talent predicament, they are going to have to do what it takes to enhance their employees' overall abilities and leadership qualities. There's no getting around it. And this may, on occasion, entail a little remedial work. Generally speaking, the leaders of tomorrow require more schooling on the job than their predecessors needed. Some individuals are ready to take the helm this very minute—and that's a very good thing. But many of tomorrow's leaders are undiscovered talents that good coaching and mentoring can both unearth and teach the requisite leadership skills.

## Let the Coaching Begin in Earnest

In the years yet to be, more and more managers on the corporate frontlines will be christened coaches. More and more of these coaches will mentor promising members of their staffs in the ABCs of both coaching and leadership. And, on top of all that, more and more coaches will find themselves being mentored from individuals above their link in the corporate chain. They will become the senior executives of tomorrow.

Not unlike educators in the world of academe, coaches and mentors desire to leave sizeable footprints in the sand. They want to make workplaces better environments all around. They want their employees to harmoniously work together as members of teams with common goals. Coaches want to make their office spaces laboratories of learning, not places where everybody's got his or her eyes on the clock and checkout time.

While coaching and mentoring is results-oriented, it is in the legacy business, too. This is precisely why more and more companies are turning to coaching in lieu of traditional managing. This is why mentoring is increasingly a player in the corporate world and, indeed, elsewhere. Coaching and mentoring embodies a guiding hand that is needed in so many different places.

Chapter 21

# The Role of a Lifetime: A Script for Mentoring

This chapter offers a mentoring script for interested parties to perform on life's multidimensional stage. It reveals the most efficient and effective routes to take in maximizing the benefits of mentoring relationships, with a special emphasis placed on adult mentors and younger mentees. Here you will see how these relationships flourish both inside businesses, as well as outside of the workplace.

# *Mentor and Mentoring: Words and Reality*

The words "mentor" and "mentoring" are loaded. That is, they are infused with a mother lode of high hopes, blue skies, and all things constructive. The onus on a mentor is to pass on wisdom of some sort to a mentee. The fulfillment of this plethora of good stuff, however, assumes that three very important factors exist:

- A mentor with wisdom to spare
- A mentor with knowledge and understanding of how to pass on wisdom to a mentee
- A mentee receptive to a mentor

Ideally, a mentor is a teacher who can teach a mentee a thing or two. But this wisdom and knowledge transfer occurs only if certain mentoring guidelines are mastered and intelligently applied. Just as teaching in a classroom setting is not a casual or haphazard undertaking, neither is mentoring. Not-for-profit mentoring organizations approach the comprehensive mentoring process and relationships between mentors and mentees with the utmost solemnity. Prospective mentors are screened, and those who make the cut are assigned mentees that best complement their backgrounds and aspirations. In this regard, it's akin to a dating service and endeavoring to ensure a compatible fit. Similarly, a mentor in business is not assigned to anyone and everyone in the workplace. A mentor-mentee relationship on the job is established only when it is believed that something significant and positive for the company—and, of course, for the mentee's career growth—can emerge from the pairing.

In parenting, too, there are particular modes of behavior that work better than others in imparting important life lessons and instilling solid values in their children. In order to be accepted as positive role models, parents must first connect with their children. They cannot be seen as lacking in moral authority. Often parents have to work very hard to get through to their offspring.

# *The Evolution of Mentoring Relationships*

All mentoring relationships are about evolution. No, this has nothing to do with Charles Darwin and his oft-debated theory. Rather, mentors are charged with the responsibility of evolving their mentees in a whole host of ways. They are not expected to realize positive results in a nanosecond. That is, they aren't expected to work miracles in one or two meetings. They are, however, counted on to move forward in these relationships, making progress all the time. Remember though that making progress doesn't preclude the inevitable setback or two—it goes with the territory.

Think about it. The very nature of mentoring implies that you're involved in somewhat complicated and layered relationships. In other words, you're mentoring individuals in need of guidance, knowledge, and skills of every imaginable hue. Mentees outside of business circles often require an all-encompassing change in the direction of their lives. And the stark reality is that such metamorphoses are more difficult to achieve than traditional, measurable work goals. This is why the emphasis is placed on the evolutionary nature of mentoring, and why it is fundamental to always remain focused on forward movement from start to finish.

**FACT**

Many business leaders promote mentoring relationships by getting their employees involved with at-risk young people. These acts of social responsibility on their parts enhance their images and help disadvantaged youngsters in need of support and tutelage in becoming the business leaders of tomorrow.

Stagnant mentor-mentee relationships fall apart because movement is critical in the relationship. Sometimes the movement won't be as swift and as smooth as you would like, but that's okay. A mentor-mentee relationship is not akin to running a 100-yard dash. It is more of a marathon—a lengthy, always forward-moving, supportive marathon.

# The Mentoring Play in Four Acts

Whether a successful mentor-mentee relationship happens between employees in the workplace or out in the community with troubled teens, it unfolds and develops in four acts. Act I is about getting acquainted. Act II is devoted to goal setting. Act III is seeing these goals through and meeting expectations. Act IV marks the closure of the mentor-mentee relationship.

## Act I: Getting Acquainted

So much hullabaloo is made about the importance of first impressions in life. Some people swear that first impressions tell them all they need to know about another person. Others say that getting to know someone gradually over time is the only way to really get to know a person. There's merit in both opinions. First impressions can make or break a relationship on the spot and in real time. Nowhere is this truer than in a mentoring relationship. This is precisely why it's vital that you move slowly at first.

**ALERT!**

Mentoring doesn't work as a crash course. Early on in mentor-mentee relationships is not the time to come on strong. The infancy of the relationship is when you informally acquaint yourself with your mentee. It's the time to put your mentee at ease.

The initial meeting between you and your mentee may be somewhat awkward. Getting to know someone usually is. Don't leap to hasty conclusions. Don't allow any negative first impressions to cloud your hopes for a brighter future. "How am I ever going to work with this punk?" "I don't see how I'll ever get through to a kid with such an attitude!" Hold on! Nobody ever said that mentoring was an easy job. It's not. It requires patience and sincere commitment. And, yes, in Act I of the mentor-mentee relationship, both patience and commitment are sometimes sorely tested.

Use your first few mentoring get-togethers to establish a bond of trust. And there's only one way to do this: Get to know your mentee as an individual. Explore the personality and interests of your mentee while withholding any value judgments. Similarly, your mentee's got to get to know you. Two people getting to know one another gradually over time is the surest route to establishing rapport. And rapport equals straightforward communication, which is essential in all successful mentoring relationships.

When setting career goals with your mentee, make sure they're your mentee's goals and not yours. Respect your mentee's interests and hopes about the future even though they may be very different from the paths that you would venture down.

In Act I of the mentor-mentee relationship, you must come to understand and appreciate your mentee's personality and temperament, and then determine the approach you're going to take to get the best out of him or her over time. For instance, you may be a person who talks about your personal feelings at the drop of a hat. Don't, however, assume that everybody else does the same thing. Don't assume that your mentee shares your penchant for getting in touch with "good stuff." The surest way to scare off mentees is to put them on the spot right away by asking them a barrage of therapist-style questions. Take it slowly—evolve.

Pay special heed to the reasons behind the goals you set in your mentor-mentee relationship. Make sure that the mentee really and truly wants to reach the goals and that they are not what he or she thinks you or a member of his or her family wants.

Earlier in the book this subject was touched on in a discussion about your role as a coach and how it was not the same as a therapist's. Similarly, your role as a mentor does not ask you to be your mentee's therapist. You're not a cable talk show host either. That is, you're not looking for a scoop in uncovering something juicy in your mentee's personal life. You're a mentor trying to help another human being be a better and more productive individual. The bottom line is, when you bond with your mentee, you'll know how he or she feels about so many different things soon enough.

Make it your purpose in life to get to know your mentee slowly but surely. Then, when you emerge from your initial mentoring meetings, you'll have achieved all of your short-term objectives. Now, move with confidence into Act II of your relationship.

## Act II: Setting Goals

Once you've cemented your mentor-mentee relationship in the get-to-know-one-another phase of Act I, it's time to advance to the goals stage. If, as the discovery process evolves, the mentor-mentee relationship is on solid ground, so too will the future expectations be on solid ground.

During Act II of the mentoring relationship both you and your mentee should discuss expectations. Work closely together in establishing real, measurable expectations—goals—that both of you have for the relationship. Keep the goals feasible and razor-sharp. Put them in writing if you have to. Encourage your mentee to verbalize the expectations that he or she has for you as a mentor beyond any high-sounding abstractions as "making a positive difference" and "providing direction." Make Act II in your mentor-mentee relationship the beginning of an intimate and productive journey. That is, trust one another and commit to seeing the relationship through to genuine results—expectations realized and goals met.

Always come prepared in your scheduled meetings with your mentees. Keep your get-togethers focused and meaningful. Know where you're headed at all times. Don't fill in the time with fluff. In fact, it's better to come overprepared than underprepared. By taking this mapped out route, you'll stave off any boredom on your mentee's part.

## Act III: Meeting Goals and Expectations

In Act III, after you've set goals and established the level of expectations that you have for your mentee and that your mentee has for you, it's time to perform—to do. It's in this phase of mentoring where you can take more liberties with your mentee, without the risk of souring or ending the relationship. It's now when you must start taking your mentee to task, if necessary, for not living up to promises, upholding your standards, and strictly abiding by your mutually agreed-upon rules for the relationship.

**FACT**

Throughout history there have been countless mentor-mentee relationships in every conceivable discipline. From philosophy to politics to psychiatry to the arts, mentoring has always played an important role. Socrates mentored Plato. Hubert Humphrey mentored Walter Mondale. Sigmund Freud mentored C. G. Jung. Ralph Waldo Emerson mentored Henry David Thoreau.

Act III is the results-oriented phase of mentoring. It's at once a time of great acceptance between you and your mentee, and a time of change. And in successful mentor-mentee relationships, we're talking about positive changes and growth as human beings. You might, for example, have extracted a goal from your mentee to do better in school during the current semester. Within the goal are expectations of better study habits and preparation for exams. Thus, you ask and expect that your mentee practice self-discipline in making the necessary changes in his or her life to accommodate the added study and overall commitment to schoolwork.

In this example, the Day of Reckoning comes with the report card. This is the ultimate measure of success. But along the way, you've got homework and exams to look over, as well as other indicators to measure your mentee's progress in reaching his or her goal. Like a coach and an employee's performance plan, you are expected to keep tabs on your mentee's performance at all times. You don't set goals together and be done with it. You don't say you want to see better grades in school and not remain focused on the road to the report card. Just as in the workplace, you cannot afford to wait until the deed is done to commence the first checkup. There need to be many checkups en route. And with periodic checkups come many opportunities to offer counsel in making corrections and overcoming obstacles. It's also the place to provide good, old-fashioned encouragement.

## Act IV: Concluding the Relationship

This is the final act in the mentor-mentee relationship. You've traveled the normal mentor-mentee path and navigated around its many potholes and slowed at its various speed bumps. First, you spent quality time getting to know one another, moving cautiously with both an open mind and an open heart. Once you bonded as a mentor-mentee pair who trusted and respected one another, you were able to sit down and discuss goals for the future and what each one of you wanted to get out of the relationship. With goals in place, you assisted your mentee in realizing them. You were there the whole time to poke and prod, to chastise when required, and to celebrate progress and legitimate achievements together.

The ending of a mentor-mentee relationship often engenders an abandonment issue in a mentee. This is why you must celebrate the ending of the formal relationship as a beginning—a beginning of many successes to come.

The last act in a mentoring relationship is the moment you put it to bed. A mentor-mentee relationship is not meant to be a lifetime proposition. It's meant to help people help themselves. Ending the mentor-mentee relationship doesn't mean you end any contact between you and your mentee. It merely means that you've done all that you can, and your mentee has positively responded and is ready to move forward on his or her own without your mentoring hand. It's up to you, in concert with your mentee, to determine the new nature of your relationship. Remaining friends is a popular next step for a mentor and mentee who have shared real successes and growth.

The reason mentor-mentee relationships are finite is the same reason kids are expected to leave the parental nest when they become adults. Ideally, they've been taught many lessons, experienced ups and downs, and are ready to go it alone. You want to give your mentee a pair of functioning wings to fly away without your assistance.

**QUESTION?**

**Is your mentee supposed to mentor you too?**
Not quite. Nevertheless, your mentee will teach you many lessons about yourself and your abilities. Courtesy of your mentee, you'll discover your aptitude for teaching, gain patience, and better understand and appreciate human nature in its infinite diversity.

# Mentoring Playbook

Throughout the mentor-mentee relationship, from Act I to Act IV, there are some very specific and useful techniques you should always keep in mind and utilize frequently.

## Give Feedback

Be generous with your feedback. That's what you're there for. Positive feedback is preferred, but even negative feedback when it's justified is helpful. However, avoid any harsh criticism of your mentee, particularly early in your relationship. Reinforce all of the positives time and again. Take note of even the minutiae in your mentee's growth and development and be sure to tell him or her about it.

## Ask Open-Ended Questions

Another important technique to employ in your mentor-mentee relationship is open-ended questioning. While you're cementing rapport and, of course, after you enter into a comfortable relationship, you want your conversations and get-togethers to be as productive as possible. A little small talk goes a long way. It's a good icebreaker, and in small doses—that's why it's called "small talk"—helps get the conversational ball rolling. But keep in mind that it's essential you make the best use of the finite time you have together.

With open-ended questioning, you encourage your mentee to reach deeper into him- or herself. You ask your mentee to think about important things like the consequences of decisions and actions. Peppering your mentee with questions such as, "Do you think you are progressing in your new job?" and then accepting a "yes" answer and moving on is not the way to go. Remember, too, you're more interested in the exposition responses to questions than you are in the anticipated first responses.

Good communication is what makes a mentor-mentee relationship work. You've got to connect with your mentee, and this entails posing a lot of open-ended questions and genuinely listening to and responding to the answers. Your mentee will know you care when he or she sees that you are reacting to the myriad answers to your open-ended questions.

You don't get much out of "yes" and "no" answers to questions. You've got to explore your relationship and know where you stand at all times. And the only way to really know where you stand is by getting real answers. "What things are you doing in your new job that you consider successes?" "Why do you feel better equipped on the job today than on your first day?" These types of questions allow mentees to expound their answers. You get the information you need and a true sense of the progress that you're making in the relationship. And what you gather about where you stand enables you to move forward from the true reality and not some perception of reality.

## Forbid the Negative

Lastly, there's a firm rule in a mentoring relationship that you must decree. That is, you need to enforce a "no negative zone." Guard it and don't permit your mentee to go near it.

Never permit your mentee to speak ill about members of his or her family, schoolmates, teachers, coworkers, and others. It's best that you always stress the positive whenever and wherever possible, and remove all of the negatives. You don't want a mentor-mentee relationship to deteriorate into a blame game, even if there is plenty of blame to go around.

Alas, even with the best of intentions, sometimes mentor-mentee relationships enter the negative zone. After all, you're working with people who need a helping hand. This often means there are persons in their lives who have not exactly done right by them. There's a lot of anger. And anger often creates a multiplier effect that lands mentees in the aforementioned negative zone.

When this happens, you've got to diffuse the anger by not permitting streams of negative references to other people. When you stamp out the negative talk early in the relationship, you set the proper tone for the long term. A tone that says, "Let's avoid playing the blame game and start looking to ourselves for answers to our own problems."

**FACT**

A mentor-mentee relationship is finite and naturally runs its course. When it's time to end the relationship, some mentors like defining their new relationships with their mentees as "associates," "partners," or "friends." When the mentor-mentee relationship ends, a new one can take flight.

## What the Right Kind of Mentoring Produces

When the mentor-mentee relationship succeeds, behaviors and attitudes change for the better. That's how success is measured. When mentees part company with their mentors, they often are more:

- Articulate in expressing themselves
- Skilled at their jobs or in school
- Focused on both the present and the future
- Trustworthy in relationships
- Self-aware regarding the consequences of their words and actions
- Resilient in recovering from setbacks
- Positive in outlook
- Sensitive to others and their problems

They are also:

- More open to differences of opinions
- More able to trust others
- Better problem solvers
- Better able to recognize opportunities
- More equipped to seize opportunities

Simply understood, the byproduct of a strong mentor-mentee relationship establishes a solid foundation that can be built upon and built upon some more. It furnishes the mother's milk for the mentors of tomorrow. The most resourceful mentors have very often been mentored at some point in their own lives.

## Mentoring: History Is on Your Side

Recorded history is replete with mentoring relationships that have shaped the world we know. From ancient times when Socrates mentored Plato to the modern day, countless prominent men and women, in every imaginable field, cite having had an important mentor in their lives. Founded in 1904, Big Brothers Big Sisters, a mentoring organization for at-risk children, champions more than a century of positive results. That is, they note thousands upon thousands of success stories under their vast umbrella—i.e., troubled youth who have seen their lives positively enriched by pairing with caring adult mentors. No matter where conscientious mentoring occurs— and no matter the ages of those in the relationship—it's a positive force for good and an absolute necessity in ensuring that human existence is more humane and that both the present and future worlds are better places to live and to work.

# Chapter 22

# Ten Myths of Coaching and Mentoring

In your travels, you might very likely encounter some misguided souls who subscribe to the more common myths out there concerning coaching and mentoring. In the final chapter, these myths will be debunked by employing the most powerful tool known to coaches and mentors: the truth.

# Myth: Capable People Don't Need Coaching

There are, in fact, coaching and mentoring practitioners who give short shrift to the importance of screening prospective employees in the interview process. It's as if employees arrive on the job by some sleight of hand. Really, though, making a thorough effort to vet job applicants should be job one of a coach and the beginning of a sweeping and conscientious coaching journey. (See Chapter 12 for an edifying glimpse at a coach's role in hiring staff.) You want to employ the best and brightest people, don't you? Down the road, it'll make your managing duties a lot less complicated and a whole lot more successful, too. This is an incontrovertible fact: One of your principal coaching duties is to find good men and women to fill any open job positions at your disposal.

**FACT**

You want to select the most capable people possible to work for you. But the reality is, because you're only human, you won't always pick perfect employees to labor under your wise and guiding hand. And, even those employees who are top-notch performers will require direction to further develop in their job roles and improve their overall skills.

As a managerial discipline, coaching and mentoring views learning as infinite and readily available to anybody and everybody. Each and every individual employee—irrespective of his or her level of knowledge and overall skills—requires a guiding hand of some kind while on the job. Just as it is for those struggling along to get tutored and acquire new skills, the support of an astute manager—a coach—is necessary for the best and brightest employees, too. You want the best and the brightest to be better and brighter.

Coaches support all of their employees—without exception—by providing hands-on managing and individual attention. Hands-on, remember, does not amount to micromanaging. The most capable people become even more capable under the smart and forward-moving leadership of coaching. And those persons who need a more thorough and recurring upgrade of their knowledge and skills often find that a good coach and coaching program delivers the goods.

It's incumbent upon you in your coaching efforts to not only reward the successes of your employees, but also to see that they appreciate the reasons for these accomplishments. Generally, success is the result of strong skills and good work habits, and not mere "luck" as some employees claim.

## Myth: Your Employees Do Most of Your Work

You've encountered continuous references throughout this book on how coaching is high on delegating more responsibilities and providing more challenges to employees in their jobs. So, does this mean you just parcel out all the work that needs to be done, put your feet up on your desk, and hit the snooze button? No, it doesn't. Sure, coaching repeatedly advocates making employees more adept by providing them job roles of real substance and furnishing them with more and more opportunities to showcase their talents and realize their possibilities. As a coach, you want to maximize your people's performances by getting them to push their potential envelopes to the limit. But you've got to do some of the pushing, too, so you delegate important jobs and responsibilities to the qualified and deserving on your staff. You increasingly challenge those you feel are most up to it. And you furnish added responsibilities to those who have earned your trust. The bottom line is that good coaches don't have the time to put their feet up on their desks, whether they are delegating a heaping helping of responsibilities or not delegating as much as they should be.

Don't ever find yourself in the guise of a managerial loomer. That is, be careful not to smother your staff by your omnipresence in watching every move they make. Use your communicative abilities to set employee performance in motion, discreetly monitor all that is transpiring, but, in the big picture, let your people get the job done.

## Myth: *You Must Be Easygoing to Coach People*

If this were the case, there would be very few coaches in management positions. Coaching and mentoring expect many things from their stable of coaches, but being perfect isn't one of them. That's a big relief! The beauty of coaching in managerial roles is its extraordinary adaptability. Thus, you can take the finest characteristics of your personality and mold them into a leadership model that works for you in getting the best possible performance results from your team. Essentially, good coaching is about influencing employees to achieve great things. And, believe it or not, you can be an influential and positive leader of people without being the warmest and fuzziest personality.

Character traits can be fine-tuned, too. If you're continually fair, candid, and communicative with your employees, a support system automatically exists in the workplace. This is a map for success. An assertive but scrupulously consistent approach to managing trumps personality quirks every time. Of course, it certainly helps to be thick-skinned, empathetic, and understanding by nature. But all sorts of personality types can thrive in coaching roles if they embrace coaching's core methodology rather than its mythology. After all, coaching in the corporate sphere is demanding. You've always got to deliver the goods by sweetening that all-important bottom line.

## Myth: *Employees Are Intimidated by Direct Communication*

Why should employees fear feedback on their performances? Who wouldn't want to know where they stand in their jobs? Granted, there are lots of folks who get overly anxious at the mere notion of constant communication and regular one-on-one meetings with their bosses. But more times than not, this internal panic is rooted in a false reality of what they think will happen rather than in what actually happens. That is, feedback in practice is nothing to fear, but a positive deliverance that should be welcomed with open arms. Coaching and mentoring's managerial methods—its various tools and techniques—are the antithesis of scary. They are in fact reassuring—as reassuring as it gets in the workplace.

> As a coach, you're continuously asked to build confidence in your employees. Let them know where they stand and what they need to do to better themselves as work entities and as human beings. The more confident your employees feel about their abilities, the more disposed they'll be to taking sensible risks and the less afraid they'll be in making mistakes.

This very direct, people-intensive approach to managing is worrisome only to those who are accustomed to working under the thumbs of dinosaur managers who dole out work assignments and then lock their office doors and throw away the keys. And the only time employees ever see these less than enlightened managers is when they've done something wrong or are about to get the old heave-ho. The unadulterated truth is that the more employees know about their jobs and their future prospects, the more relaxed they feel and the more productive they are. Coaching and mentoring puts a premium on honesty and being up-front with employees at all times, rain or shine. This reality is nothing to be intimidated by. Quite the contrary.

## Myth: Coaches Don't Need Technical Qualifications

Of course coaches need technical qualifications! In fact, a key factor in cementing a bond of respect between you and your employees is deeply rooted in your competence. There is this curious opinion held by some misinformed souls that coaches are placed in managerial positions by rote. That is, they are somehow interchangeable and solely on the job to inspire their staff to perform and to achieve at the highest levels possible. These misguided minions see coaches as merely inspirational talking heads put in positions of authority to deliver motivational speeches and offer "you can do it" encouragement to employees.

Ah, but the truth is, coaches need to know all the ABCs of the department they're managing—and then some. This is common sense and applies to managers of all stripes, including those dinosaurs. For a moment, imagine laboring in the engineering department of a company supervised by a manager whose educational expertise lies in social work. Suffice it to say, there's not going to be a whole lot of respect and trust for this particular person emanating from a staff of trained engineers. How could they possibly admire and follow the lead of a manager who tells them what to do and grades their performances, but doesn't know beans about the technical intricacies of engineering?

Because coaching utilizes performance plans and regular measurement of performance, it's more than imperative that coaches display technical competence in the areas they manage. In fact, they should exhibit more than mere competence, but a great deal of expertise. They should have the intellectual and educational capacities to fully comprehend all that's going on around them and all that characterizes the various performance results of their employees. The coach should have know-how that she can pass on to her employees. She should be able to detect mistakes. She should be ready to alter course at a moment's notice based on her vast knowledge of what needs to be accomplished and how best to get there.

## Myth: Only Employees Who Want Coaching Are Coachable

Coaching and mentoring are comprehensive managerial methodologies that apply across the board to each and every employee on the job. You can, of course, bring in external and personal coaches to work one-on-one with individuals for specific reasons or to solve certain problems beyond your ken. But day-to-day managing as a coach means that you are coaching everybody on your staff without exception.

Let's bring this point to the football field to further drive it home and kick a field goal. You wouldn't try out for a football team, make the cut, and then inform the coach you don't desire any of his coaching. If you did, he'd tell you where to go. You wouldn't tell him that you know all there is to know about the game and that you'd appreciate if he would leave you alone, refrain from telling you what to do, and just let you play. That's not how the football bounces. A football coach coaches a team of individuals. And a team is all about teamwork, where every single person's performance contributes to the final results. Ditto in the workplace. A coach on the football field or in the office doesn't wait for invitations to coach. He is expected to coach everybody on his team, whether they think they need coaching or not.

You want to get the best performance out of every one of your employees. And that means that you want to maximize the performances of the best performers just as much as you do the lesser performers. Coaching places no restrictions on performance or on the potential of individuals. This is precisely why every single person is a candidate for coaching. There isn't anybody alive who can't do better and move to the next level.

This discussion doesn't mean that each and every individual will respond well to coaching, or that everybody and anybody will respond the same way to it. But in most cases, coaching methodologies get more out of employees than do other managerial approaches. Coaching and its uniquely personal touch gets more out of people both in job performance and in job satisfaction. And that's a winning combination, most especially in this dog-eat-dog day and age.

## Myth: Close Working Relationships Make Conflicts Impossible to Rectify

Just the opposite is the case. To some people, a close working relationship with employees on an individual basis is a ticking time bomb waiting to explode when a daunting problem or obstacle comes down the work pike. These folks see coaching and its support system as an employees' insurance program. They view coaches as something akin to union bosses who will defend their employees come hell or high water, and therefore gloss over problems and mitigate disagreements without necessarily righting things. This is far from the reality of what coaches do. The very fact that coaches get to know their employees and candidly communicate with them on a regular basis means that all sorts of job snafus are likely to be caught early in their development and dealt with expeditiously and openly.

As a coach, you're not there to be your employees' best buddy or guardian angel. You're their coach, which means that you're their manager in a work setting. You're seeking the best bottom line for the company that pays your salary. You're a professional who expects professionalism in the job performances of your people. You expect that your staff of men and women will always be responsible for their words and actions, and do their jobs to the best of their abilities. With all of your expectations out in the open, coupled with performance goals set by each one of your employees, you ensure that problems—from performance breakdowns to employee-versus-employee conflict—are easier to address and rectify because the atmosphere in your office is, above all else, aboveboard.

## Myth: Coaching Works Only in Office Jobs

Coaching and mentoring know no boundaries. Their tools and techniques, with a little situational fine-tuning, of course, work in the offices of the corporate world, non-profit enterprises, government agencies, and in the hustle and bustle of retail and service business environments, too. In fact, the principles of coaching and mentoring are most welcome in the business venues with the poorest employee morale and the highest turnover. That is, in businesses perceived as offering drudgework, poor pay, and dead-end jobs, the need for an uplifting and enlightening managerial approach is self-evident.

One of the chief factors in the current business climate that's given rise to coaching and mentoring is the reality that today's jobs—and jobholders—are so often transient. That is, there's more voluntary and involuntary movement in the labor force than ever before. And coaching employees takes this fact of modern life into account by scrupulously working on the job at hand, yes, but simultaneously recognizing that tomorrow's job is also an important consideration. What this means is that coaching and mentoring want to fashion knowledgeable and better-skilled workers, and hence employees who are more resilient and ready to move on to new and better jobs when the opportunities arise.

Even in seemingly unskilled jobs, good coaching extracts lessons to be learned and in so doing creates better-prepared workers who are more apt to go on to bigger and better things. Coaching and mentoring zero in on skills beyond the hard technical kinds and impart the softer varieties involved with dealing with people, accepting responsibility, maintaining a good attitude, and establishing a firm work ethic. These invaluable "other" skills need to be taught and applied in the restaurant and the record store, just as much as in the office place.

## Myth: A Coach Meets with Employees as a Therapist Meets with Patients

No way. In fact, you're not hired as a coach to be all knowing and solve problems unrelated to the job. The time we live in often brings psychotherapy into places it doesn't belong. And it doesn't belong in the workplace. Some companies refer employees with psychological or personal problems of a great magnitude to trained and licensed professionals. And this is good. But you're a coach, so coach. Leave the head shrinking, as it were, to the head shrinkers.

Coaches maximize the performance of their employees by, among other things, maximizing the use of their time. A coach works with the facts of life that office hours are finite and that time spent in the office needs to be quality time—no wasted minutes from morning bagel to evening yawn.

That said, coaches nevertheless are expected to have a good grip on human nature and how people motivate themselves. But this isn't something you have to sport a degree in to know the score. For coaches, it's often a matter of being more patient and empathetic than traditional managers that ratchets up their employees' performances. You need to approach each one of your people in a distinct manner to spur them on to perform. This isn't therapy by any stretch of the imagination. It's being thoughtful and wise. Parents know that their children are unique individuals with different personalities. And the best parents don't raise their children in a restraining, one-size-fits-all mold. Well, the best coaches look upon their employees in much the same light. And you don't have to be a psychologist to be a good parent, or a good coach.

## Myth: Coaches Make All Decisions in Concert with Employees

Yes, it's true that coaching and mentoring encourage coaches to rather extensively consult with their employees on job-related matters. But, no, coaches aren't bound by consensus decision making. Nevertheless, there is this pervasive myth that portrays coaches as somewhat impotent leaders presiding over something more akin to a focus group than a staff of employees.

The confusion here rests in the reality of employees playing important roles in shaping their job responsibilities and—by extension—their future careers. And this is what coaching and mentoring bring into management—a partnership of sorts between coaches and employees. But this partnership doesn't relegate the coach to titular head status. There must always be one leader who sets the tone and direction of the office. There must be one leader who monitors what's going on in the office by measuring performance and doing what it takes to remain productive and forward moving. Coaches, in fact, are asked to be more informed, more understanding, and more aware of the work in progress in the office than other managers. It's true. This does not mean micromanaging every detail and looking over every employee's shoulder all day long, but it is this awareness that enables coaches to do the job of helping employees to thrive and produce in an atmosphere of continual growth and skill development.

# Glossary

**action plans**
Clearly defined directions inserted in individual job performance plans that meticulously itemize what employees must do—the actions that they need to take—to reach their goals and meet their standard of performance. There are usually several action plans within distinct performance plans.

**anticipated first response**
An answer to a question that is both expected and unenlightening. Coaches are more interested in exposition responses to their queries, which are ordinarily more illuminating and advance their capacities to effectively lead a team of individuals.

**assumption function**
The erroneous supposition that each and every individual from a particular group is somehow a clone of one another with identical work habits and abilities. This mode of thinking often engenders employment discrimination and runs completely counter to coaching and mentoring.

**attitude**
The embodiment of an individual's overall thought process and the precursor of actions. Thus, attitude is usually the harbinger of job performance.

**attitudinally disabled employees**
Individuals who possess unfavorable attitudes 24/7.

**baby boomer generation**
Men and women born between the years 1946 and 1964. Approximately 78 million "boomers," as they are sometimes called, were born in that time period.

**blame game**
The practice of managers and/or employees not accepting responsibility for their own actions and shifting the accountability onto others. Sometimes referred to as "passing the buck."

**boredom bomb**
Unchallenging, intellectually unfulfilling, or uninteresting job roles and work responsibilities that are poised to detonate and explode into employee performance drop-offs, general discontent, and personnel turnover.

**brainstorming sessions**
A tried-and-true coaching and mentoring technique of permitting employees or mentees to altogether express themselves by offering ideas and suggestions on important matters without fear of ridicule or worse.

**close-ended questions**
Queries posed to provoke definitive, short, often "yes" or "no" responses.

### coach

A manager in a business setting who endeavors to fashion an optimum work environment by emphasizing the continual growth and development of employee knowledge and skills. A coach communicates with and encourages employees on a one-on-one basis to maximize their job performances and to realize their full potential both personally as well as professionally.

### coaching

A managerial methodology that seeks to maximize employee performance by conscientiously considering employees as individuals with unique talents and possibilities. Coaching is rooted in consistent and up-front communication between coaches and employees.

### compartmentalization

The deliberate act of an individual who wholly and successfully detaches a set of circumstances or attitude from another set of circumstances or attitude in order to focus on a goal and/or make forward progress. Often discussed in terms of leaving personal problems at home when on the job.

### corrective coaching

A designation applied to particular coaching efforts in situations where employee attitudes and behaviors indicate serious problems and workplace disruptions unless rectified.

### critical talent

The men and women who are the lifeblood of a business organization's core success. That is, the key personnel behind businesses' basic functioning, as well as their stellar performances.

### delegating

An essential coaching technique that affords deserving employees more responsible and challenging job roles.

### dinosaur managers

The so-called doer, directive-style, traditional managers who do not work with employees on a person-to-person basis, and do not collaborate with them in shaping their jobs and futures. Sometimes called "fossil managers."

### enlightened scrutiny

A coaching and mentoring technique that entails the continual surveying and evaluation of employees to maximize their productivity in the most optimum of possible work environments.

### equality doctrine

Office standards that each employee—without exception—is expected to uphold and abide by. These standards include clearly enunciated rules of conduct, ethical boundaries, and performance level expectations. On the other hand, equivalence in employee treatment is not part of coaching, which views workers as individuals with unique temperaments and backgrounds and adjusts coaching methods accordingly, and as needed, on a one-on-one basis.

### exposition response

An answer to an open-ended question that is generally more enlightening than a predictable or rehearsed answer. Coaches rely heavily on open and in-depth communication with their staff members, and on understanding what they are truly thinking and feeling.

### external coach

A consultant from outside a company brought in to troubleshoot particular problems and remove workplace obstacles by working intimately with individuals or groups and utilizing the tools and techniques of coaching. This slice of coaching is not the same as day-to-day managing, but is highly specialized and usually short term.

### feedback

A fundamental coaching and mentoring communication technique and information dispenser frequently utilized to pass on observations to employees regarding their performances or other workplace concerns. It can be either positive or negative in nature, but it shouldn't be praise or criticism. Feedback is wholly constructive in practice. That is, it is parceled out in the hopes of finding solutions and realizing positive outcomes in any and all situations.

### five points of professionalism

Integrity, initiative, resilience, positive attitude, and teamwork.

### glass ceiling

The term used to characterize the intangible barrier preventing women and minorities from breaking into corporate senior management positions in numbers commensurate with their percentages in the workforce at large.

### goals

Performance expectations established in collaboration between coaches and employees in the initial phase of performance planning. Also called "objectives." Setting goals also plays an important role in mentor-mentee relationships.

### hard skills

Knowledge and technical skills that are measurable in aptitude and performance. Sometimes called "hands-on skills."

### high-octane coaching

An appellation applied to coaching efforts where special employee training is required, such as grooming a new employee, upgrading skills, preparing an individual for a job promotion, and so on.

### internal coaching

Managing as a coach on an everyday basis within a company. This role is in contrast to external coaching, which is brought into organizations from the outside for specific problem solving, skills upgrading, and so on.

### invisible hand

The term given to the ambiguous cultural reasons that keep women and minorities from cracking into senior management positions in large numbers. More specifically, it refers to the common practice of persons grooming as their successors those with whom they feel most comfortable, thus perpetuating a cycle of exclusion.

### knowledge transfer facilitator

The term applied to coaching and mentoring and its important legacy role in business settings. That is, coaching and mentoring passes on crucial knowledge and vital skills from those on higher rungs in an organization to those in lower positions.

**look-out-for-them principle**

A doctrine that coaches conscientiously abide by in providing perpetual on-the-job and career development opportunities for their employees.

**measures**

The standards by which job performance is judged. Periodic monitoring and verification of performance plans via mutually agreed upon (coach-employee) measures ensure that standards are being met. Examples of measures include audits, status reports, physical observations, and so on.

**mentor**

An individual in a business setting who assumes a relationship with an employee on a lower rung of the organizational hierarchy for the purpose of grooming the employee for job and career growth and development. Also, outside of the workplace, a mentor can be an adult individual who tutors a younger person in need of guidance.

**mentoring**

A more informal relationship than coaching, rooted in passing on wisdom and know-how from one person to another, mentor to mentee. Mentoring is applicable in business environments as well as on the outside, including organizations devoted to helping at-risk young persons.

**mini-mentoring**

An appellation affixed to in-house business relationships, usually established between two employees, where one helps another. A coach often initiates this relationship by having an employee with stellar knowledge and skills tutor a peer in need of improvement in certain areas.

**mini-vision**

A coach's microcosmic goals for the particular niche of the company that he or she manages. A mini-vision is transposed from the company's broader, long-term vision, and it is more meaningful for employees laboring in the here and now.

**mirroring feelings**

An empathetic coaching technique whereby coaches observe and appreciate an employee's state of mind, and accordingly adjust their approach in any conversations or meetings with the individual.

**objective ear**

The completely unbiased position assumed by both coaches and mentors who need to be fair and honest at all times with their employees or mentees. This stance is in stark contrast to sycophantic cheerleading, which is not the role of coaches and mentors, on or away from the job front.

**open-ended questions**

Queries regularly posed by coaches and mentors to draw out extended, thoughtful responses from employees or mentees. There are no right and wrong answers attached to these questions.

**paraphrasing**

An essential listening skill in coaching whereby coaches let their employees know that they are hearing what is being said to them by repeating the sum and substance of it in their own words.

**performance plans**

A coach's tool and the centerpiece of each employee's work life. These plans, crafted by the coach in concert with the employee, consist of goals/objectives, standards of performance, action plans, and measures. Employees usually work with several performance plans simultaneously. Sometimes called "work plans."

### performance review
A coaching tool prepared for employees on an individual basis that documents their overall job performances. Contained in these reviews are specific details of each employee's efforts—solid or otherwise—and their achievements or lack thereof.

### planned mentoring
Mentoring in business circumstances whereby a higher-up in an organization is paired with an employee being groomed for new job responsibilities or a promotion. Also refers to the not-for-profit outfits in which adult mentors are matched with younger mentees.

### positive reinforcement
A coaching and mentoring technique that identifies and lauds the right behaviors of employees and mentees on the spot, ideally leading to more of the same.

### principled coherence
The coaching and mentoring standard that asks coaches and mentors to do what they say they're going to do, when they say they are going to do it.

### productive confrontation
Conflicts in the workplace converted into positive lessons learned and forward movement.

### professionalism
The conscientious behaviors expected of all individuals in a workplace environment. Encompasses how the job is done, not the end-results.

### reality laboratory
A metaphorical place where employees go to participate in role reversal. This important work function allows employees to think in entrepreneurial ways, empathize with customers, fashion flexibility, and sharpen self-awareness.

### role
A group of work responsibilities and job expectations—i.e., what an employee is hired to undertake.

### self-motivation
An individual's embracing of commitment to the job coupled with the personal desire to perform well and to continuously learn. Applicable outside the workforce in countless circumstances, but always with the same bedrock principles in place—steadfastness and a desire to always gain knowledge and new skills.

### sensitivity-plus
A coaching communication technique for handling thin-skinned, overly sensitive employees, which entails coaches modulating their tone to suit the circumstances. Often applied to soften the delivery of negative feedback and to get through to employees without generating a defensive, antagonistic, and unproductive reaction.

### skills
Distinctive competencies in particular fields and disciplines, including technical skills and the so-called softer skills, a.k.a. "people skills."

### soft skills
Communication and interpersonal skills that are behavioral and abstract in nature, but nevertheless essential to performing most jobs.

**standards of performance**
The expectations of the quality of results in performance plans. Sometimes shortened to "standards."

**three Bs of coaching and mentoring**
Be aware, be fair, and be there.

**three Ps of coaching and mentoring**
People, performance, and positive outcomes.

**time management**
The meticulous management of individuals and what they can do in the finite constraints of time.

**tone setting**
A coach's words and actions that define the culture of the workplace and the nature of all on-the-job relationships. Tone setting is derivative of leadership by example.

**vision**
Noble, aggressive goals for a company's short-term and long-term future.

**work ethic**
The overall work habits of men and women on the job.

# Appendix B

# Resources

## Books

Belker, Lorin B. and Gary S. Topchik. *The First-Time Manager*. (AMACON, 2005).

Cook, Marshall J. *Effective Coaching*. (McGraw-Hill, 1998).

Flaherty, James. *Coaching: Evoking Excellence in Others*. (Butterworth-Heinemann, second edition, 2005).

Fournies, Ferdinand F. *Coaching for Improved Work Performance*. (McGraw-Hill, third edition, 1999).

Hudson, Frederic M., Ph.D. *The Handbook of Coaching*. (Jossey-Bass, 1999).

Logan, David, Ph.D., and John King. *The Coaching Revolution*. (Adams Media Corporation, 2001).

Maxwell, John C. *The 21 Indispensable Qualities of a Leader*. (Nelson Business, 1999).

McClain, Gary R., Ph.D., and Deborah S. Romaine. *The Everything Managing People Book*. (Adams Media Corporation, second edition, 2007).

Morgan, Howard, Phil Harkins, and Marshall Goldsmith. *The Art and Practice of Leadership Coaching*. (John Wiley & Sons, 2004).

Stoddard, David A. *The Heart of Mentoring*. (Navpress Publishing Group, 2003).

Stone, Florence. *The Essential New Manager's Kit*. (Kaplan Business, 2003).

Whitmore, John. *Coaching for Performance*. (Nicholas Brealey Publishing, third edition, 2002).

Zachary, Lois J. *Creating a Mentoring Culture*. (Jossey-Bass, 2005).

## Web Sites

**Action Coach**
*www.actioncoaching.com*
Business coaching service with onsite resources, newsletter, store, and more.

**BusinessCoach.com**
*www.businesscoach.com*
Business coaching service with general information and free resources onsite.

**Center for Coaching & Mentoring (CCM)**
*www.coachingandmentoring.com*
Consulting service with free resources on the subject matter available onsite.

### The Coach Connection

✐*www.findyourcoach.com*

Coach matchmaking service in the broadest range of areas: life, business, career, executive, personal, sales, transition, leadership, ADD, mentor, management, real estate, and retirement.

### The Coaches Training Institute

✐*www.thecoaches.com*

ICF accredited training program.

### Coaching for Success, Inc.

✐*www.coach.net*

Coaching service with general information and topical links on both business and life coaching.

### International Business Coach Institute (IBCI)

✐*www.businesscoachinstitute.org*

International association with membership available only to professionally trained and accredited business coaches.

### International Coach Federation (ICF)

✐*www.coachfederation.org*

World recognized service and accrediting organization in the area of business and personal coaching.

### The Worldwide Association of Business Coaches

✐*www.wabccoaches.com*

International professional association serving the business coaching trade.

# Appendix C

# Case Studies

This appendix furnishes a group of case studies from the vast and varied business world, with each one revealing how coaching and mentoring methodologies play (or can play) positive roles in ameliorating unhealthy work situations and suffering bottom lines.

## Food for Thought

Neighborhood diners are scattered all across the American landscape. You might say they are as American as the apple pie they serve. And the food and customer service received in them varies considerably. The particular diner we will patronize for our case study is a badly managed mid-sized eatery. This once popular eatery, with a long, prosperous history in the neighborhood that it served for many years, changed ownership for the first time. The switch immediately generated the usual problems that such a stark and sudden transformation brings to customer-intimate businesses like diners.

When the new management team grabbed the baton—or spatula in this instance—they made a colossal miscalculation. That is, they mistakenly assessed their market standing and disregarded the loyal customer base already in place. They assumed ownership with the mindset that the former proprietors didn't know what they were doing all across the board. They sniffed their noses at the past owners and their lagging so far behind the times in areas ranging from cooking equipment to employee perks to the menu (no cappuccino maker). They also branded the loyal legions of regular customers as a bunch of yahoos.

Wise management, however, doesn't throw the baby out with the bathwater, or, in a diner's case, their industrial refrigerator out with the rancid rice pudding. Yes, it was shrewd for the new ownership to upgrade equipment and add a few yuppie dishes to the menu, but very shortsighted to neglect both employee satisfaction and customer service, which is what they did. The new diner management, in fact, replaced all the wait staff with new faces, even though many of the waiters and waitresses let go had worked there for many years, and were well-known and liked by the clientele. The new management reasoned that fresh faces could be easily instructed in the new ways of doing things. To them, the old wait staff was hopelessly lost in the past. This rather common business posture makes sense in some instances, but only if the new ways are a marked improvement over the old ways.

But, in this case, the new help was directed to get patrons in and out of the diner posthaste. In no uncertain times, they were told that speedy customer turnover was essential in generating more business at the brisk breakfast, lunch, and dinner hours. Management, in fact, instituted all kinds of employee rules and regulations, including directives regarding coffee cup refills—only one and then only when requested. The diner's once-upon-a-time bottomless coffee cup was sealed tight, much to the dismay of caffeine-craving customers. In addition, strict codes regarding fraternizing with customers were also enforced. No personal conversations of any sort were permitted with them at the dining room's booths and tables outside of "hello" and "goodbye." Waiters and waitresses were advised—in written policy, by the way—to take customers' orders and deliver their food.

Predictably, the entire diner staff felt strangled by these very short leashes. And the icing on the chocolate layer cake was that they were compelled to listen to increasing numbers of customer complaints concerning the new management policies. If they wanted to keep their jobs, however, the staff had little choice but to remain silent and smile through it all. By any measurement, the newly managed diner was not a healthy environment—and that's leaving the quality

of the food out of the equation. Customers were unhappy. Employees labored in the antithesis of a learning atmosphere. Predictably, the constrictive work conditions manifested themselves in perpetual employee turnover. And in diner environs, revolving-door employees are regular customers' worst nightmares.

Needless to say, the diner managerial methods did not amount to anything resembling coaching. The owners desired maximizing employee performance—yes—but not by respecting the staff on a person-to-person basis. On the contrary, they put them all in a job straightjacket and asked that employees maximize diner profits by strictly adhering to a surplus of rules and regulations. The result was that there was no personal approach to service, and—surprise—no maximization of profits. Management viewed the diner business only in terms of dollars and cents and superimposed this bloodless attitude onto their employees. They didn't recognize the human potential of their workforce and therefore did not try to tap into it.

The bottom line is that the bottom line suffered. It suffered because the purported farsightedness in upgrading equipment, menu, and so on, as well as bringing the eatery into the twenty-first century was not commingled with foresight in the key areas that coaching and mentoring managerial methodologies address. The diner desperately needed a people approach to managing with strong communication between management and employees and, on the other end of the spectrum, strong communication between employees and customers.

## Stagnant Waters

For her annual performance assessment, Martha reported to her immediate superior, Ken, who told her in no uncertain terms that he thought she was stagnating in her role as team leader. Ken didn't mince his words, informing Martha that she managed with a detached, almost haughty style that was turning off members of her staff. He concluded that this serious disconnect between manager and employees contributed to performance drop-offs all across the board.

Ken further explained to Martha that she was seen as unapproachable, and that this aloofness signified a snowballing problem. In her position in the organization (a large insurance company), she needed to convey information to and upgrade the skills of her staff on a recurrent basis. And because of her standoffishness, a conspicuous communication barricade had arisen, making the essential flow of information and the enhancing of skills both slow and incomplete.

Martha wasn't surprised by her performance review. Deep down she knew her remote persona had caused a rift to develop between herself and the staff. She freely agreed to make some necessary adjustments to her managerial style. She didn't tell Ken exactly how she planned on seeing this metamorphosis through, only that she was definitely going to connect better and forge a stronger working relationship with those under her thumb. Martha didn't tell Ken that she intended on working with an external coaching consultant who specialized in managerial behavior modifications. Paying for the service out of her own pocket, she hired a personal coach and initiated a coaching relationship via the telephone. This is not an uncommon arrangement.

Martha quickly appreciated that she could unburden herself to her coach. She laid out all the pertinent details of her job situation. In return, she was afforded counsel on behavioral adjustments that would place her on the fast track to a more productive brand of managing.

Martha's coach advised her in a wide range of areas, including mode of dress. Yes, there are certain styles and colors of clothing that are more open and less forbidding. She was told that everything mattered, including putting the right clothes on in the morning. In Martha's managerial makeover, she now met with her employees on a one-on-one basis and began leaving her office door open. This is the literal interpretation of the open door policy—symbolic, yes, but very effective in Martha's particular circumstances. For a long time her office door was so tightly shut that employees needed dynamite to blow it open! The dramatic change in managerial style assumed by Martha didn't go unnoticed. Not only did her team feel more comfortable with the new and improved Martha as their superior, but also others in similar management positions throughout the organization appreciated the better performance results she was extracting from her people.

Martha worked for an organization that didn't have coaching in its managerial chain—either internal or external. So she took it upon herself to hire a personal coach to improve her managerial abilities. By traveling down this route, she also upgraded her employees' skills, their overall job satisfaction, and performance levels. By utilizing this outside coaching assistance, Martha not only bolstered her present job position, but also made her career shine brighter. The knowledge and skills that she gathered from her coach and, more importantly, that she experimented with in the reality laboratory called the workplace, made positive differences for both her today *and* for her tomorrow. And that's what good coaching is all about. It's grounded in the present with clear eyes peeled on the future.

## Workplace Vacuum

Ricky was a technical whiz who knew his way around a keyboard and hard drive. He also had a penchant for shooting off his mouth. In fact, he couldn't keep quiet about his after-hours moonlighting. That is, Ricky clued his coworkers in on exactly how he was supplementing his office job income. And how he was earning a few extra dollars was—for lack of a better word—illegal.

Ricky was, in fact, stealing merchandise from big-box retailers. But he wanted his peers to appreciate his ingenious thievery. In a nutshell, Ricky would switch barcodes from cheaper store products with more expensive alternatives. His preferred item was the vacuum cleaner. He'd clip barcodes from $75 machines and affix them to $400 machines. And when he checked out, cashiers noticed nothing untoward. He was purchasing vacuum cleaners and had vacuum cleaners. Ditto the security people who looked at his receipts. Ricky subsequently sold his ill-gotten gains—new in box—on eBay. Ouch!

Naturally, word of Ricky's antics quickly spread through the office tiers, reaching the ears of Caitlin, his manager and coach. She was confronted with an awful dilemma. Were Ricky's actions outside her purview—a personal matter, even though they were plainly illegal and could land the man in jail? In fact, she reasoned it would eventually come to that because surveillance cameras and other security measures are always on the lookout for these kinds of scams. But what exactly could Caitlin say or do in her standing as Ricky's boss?

She couldn't deliver an ultimatum—stop your outside thievery or you're fired, because it was essentially an empty threat. How could she really know that he wasn't engaging in the practice anymore? Caitlin could, however, call Ricky into her office and talk it out. And that's what she did. She expressed disbelief at what she was hearing and hoped that it wasn't true. She asked Ricky to cease and desist from his felony moonlighting—if, in fact, it was the case—and told him to put a lid on his flapping tongue. She also made it clear how much she valued Ricky's job performance and asked that he not do anything to jeopardize his position. Lastly, Caitlin made it known that she couldn't tolerate any more of such office gossip, because it was fast becoming a larger workplace issue. She told Ricky that if it didn't stop—and right away—it would be a morale matter of great import that she would have to deal with accordingly. Not another word from Ricky's mouth was ever uttered on this subject again. Coach Caitlin prayed that Ricky was indeed on the straight and narrow, putting a premium on his highly paid office job.

## Two-Headed Monster

Two managers, Scott and Andrea, were on the same plane in the organizational hierarchy. They had different managerial roles but encountered some overlap in their job responsibilities. In one peculiar instance, they even shared the same employee for a period of time. Having two managers to report to was the unusual dilemma that confronted Jim, who served as an assistant to both Scott and Andrea.

At the beginning of his job stint, Jim generally liked working for both his superiors. However, Scott and Andrea didn't care for one another. Their distaste was both personal and professional, and they made no bones about it. Their cross working relationship was competitive and contentious. In essence, Jim was compelled to serve two masters at odds with one another much of the time.

Scott thought very highly of Jim. He believed that his employee's future shined brightly. He hoped to groom him for an important sales rep position in the company. Scott felt Jim possessed the strong verbal communication skills required for success in such a position. He saw in him a vast reservoir of human potential and hoped to tap into it over time. Scott, in effect, assumed the role as Jim's more experienced mentor.

Andrea, on the other hand, saw Jim in a decidedly different light. To her, he was a capable assistant and not much more than that. She didn't view him as a man with great potential beyond his rather ordinary office job. Yes, she considered Jim highly intelligent, a witty conversationalist, and a treasure trove of knowledge. But in her opinion, he sorely lacked what she considered to be the key to success—an ambitious soul married to a robust work ethic.

When Scott informed Andrea of his plans for Jim, she vetoed the idea with great alacrity. This only worsened the already strong antipathy the two managers felt toward one another. And, naturally, this impasse did nothing to uplift Jim's on-the-job spirits. Scott's mentoring of Jim ran headfirst into an impenetrable roadblock. Coaching and mentoring in management put no such obstacles in employees' ways. And while coaching champions a meritocracy, it never consigns employees to fixed job roles and doesn't impede, in any way, their forward career movement. The employment circumstances that confronted Jim violated these core principles.

Of course, Jim was not working for a company with a formal coaching apparatus in place. And although Scott adopted bits and pieces from coaching and mentoring methodologies, they need to be wholly embraced and supported to get the best possible results. The rancorous relationship between Scott and his colleague in management, Andrea, imploded what was a good-faith attempt on his part to grow the skills of the employee who worked for both of them.

Jim, meanwhile, was caught in the crossfire and saw the handwriting on his cubicle wall. He concluded that he was in a dead-end job and wrote a strongly worded memo to both of his superiors—Scott and Andrea—citing his inert position as beneath his talents and abilities. He eloquently grumbled that he was not being afforded opportunities for career growth in his current job role.

Immediately upon receiving his copy of the memo, Scott raced over to Andrea's mailbox like a gazelle. He wanted to spare Jim, whom he still liked and maintained high hopes for, the wrath of boss number two, Andrea. Looking out for Jim the whole time, Scott viewed Jim's no-holds-barred memo as counterproductive in the big picture. He saw it as injurious to both Jim's present job status and future possibilities.

Unfortunately, the fleet feet of Scott were no match for Andrea's attention to detail, as she was already reading Jim's memo when he arrived to intercept it. Jim's memo, among many things, compared his job tasks to that of a houseboy—i.e., making power lunch reservations, travel arrangements, and even picking up his boss's laundry. Andrea didn't appreciate the tone of her employee's missive, nor did she accept its pessimistic premise. She promptly put her disgruntled employee on a ninety-day probation, telling him that he either ratchet up his increasingly lackluster work habits and realign his attitude, or face termination. Scott, meanwhile, was powerless to intercede. He encouraged Jim to pick up his work pace to placate Andrea. And although he continued to believe in Jim's overall intellect and potential, he couldn't in good conscience defend Jim's increasingly lifeless work ethic and poor attitude.

In the end, Jim looked at the probation period as the last straw and decided he had no future in the company. He deliberately didn't do what was necessary to save his job, figuring that termination would get him an unemployment check while he looked for another, more challenging position.

## The Calling

Kathy considered herself a burnout case in the making. Courtesy of her many years in the increasingly dog-eat-dog corporate world in which she labored, she was developing stomach ulcers. Kathy had long heard whispers of this new approach to managing called "coaching" and started to look into what all the fuss was about. In her research, she concluded that coaching methods in managing were just what the doctor ordered. She wanted to incorporate the many tools and techniques of coaching in her own day-to-day managing. For her own psychological and physical well-being and for the benefit of both her employees and the company's bottom line, she felt coaching was worth trying.

A product manager, Kathy took her coaching idea to the head of her division. She explained the changes in managerial methods she envisioned. She said she anticipated that such new-fashioned approaches

would obtain significantly better results than she was getting. Kathy's superior considered her idea and got back to her with the good news. She had the green light to proceed in what was dubbed a "pilot project." That is, if her trailblazing coaching methods got the results she anticipated, the company would consider adapting coaching throughout its entire organization.

Kathy immediately set about changing the way things worked in her office. Communicating on a one-on-one basis was the first change she inaugurated. She brought each of her employees individually into her office for a chat. She wanted to get a fix on where they felt they stood in their job roles and what they thought could improve their performances and overall satisfaction with their work. She queried them on whether they felt sufficiently challenged, what their future plans included, and if they saw their present jobs as key to their long-term careers.

By undertaking this thorough personnel inventory of her employees, Kathy culled many useful things. She learned that some of her employees were unhappy, feeling that they were being underutilized or, in some cases, had responsibilities altogether mismatched with their abilities. With this wealth of information now at her disposal, Kathy made personnel shifts in job responsibilities and roles, putting the right people in the right jobs as never before. It was like piecing together a puzzle.

In a short span of time, the results Kathy got out of her team were demonstrably positive. The regular communication that Kathy instituted as office policy not only improved the morale and productivity of her team, but she herself felt less stress in her own life. She was a happier camper all around and kept her blossoming ulcers at bay. The new rapport she generated with her employees was a real eye-opener. She described this new relationship as a revelation—life-changing. Because her huge workload was previously bringing her down—both on the job and in her personal life—she discovered that coaching tools and techniques were totally effective in minimizing anxiety.

By developing a bond of trust between her and her employees that didn't exist before, Kathy gave her employees real wings for the first time. Wings to do the jobs that they were most capable of doing, as well as wings to do them better than ever before because of the new support system in the office. Prior to coaching, Kathy was a worrywart extraordinaire, who never felt comfortable delegating responsibilities to her employees. And when she did delegate tasks, she did not feel confident that all would turn out well. In her coach's role, however, Kathy felt that because she was armed with so much more information about her people and what they could do, she could delegate with confidence and bring her employees into the planning processes of their own jobs.

The pièce de résistance, as far as Kathy was concerned, was that her coaching pilot project was considered a resounding success throughout the company. She was thus promoted and given the important job role of converting the entire organization into the coaching mode. This was the ultimate in jobs as far as she was concerned because she believed in what she was doing as never before. She believed that teaching the ways and means of coaching and mentoring was more than just important, but apocalyptic in altering business environments for the better, in a time when such changes are desperately needed.

## Table Talk

The first thing Jen noticed when she assumed her "desk" in her new job was that she was afforded little privacy. In fact, everybody in her particular department of the company worked at the same long table. They worked in the same large room taking and executing real-time stock trades via the telephone. Jen compared the look of the office to a cafeteria. However, her job role wasn't about a sandwich and cup of coffee, but high finance.

When Jen accepted the job, she did so with some trepidation. It wasn't the type of job that she wanted. It was work unlike anything she'd ever done before, but she was—in the common parlance—"desperate" and had "bills to pay." Jen was unnerved when she saw the office setup for the first time. She had been apprised of her job tasks, but nobody had told her about the long table and constantly ringing telephones, with everybody aware of what everybody else was doing. It looked very frenetic and intimidating. Jen would have preferred to work behind a cubicle wall while getting her feet wet. Nevertheless, she kept her apprehension to herself.

Steve, her manager, oriented her as best he could. He was warm and reassuring, Jen thought, and she appreciated the way he highlighted—without her having to say anything—the office setup and seemingly stress-filled, scary work atmosphere. Because of Steve's openness, Jen began her first day on the job nervous, but not nearly as nervous as she thought she might be. Steve told her to remain calm at all times and expect to make some initial mistakes. He told her never to hesitate coming to him with any questions about job-related issues and concerns.

Steve, in fact, made himself highly visible. He worked the big room and made everyone feel a part of something important; made everyone feel that they were contributing to a final product. And this was no small accomplishment, considering that the work they were doing involved busily answering telephones and typing in stock orders for people with a lot of dollars and very little patience. This type of work was ripe for resentment and meltdown, as many employees dealt with snippy, condescending customers who didn't have much use for them beyond their fingers typing in the right numbers and right away. Almost to a person in the office, though, there were few complaints about the frenzied work. Steve managed to make his staff take the work seriously—because it was serious business—but not take to heart the gruffness and curtness of the phone callers. By separating the two things, Steve fashioned remarkable loyalty from his team. He was respected and liked because he was always aware, always fair, and always there for his troops.

After only a few days on the job, Jen's high anxiety was a thing of the past. She was also pleasantly surprised that she enjoyed the fast-paced work. The big long table in the open office now appeared welcoming and nurturing. However, one fateful day, a major faux pas on Jen's part tested the mettle of both her and her manager. During her transcribing of the order information from one caller, she somehow missed an important zero in a keystroke. A $100,000,000 stock trade typed in as $10,000,000 may be one keystroke off, but it's also $90,000,000 off. Not chump change!

Jen was not only embarrassed, but a little frightened, too. It's not everyday that $90,000,000 goes missing and you're the guilty party. Although alarmed, Steve maintained calm and set to rectify the situation by retracing the steps leading up to the transaction gone awry. Thanks to his diligence and equanimity, the error was found and fortunately no long-term damage was done. It was a happy ending for all concerned. Jen thought that she might get the boot for her $90,000,0000 blunder, but Steve took her aside and explained exactly what went wrong, and how such a mistake was to be avoided in the future. Jen described the meeting with her boss as amiable but firm, with Steve telling her with something of a smile, "Don't do that again." Steve didn't gloss over the momentousness of what had happened. Yes, he said, everybody would make mistakes from time to time, but there are mistakes and then there are Mistakes!

Steve proved himself a fine coach-manager. He presided over a healthy and productive workplace. The people who worked for him learned a lot on the job. They learned how to work under extreme pressure—so much so that after a short span of time, it didn't seem like so much pressure at all. And, as for Jen's mistake, Steve followed the coaching script. He didn't bawl out Jen or fire her on the spot to set an example for others, but he expected her to learn from the mistake and not make anything resembling such a big blunder again.

## Double Life

Sheila managed an office with fifteen employees. Because Sheila was a coach, she always made it a point to get to know her people inside and out, including tidbits of their personal lives. No, she wasn't a busybody who wanted to exhume all of the dirt from their closets. She merely wanted to know what made her employees the people they were and what motivated them to behave as they did.

One of her best employees was a man named Michael, who since he joined her team had significantly elevated its overall performance. Sheila knew that Michael was married with two kids. By all indications, he had a very happy home life, and he never tired of pulling out his wallet full of snapshots of his young boy and girl doing everything from trick-or-treating on Halloween to learning to ride a bicycle. After about eight months on the job, however, Michael's cheery demeanor changed. At first, his coworkers noticed only subtle differences in the way he went about his work. Then more overt changes became evident, as Michael began snapping at his colleagues. He even looked unkempt on occasion. Eventually, his performance slowed, impacting everyone on his team who depended on him.

Sheila met regularly with all of her employees, including Michael. At first she was unable to get anything out of him. He said that all was well and she didn't press him any further. When his performance slipped further, she could no longer accept the "everything is fine" line, because she knew it wasn't. So, Sheila pressed on, expressing her disappointment at his on-the-job regressing. She also noted the changes in his temperament and even in his appearance. Why was this formerly easygoing, neatly dressed, and punctilious fellow no longer any of these things? There had to be a reason or reasons behind the transformation.

With patient but persistent questioning, Sheila finally got Michael to unburden himself. He told her that his little daughter had been diagnosed with a serious, possibly life-threatening illness, and that he and his wife had been spending much of their time running back and forth to doctors and hospitals, getting very little sleep, and sometimes not even changing out of their clothes from one day to the next. Surprised, Sheila offered her complete sympathy, and wondered why Michael hadn't told her or any of his coworkers sooner. He said that he considered it a personal matter and didn't want to bring his problems from home into the workplace.

Sheila informed him that many of his coworkers were worried about him and had expressed their concerns to her. She offered him time off if he needed it. Michael said that he thought it was best that he keep working, but appreciated the offer and Sheila's understanding. He did, however, accept Sheila's offer to rearrange his work schedule to accommodate his home needs, which she insisted must always take precedence.

She further suggested that he tell his colleagues what was going on in his life. First, she told him it would be better if he got it off his chest. After all, his coworkers were asking him time and again if anything was wrong, and his snippy responses were only exacerbating things. Second, Sheila felt that teamwork required openness, and if his work schedule and job assignments were adjusted to balance his home situation, it was important that his coworkers knew the reason why. If they didn't know the explanation behind the changes, they might feel he was getting special treatment and resent it, leading to morale problems. And, of course, it would create a leadership problem, with Sheila being seen as favoring one employee above all the others.

Sheila always preached that it was in the team's best interests if everybody's cards were on the table. She firmly believed that Michael would get support from his coworkers that would help him get through his trying personal crisis, and assist him, too, in doing his job better under difficult circumstances.

# Index

# The EVERYTHING Series!

## BUSINESS & PERSONAL FINANCE

Everything® Accounting Book
Everything® Budgeting Book
Everything® Business Planning Book
**Everything® Coaching and Mentoring Book, 2nd Ed.**
Everything® Fundraising Book
Everything® Get Out of Debt Book
Everything® Grant Writing Book
**Everything® Guide to Foreclosures**
Everything® Guide to Personal Finance for Single Mothers
Everything® Home-Based Business Book, 2nd Ed.
Everything® Homebuying Book, 2nd Ed.
Everything® Homeselling Book, 2nd Ed.
Everything® Improve Your Credit Book
Everything® Investing Book, 2nd Ed.
Everything® Landlording Book
Everything® Leadership Book
Everything® Managing People Book, 2nd Ed.
Everything® Negotiating Book
Everything® Online Auctions Book
Everything® Online Business Book
Everything® Personal Finance Book
Everything® Personal Finance in Your 20s and 30s Book
Everything® Project Management Book
Everything® Real Estate Investing Book
Everything® Retirement Planning Book
Everything® Robert's Rules Book, $7.95
Everything® Selling Book
Everything® Start Your Own Business Book, 2nd Ed.
Everything® Wills & Estate Planning Book

## COOKING

Everything® Barbecue Cookbook
**Everything® Bartender's Book, 2nd Ed., $9.95**
**Everything® Calorie Counting Cookbook**
Everything® Cheese Book
Everything® Chinese Cookbook
Everything® Classic Recipes Book
Everything® Cocktail Parties & Drinks Book
Everything® College Cookbook
Everything® Cooking for Baby and Toddler Book
Everything® Cooking for Two Cookbook
Everything® Diabetes Cookbook
Everything® Easy Gourmet Cookbook
Everything® Fondue Cookbook
Everything® Fondue Party Book
Everything® Gluten-Free Cookbook
Everything® Glycemic Index Cookbook
Everything® Grilling Cookbook
Everything® Healthy Meals in Minutes Cookbook
Everything® Holiday Cookbook

Everything® Indian Cookbook
Everything® Italian Cookbook
Everything® Low-Carb Cookbook
**Everything® Low-Cholesterol Cookbook**
Everything® Low-Fat High-Flavor Cookbook
Everything® Low-Salt Cookbook
Everything® Meals for a Month Cookbook
Everything® Mediterranean Cookbook
Everything® Mexican Cookbook
Everything® No Trans Fat Cookbook
Everything® One-Pot Cookbook
Everything® Pizza Cookbook
Everything® Quick and Easy 30-Minute,
    5-Ingredient Cookbook
Everything® Quick Meals Cookbook
Everything® Slow Cooker Cookbook
Everything® Slow Cooking for a Crowd Cookbook
Everything® Soup Cookbook
Everything® Stir-Fry Cookbook
**Everything® Sugar-Free Cookbook**
**Everything® Tapas and Small Plates Cookbook**
Everything® Tex-Mex Cookbook
Everything® Thai Cookbook
Everything® Vegetarian Cookbook
Everything® Wild Game Cookbook
Everything® Wine Book, 2nd Ed.

## GAMES

Everything® 15-Minute Sudoku Book, $9.95
Everything® 30-Minute Sudoku Book, $9.95
**Everything® Bible Crosswords Book, $9.95**
Everything® Blackjack Strategy Book
Everything® Brain Strain Book, $9.95
Everything® Bridge Book
Everything® Card Games Book
Everything® Card Tricks Book, $9.95
Everything® Casino Gambling Book, 2nd Ed.
Everything® Chess Basics Book
Everything® Craps Strategy Book
Everything® Crossword and Puzzle Book
Everything® Crossword Challenge Book
Everything® Crosswords for the Beach Book, $9.95
**Everything® Cryptic Crosswords Book, $9.95**
Everything® Cryptograms Book, $9.95
Everything® Easy Crosswords Book
Everything® Easy Kakuro Book, $9.95
Everything® Easy Large-Print Crosswords Book
Everything® Games Book, 2nd Ed.
Everything® Giant Sudoku Book, $9.95
Everything® Kakuro Challenge Book, $9.95
Everything® Large-Print Crossword Challenge Book
Everything® Large-Print Crosswords Book
Everything® Lateral Thinking Puzzles Book, $9.95

Everything® Literary Crosswords Book, $9.95
Everything® Mazes Book
**Everything® Memory Booster Puzzles Book, $9.95**
Everything® Movie Crosswords Book, $9.95
**Everything® Music Crosswords Book, $9.95**
Everything® Online Poker Book, $12.95
Everything® Pencil Puzzles Book, $9.95
Everything® Poker Strategy Book
Everything® Pool & Billiards Book
**Everything® Puzzles for Commuters Book, $9.95**
Everything® Sports Crosswords Book, $9.95
Everything® Test Your IQ Book, $9.95
Everything® Texas Hold 'Em Book, $9.95
Everything® Travel Crosswords Book, $9.95
**Everything® TV Crosswords Book, $9.95**
Everything® Word Games Challenge Book
Everything® Word Scramble Book
Everything® Word Search Book

## HEALTH

Everything® Alzheimer's Book
Everything® Diabetes Book
Everything® Health Guide to Adult Bipolar Disorder
**Everything® Health Guide to Arthritis**
Everything® Health Guide to Controlling Anxiety
Everything® Health Guide to Fibromyalgia
**Everything® Health Guide to Menopause**
**Everything® Health Guide to OCD**
**Everything® Health Guide to PMS**
Everything® Health Guide to Postpartum Care
Everything® Health Guide to Thyroid Disease
Everything® Hypnosis Book
Everything® Low Cholesterol Book
Everything® Nutrition Book
Everything® Reflexology Book
Everything® Stress Management Book

## HISTORY

Everything® American Government Book
Everything® American History Book, 2nd Ed.
Everything® Civil War Book
Everything® Freemasons Book
Everything® Irish History & Heritage Book
Everything® Middle East Book
Everything® World War II Book, 2nd Ed.

## HOBBIES

Everything® Candlemaking Book
Everything® Cartooning Book
Everything® Coin Collecting Book
Everything® Drawing Book

Everything® Family Tree Book, 2nd Ed.
Everything® Knitting Book
Everything® Knots Book
Everything® Photography Book
Everything® Quilting Book
Everything® Sewing Book
Everything® Soapmaking Book, 2nd Ed.
Everything® Woodworking Book

## HOME IMPROVEMENT

Everything® Feng Shui Book
Everything® Feng Shui Decluttering Book, $9.95
Everything® Fix-It Book
**Everything® Green Living Book**
Everything® Home Decorating Book
Everything® Home Storage Solutions Book
Everything® Homebuilding Book
**Everything® Organize Your Home Book, 2nd Ed.**

## KIDS' BOOKS

All titles are $7.95
Everything® Kids' Animal Puzzle & Activity Book
Everything® Kids' Baseball Book, 4th Ed.
Everything® Kids' Bible Trivia Book
Everything® Kids' Bugs Book
Everything® Kids' Cars and Trucks Puzzle and Activity Book
Everything® Kids' Christmas Puzzle & Activity Book
Everything® Kids' Cookbook
Everything® Kids' Crazy Puzzles Book
Everything® Kids' Dinosaurs Book
**Everything® Kids' Environment Book**
**Everything® Kids' Fairies Puzzle and Activity Book**
Everything® Kids' First Spanish Puzzle and Activity Book
Everything® Kids' Gross Cookbook
Everything® Kids' Gross Hidden Pictures Book
Everything® Kids' Gross Jokes Book
Everything® Kids' Gross Mazes Book
Everything® Kids' Gross Puzzle & Activity Book
Everything® Kids' Halloween Puzzle & Activity Book
Everything® Kids' Hidden Pictures Book
Everything® Kids' Horses Book
Everything® Kids' Joke Book
Everything® Kids' Knock Knock Book
Everything® Kids' Learning Spanish Book
**Everything® Kids' Magical Science Experiments Book**
Everything® Kids' Math Puzzles Book
Everything® Kids' Mazes Book
Everything® Kids' Money Book
Everything® Kids' Nature Book
Everything® Kids' Pirates Puzzle and Activity Book
Everything® Kids' Presidents Book
Everything® Kids' Princess Puzzle and Activity Book
Everything® Kids' Puzzle Book
**Everything® Kids' Racecars Puzzle and Activity Book**
Everything® Kids' Riddles & Brain Teasers Book
Everything® Kids' Science Experiments Book
Everything® Kids' Sharks Book

Everything® Kids' Soccer Book
**Everything® Kids' Spies Puzzle and Activity Book**
Everything® Kids' States Book
Everything® Kids' Travel Activity Book

## KIDS' STORY BOOKS

Everything® Fairy Tales Book

## LANGUAGE

Everything® Conversational Japanese Book with CD, $19.95
Everything® French Grammar Book
Everything® French Phrase Book, $9.95
Everything® French Verb Book, $9.95
Everything® German Practice Book with CD, $19.95
Everything® Inglés Book
Everything® Intermediate Spanish Book with CD, $19.95
**Everything® Italian Practice Book with CD, $19.95**
Everything® Learning Brazilian Portuguese Book with CD, $19.95
**Everything® Learning French Book with CD, 2nd Ed., $19.95**
Everything® Learning German Book
Everything® Learning Italian Book
Everything® Learning Latin Book
**Everything® Learning Russian Book with CD, $19.95**
Everything® Learning Spanish Book with CD, 2nd Ed., $19.95
Everything® Russian Practice Book with CD, $19.95
Everything® Sign Language Book
Everything® Spanish Grammar Book
Everything® Spanish Phrase Book, $9.95
Everything® Spanish Practice Book with CD, $19.95
Everything® Spanish Verb Book, $9.95
Everything® Speaking Mandarin Chinese Book with CD, $19.95

## MUSIC

Everything® Drums Book with CD, $19.95
Everything® Guitar Book with CD, 2nd Ed., $19.95
Everything® Guitar Chords Book with CD, $19.95
Everything® Home Recording Book
Everything® Music Theory Book with CD, $19.95
Everything® Reading Music Book with CD, $19.95
Everything® Rock & Blues Guitar Book with CD, $19.95
Everything® Rock and Blues Piano Book with CD, $19.95
Everything® Songwriting Book

## NEW AGE

Everything® Astrology Book, 2nd Ed.
Everything® Birthday Personology Book
Everything® Dreams Book, 2nd Ed.
Everything® Love Signs Book, $9.95
**Everything® Love Spells Book, $9.95**
Everything® Numerology Book
Everything® Paganism Book
Everything® Palmistry Book
Everything® Psychic Book
Everything® Reiki Book
Everything® Sex Signs Book, $9.95

**Everything® Spells & Charms Book, 2nd Ed.**
Everything® Tarot Book, 2nd Ed.
Everything® Toltec Wisdom Book
Everything® Wicca and Witchcraft Book

## PARENTING

Everything® Baby Names Book, 2nd Ed.
**Everything® Baby Shower Book, 2nd Ed.**
Everything® Baby's First Year Book
Everything® Birthing Book
Everything® Breastfeeding Book
Everything® Father-to-Be Book
Everything® Father's First Year Book
**Everything® Get Ready for Baby Book, 2nd Ed.**
Everything® Get Your Baby to Sleep Book, $9.95
Everything® Getting Pregnant Book
**Everything® Guide to Pregnancy Over 35**
Everything® Guide to Raising a One-Year-Old
Everything® Guide to Raising a Two-Year-Old
**Everything® Guide to Raising Adolescent Boys**
**Everything® Guide to Raising Adolescent Girls**
Everything® Homeschooling Book
Everything® Mother's First Year Book
Everything® Parent's Guide to Childhood Illnesses
Everything® Parent's Guide to Children and Divorce
Everything® Parent's Guide to Children with ADD/ADHD
Everything® Parent's Guide to Children with Asperger's Syndrome
Everything® Parent's Guide to Children with Autism
Everything® Parent's Guide to Children with Bipolar Disorder
Everything® Parent's Guide to Children with Depression
Everything® Parent's Guide to Children with Dyslexia
Everything® Parent's Guide to Children with Juvenile Diabetes
Everything® Parent's Guide to Positive Discipline
Everything® Parent's Guide to Raising a Successful Child
Everything® Parent's Guide to Raising Boys
Everything® Parent's Guide to Raising Girls
Everything® Parent's Guide to Raising Siblings
Everything® Parent's Guide to Sensory Integration Disorder
Everything® Parent's Guide to Tantrums
Everything® Parent's Guide to the Strong-Willed Child
Everything® Parenting a Teenager Book
Everything® Potty Training Book, $9.95
Everything® Pregnancy Book, 3rd Ed.
Everything® Pregnancy Fitness Book
Everything® Pregnancy Nutrition Book
Everything® Pregnancy Organizer, 2nd Ed., $16.95
Everything® Toddler Activities Book
Everything® Toddler Book
Everything® Tween Book
Everything® Twins, Triplets, and More Book

## PETS

Everything® Aquarium Book
Everything® Boxer Book
Everything® Cat Book, 2nd Ed.
Everything® Chihuahua Book

Everything® **Cooking for Dogs Book**
Everything® Dachshund Book
Everything® Dog Book
Everything® Dog Health Book
Everything® Dog Obedience Book
Everything® Dog Owner's Organizer, $16.95
Everything® Dog Training and Tricks Book
Everything® German Shepherd Book
Everything® Golden Retriever Book
Everything® Horse Book
Everything® Horse Care Book
Everything® Horseback Riding Book
Everything® Labrador Retriever Book
Everything® Poodle Book
Everything® Pug Book
Everything® Puppy Book
Everything® Rottweiler Book
Everything® Small Dogs Book
Everything® Tropical Fish Book
Everything® Yorkshire Terrier Book

## REFERENCE

Everything® American Presidents Book
Everything® Blogging Book
Everything® Build Your Vocabulary Book
Everything® Car Care Book
Everything® Classical Mythology Book
Everything® Da Vinci Book
Everything® Divorce Book
Everything® Einstein Book
Everything® Enneagram Book
Everything® Etiquette Book, 2nd Ed.
Everything® **Guide to Edgar Allan Poe**
Everything® Inventions and Patents Book
Everything® Mafia Book
Everything® **Martin Luther King Jr. Book**
Everything® Philosophy Book
Everything® Pirates Book
Everything® Psychology Book

## RELIGION

Everything® Angels Book
Everything® Bible Book
Everything® **Bible Study Book with CD, $19.95**
Everything® Buddhism Book
Everything® Catholicism Book
Everything® Christianity Book
Everything® Gnostic Gospels Book
Everything® History of the Bible Book
Everything® Jesus Book
Everything® Jewish History & Heritage Book
Everything® Judaism Book
Everything® Kabbalah Book
Everything® Koran Book

Everything® Mary Book
Everything® Mary Magdalene Book
Everything® Prayer Book
Everything® Saints Book, 2nd Ed.
Everything® Torah Book
Everything® Understanding Islam Book
Everything® **Women of the Bible Book**
Everything® World's Religions Book
Everything® Zen Book

## SCHOOL & CAREERS

Everything® Alternative Careers Book
Everything® Career Tests Book
Everything® College Major Test Book
Everything® College Survival Book, 2nd Ed.
Everything® Cover Letter Book, 2nd Ed.
Everything® Filmmaking Book
Everything® Get-a-Job Book, 2nd Ed.
Everything® Guide to Being a Paralegal
Everything® Guide to Being a Personal Trainer
Everything® Guide to Being a Real Estate Agent
Everything® Guide to Being a Sales Rep
Everything® **Guide to Being an Event Planner**
Everything® Guide to Careers in Health Care
Everything® Guide to Careers in Law Enforcement
Everything® Guide to Government Jobs
Everything® **Guide to Starting and Running a Catering Business**
Everything® Guide to Starting and Running a Restaurant
Everything® Job Interview Book
Everything® New Nurse Book
Everything® New Teacher Book
Everything® Paying for College Book
Everything® Practice Interview Book
Everything® Resume Book, 2nd Ed.
Everything® Study Book

## SELF-HELP

Everything® **Body Language Book**
Everything® Dating Book, 2nd Ed.
Everything® Great Sex Book
Everything® Self-Esteem Book
Everything® Tantric Sex Book

## SPORTS & FITNESS

Everything® Easy Fitness Book
Everything® **Krav Maga for Fitness Book**
Everything® Running Book

## TRAVEL

Everything® **Family Guide to Coastal Florida**
Everything® Family Guide to Cruise Vacations
Everything® Family Guide to Hawaii
Everything® Family Guide to Las Vegas, 2nd Ed.
Everything® Family Guide to Mexico
Everything® Family Guide to New York City, 2nd Ed.
Everything® Family Guide to RV Travel & Campgrounds
Everything® Family Guide to the Caribbean
Everything® **Family Guide to the Disneyland® Resort, California Adventure®, Universal Studios®, and the Anaheim Area, 2nd Ed.**
Everything® **Family Guide to the Walt Disney World Resort®, Universal Studios®, and Greater Orlando, 5th Ed.**
Everything® Family Guide to Timeshares
Everything® Family Guide to Washington D.C., 2nd Ed.

## WEDDINGS

Everything® Bachelorette Party Book, $9.95
Everything® Bridesmaid Book, $9.95
Everything® Destination Wedding Book
Everything® Elopement Book, $9.95
Everything® Father of the Bride Book, $9.95
Everything® Groom Book, $9.95
Everything® Mother of the Bride Book, $9.95
Everything® Outdoor Wedding Book
Everything® Wedding Book, 3rd Ed.
Everything® Wedding Checklist, $9.95
Everything® Wedding Etiquette Book, $9.95
Everything® Wedding Organizer, 2nd Ed., $16.95
Everything® Wedding Shower Book, $9.95
Everything® Wedding Vows Book, $9.95
Everything® Wedding Workout Book
Everything® **Weddings on a Budget Book, 2nd Ed., $9.95**

## WRITING

Everything® Creative Writing Book
Everything® Get Published Book, 2nd Ed.
Everything® Grammar and Style Book
Everything® Guide to Magazine Writing
Everything® Guide to Writing a Book Proposal
Everything® Guide to Writing a Novel
Everything® Guide to Writing Children's Books
Everything® Guide to Writing Copy
Everything® **Guide to Writing Graphic Novels**
Everything® Guide to Writing Research Papers
Everything® Screenwriting Book
Everything® Writing Poetry Book
Everything® Writing Well Book